THE LITERARY
LABYRINTH

THE LITERARY LABYRINTH

Contemporary Critical Discourses

Bernard Sharratt

Lecturer in English
University of Kent

THE HARVESTER PRESS · SUSSEX

BARNES & NOBLE BOOKS · NEW JERSEY

First published in Great Britain in 1984 by
THE HARVESTER PRESS LIMITED
Publisher: John Spiers
16 Ship Street, Brighton, Sussex
and in the USA by
BARNES & NOBLE BOOKS
81 Adams Drive, Totowa, New Jersey 07512

© Bernard Sharratt, 1984

British Library Cataloguing in Publication Data
Sharratt, Bernard
    The literary labyrinth.
    1. Criticism
    I. Title
    801'.95   PN81

        ISBN 0-7108-0902-6
        ISBN 0-7108-0966-4 Pbk

Library of Congress Cataloging in Publication Data
Sharratt, Bernard.
    The literary labyrinth.

    1. Literature.   2. Reading.   I. Title.
PN45.S379   1984   809   84-16726
ISBN 0-389-20526-5

Typeset in 11/12 point Garamond by
Alacrity Phototypesetters,
Banwell Castle, Weston-super-Mare
Printed in Great Britain by
Whitstable Litho Ltd, Whitstable, Kent

For Marion and Nicola

who gave me the time
in which to write it

NEW CRISIS QUARTERLY

One takes a long time to outline the sketch of a work which, once completed, would be returned to oblivion and nothingness. But this is all wrong, for the sketch already contains the whole work, and this alone is the work.

(Jean Baudrillard, *The Mirror of Production*)

Our literature is characterised by the pitiless divorce which the literary institution maintains between the producer of the text and its user, between its owner and customer, between its author and its reader. This reader is thereby plunged into a kind of idleness — he is intransitive; he is, in short, *serious*: instead of functioning himself, instead of gaining access to the magic of the signifier, to the pleasure of writing, he is left with no more than the poor freedom either to accept or reject the text: reading is nothing more than a *referendum*.

(Roland Barthes, *S/Z*)

This man hath left me in a Laborinth.

(George Peele, *The Old Wives' Tale*)

New Crisis Quarterly

Tenth Anniversary Issue

Contents

Editorial : Valediction

'As I write, highly civilised human beings are flying overhead, trying to kill me.' I appropriate George Orwell's remark, from 1941, because at the moment it is true. Some time during the next few years I shall probably be murdered by an American President. I understand there will be no personal animosity, of course. The same fate is likely to befall the contributors to this periodical (and, incidentally, its readers). Some contributors do not share my view. They take seriously the claim, often implied in speeches by the current American President, that they will be murdered by a Soviet President. They agree, however, that the difference is not materially significant. Two contributors believe that they personally will not be murdered. One of these is a pessimist.

In the light of these considerations we have decided to bring forward this Tenth Anniversary issue of *New Crisis Quarterly*, and to alert our subscribers that this number is also the last *NCQ*. We take this opportunity of thanking them for their support, short-lived as it may have been in some cases.

Even a slightly premature anniversary is, nevertheless, a useful occasion for retrospection, and this editorial — rather longer than usual — glances back, with a forgiveable nostalgia, at the origins and intentions of *NCQ* in its early days, to remind us of how far we might have succeeded in our aims.

* * * *

New Crisis Quarterly emerged from a particular convergence of trends in the mid-1980s, familiar perhaps to some of our older readers but worth schematically recalling. The 'information explosion' was naively attributed at the time to a 'wave of new technology' (those quaintly dated phrases!) —

3

remember microfiche, word-processors, videodiscs, teletexts, viewdata, electronic mail, EFT, ETC., etc.! But the almost universal jettisoning of their print-publishing sub-branches by the major I.T. conglomerates still operating left a curious vacuum — which turned out to have been there for some time. It became widely apparent that for many years very few actual people had actually been reading actual books. Books were, of course, still in many ways central to our literate culture: readers still habitually read reviews, publishers' adverts and catalogues, cover-blurbs and contents-pages. Bookshop-browsing and even book-buying were buoyant, as was the output of publishers — the UK trade finally topped 50,000 new titles in a single year. Book-clubs and TV book-programmes abounded. But a spate of sober investigations finally showed that for most readers the majority of actual pages in the books they 'read' were regarded as superfluous. Readers of 'serious non-fiction' (to recall a disused category) would normally 'skip' prefaces, introductions and preliminary chapters and then rapidly 'sample' the rest, quickly compiling a slender card-file of the results. The more hard-pressed simply used the index to locate the references they wanted, or flicked through footnotes and bibliography to assemble their own perpetually on-going reading-lists. Readers of 'non-serious fiction' tended to focus, as the many pages turned of that week's best-selling blockbuster, upon immediately 'significant' passages, quotable extracts, episodes prominent in TV adaptations, or, in some sad cases, only the more titillating 'moments'. The publicity given to these findings, in press-summaries and news-bulletins, was of course exploited by a combination of electronics manufacturers and tree-conservationists.

Counter-campaigns to mobilise 'the general reader' encountered serious difficulties, as sectional trade-offs and competing specialist sacrifices were negotiated. One mildly memorable I.T. advert satirised the very basis of the campaign: 'The last guy to have read everything was Adam.' In a dignified, though indeterminate, editorial the *Sun-Times* reminded us that the problem of too much reading-matter — and its truly terrible price — had been with us certainly since

4

sixth-century China, contriving rather majestically to quote one of the better-known passages from the great Liu Hsieh:

The worthies of old, wishing to spread abroad benevolence and righteousness in the world were always struggling against time. They set no value on whole foot-lengths of jade, but a tenth of an inch of shadow on the sundial was as precious as pearls to them. Thus it was that Yü the Great raced with time to finish his work ... Thus it was ... that Confucius grudged every moment lost from reading, and Mo Ti was up and about again before his bed had had time to get warm. All these applied their virtue and genius to relieve the miseries of their times, so that they have left a good name behind them through a hundred generations.

Up till now, that is. In somewhat more recent years the 'general reader' has often, at best, felt like Mr Pickwick's friend, who sought illumination on Chinese metaphysics by consulting the separate entries in the encyclopaedia under the headings 'China' and 'Metaphysics'. The possibility of approaching a life-time of reading with even the faintest promise of accumulated wisdom or culminating synthesis has seemed increasingly remote. Conversely, the serious writer has frequently despaired of even the modest cohesion and inter-connection between his or her various writings ever impinging upon any particular individual within an eclectic, fragmented and overwhelmed 'reading public'. Even the specialist has learned to forgo that generous but futile gesture of referring the results, or problems, of his labours to the kind attention of 'colleagues in neighbouring disciplines'. They, regrettably, no longer have the time even to read his offer of cooperation.

It was perhaps ironic therefore that from the 1960s through to the 1980s, precisely as the efficacy of print began to fade, the most remarkable productivity of production stemmed from those most overtly concerned to 'relieve the miseries of their time': the revolutionary socialists. The extraordinary efflor-escence of 'Left' publications, especially periodicals, pro-duced, however, very few 'names' which lasted even a hundred months. Who now remembers such resonantly defiant titles as *Left Quarter, Red Reader, Socialist Text*, the more earthy *Crunch, Wrangle* and *Bias*, or the coolly ambivalent *Capital*

Gain and *Prison Notebooks*? Yet they were indeed contemporaries of the early *NCQ*. We too were part of that 'back to the printing press' phase — though, like others, we also participated in the more activist interventions and campaigns: Rock Against Racism, Poets Against Poverty, Film Theorists Against Imperialism, Cyclists Against Nuclear Power, and even occasionally Shop Stewards Against Capitalism. Looking back, one realises the double-edged truth of a remark in a now-forgotten predecessor, the formidable *Cornhill*, in September 1861:

The great peculiarity of periodical literature is that it reflects, with minute exactness, the moral and intellectual features of the society in which it exists; and there is no particular in which it does this more precisely than in respect of the different degrees of earnestness and power with which different subjects are discussed.

One is reminded too of the verdict of the *Wellesley Index* editor upon a critical moment in the career of another great periodical, one of our revered ancestors and partial namesakes:

In the last decade of the century, as causes and crises succeeded each other with ever-increasing speed and complexity, it became well-nigh impossible for either the Conservative Party or the *Quarterly* to take a consistent stand on any one body of political doctrine.

— Digression is the risk nostalgia takes. Our own specific origins within this ephemeral flowering were entirely accidental. A record £3 million win on Littlewoods Pools for an elderly eccentric socialist endowed us unexpectedly with our own printing press in Reading and adequate initial capital (sadly, this final issue also sees the last cheque drawn on that account).

Here, a third strand in the early 1980s intersected with our political commitments and deeply shaped the formal policy of *NCQ*. The construction of 'imaginary' works within literature had not been unknown previously. Even in this century one thinks immediately of Borges and Calvino, of Stanislav Lem and Thomas Mann. But what had been an occasional *jeu d'esprit* or local device became in the 1980s an intellectual fashion, even a major genre. The early signs were present in, for example, the *TLS*'s rather transparent celebration of the work

of Mstislav Bogdanovitch (19 December 1975) and subsequently of Hendrik de Stijl (21 April 1978); but a subtler
formula was soon found, with Ernst Gelner's diagnosis of the
shortage of the letter L in Poland (*TLS* 31 July 1981) and
David Lodge's imaginative review of a wholly preposterous
but almost plausible 'text-book' (23 April 1982). Radio 3 also
fostered the mode, cautiously at first with a programme
devoted to Adrian Leverkühn's music (9 March 1980) and then
more impishly with the angry exchanges over H. A. Dash's
biography of Sterne, *Yorick before Tristam* (12 April 1981). As
usual, German radio provided its own entertaining variation
on this emerging trend, with its broadcast of a brilliantly
imaginative *silent* Act III of *Meistersingers* in August 1981,
performed by the normally staid Bavarian State Opera in
Munich. The subsequent proliferation of purely imaginary
works needs no documentation. It is impossible, by now, to
open a journal or read a reviews page without being aware that
the fashion has stayed firmly with us, and has even to some
extent mitigated the problem of maintaining the cultural
function of 'books' long after the collapse of actual publishing.

    NCQ was founded just as this fashion was forming —
though our more conscious debt was at least equally to the
pioneering experiment of Miss Fiona Macleod in the 1890s (her
magnificent editorship of *The Pagan Review*). Our policy,
then as now, was to invite contributors to imagine the works
they would not have time to write (nor, obviously, readers to
read) and, pseudonymously, to review them for us. For some
this was a welcome relief from the normal requirement to re-
write the same book yet again. For others it served as a release
from compositional constipation. A few, with poignant
honesty, declined for fear that in this short-circuiting of the
'necessary' labours of actual writing they would be forced to
face a too-early expulsion from the protective libraries in
which they were seeking refuge from the mounting nightmare
of history. By offering space for each review on a scale not
common since the great Victorian periodicals and by encouraging, like them, extensive quotation, we hoped to deter mere
précis or prospective outline, while still leaving a critical, and
often self-critical, gap between conception and putative per-

formance which would stimulate our readers to participate themselves in the process of imagined production. It was, indeed, a condition of contribution that any readers were free (in terms of copyright) actually to write the works reviewed, if they had both inclination and time. A further condition — perhaps unnecessary in the early days — was that the review should make clear the political intent or implication of the book discussed. These simple aims were summarised in the first two mottoes on our masthead (a third was later added).

In other respects, too, we originally sought to emulate some of the 'general' periodicals of the Victorian period: to cater mainly for readers whose primary mode of access to the contemporary was in terms of the 'literary' but whose concerns stretched across politics, philosophy, history, religion, science and economics. Though there are indeed more urgent and more important things to think about than 'literature', 'literature' may provide an important *way* of thinking urgently about them. For a brief time we even included a fiction serial (*A Trance in the Museum of Time*), each 'number' being reviewed in consecutive issues — but the lurking dangers of mere parody, always implicit in our overall project, were rather too quickly realised in that instance. However, we also took seriously Tennyson's laconic stricture: 'Reading magazines breaks one's mind all to bits.' Each issue, therefore, was organised upon a latent common theme, though admittedly rather in the spirit of the jazz-critic André Hodeir's comment that:

The form of a work is that mode of being which ensures its unity while tending to promote at the same time the greatest possible diversity.

As to how far we might have succeeded in these various aims, our back numbers will have to speak for themselves.

* * * *

It is apposite that two interlinked themes should latently unify this final issue: politics and time, or perhaps the politics of time. The preoccupation of some reviewers is clearly the problem of finding appropriate (or exorcising inappropriate) bases for, or modes of, political authority and political thinking — after the repeated crises of rationality, of credibility, of expertise, the recurrent impasses of strategy, motivation and perspective. Central to some works under review are various forms, or modes, of time — from the nine months of the womb to the instant of death, from the odd immeasurableness of reading-times to that peculiarly a-temporal moment, in and out of time, in which conversions occur, ideas happen and decisions are taken. The often disturbingly palpable relation between present transient politics and the permanent proximity of the past, through its perpetuation in art, literature, music, is an indirect concern of other contributions. These themes converge, elliptically or polyphonically, to suggest that the politics of time itself may be at the deepest core of our own historical crisis. Yet though the profoundly political implications of our various temporal modalities are perhaps sufficiently indicated by the individual reviewers themselves not to need further comment here, I cannot quite resist the temptation — from my privileged valedictory position — to remark on two additional facets which have increasingly concerned me, precisely as editor of this periodical.

Jenny Hutton's rightful insistence, for example, that reading and, even more so, writing constitute a curious fusion of 'mental' *and* 'manual' labour (a strand in her argument strangely missed by the normally perceptive Mr Ford) has been brought painfully home to me by my editorial duties. Yet comparatively few of our readers seem to appreciate the point. It has indeed been a regular complaint that our readers are expected to *have read* the works discussed, and this has apparently aroused resentment. While acknowledging that it is normally unreasonable to demand an intimate prior acquaintance with the purely imaginary books we review, may I patiently remind such readers that the deliberately very high price of this periodical was originally adopted for the very purpose of excluding those not prepared to *work* for their pleasures. Our consistent policy has been to recognise that reading is *not* a matter of mere continuous and passive 'flow', and while we make every effort to eradicate any mere *waste* of reading-time, we do expect our subscribers to remain faithful to their own participatory duties.

A second, but related, problem has often been posed by new readers, and is latent in a number of contributions to this issue. Put crudely: why should we continue writing at all, any more? We can hardly, it is said, hope to influence those with any real power: no President or Prime Minister, still less an international banker or NATO general, has ever figured among our subscribers — though some of their less publicised servants have regularly perused us. One might once have replied that even such people have to have been young some time, and there is always the future — but that would perhaps be a singularly misplaced or even over-optimistic remark, at present. Surely, however, this is always an inappropriate objection: 'political power' is not only a matter of formal authority, overt manipulation, concentrated privilege, military force, media control and rapacious private possession. It is also, quite massively, a matter (literally) of how our *time — our* time — is controlled, organised, appropriated, constructed, used up, not least by ourselves: the habits and presuppositions which deeply shape our relation to our own location within and activation of complexly overlapping series and conjunctures of temporalities. If we can dislodge even a few of those constitutive components of our present 'crisis' (in Chinese, the ideogram combines 'danger' and 'opportunity') then we may have contributed something, and a modal shift or formal intervention, even at a primarily conceptual level, should not be underestimated, however restricted the area in which it initially appears. Few could have predicted the consequences, or even appreciated the real determinants, of a scholastic reconsideration of the ethics of usury.

* * * *

We would normally, of course, conclude our editorial comment with an updated list of 'current crises' — and our cumulative tally now makes very sober reading indeed for those with courage enough to consult the entire span of our quarterly surveys — but in the spirit of retrospection which has marked this final editorial, we will offer instead only a micro-sample, taken not from today but — quite literally — from the very day on which we wrote our first editorial. The following sixteen items are therefore all from a single day's newspaper-reading. They may serve to remind us that the crisis is new in every moment but that not all crises can continue indefinitely:

President Reagan is to recall his ambassador to London, Mr John J. Louis, one of his old cronies and a major contributor to his successful election campaign in 1980. Mr Louis, heir to the Johnson's Wax fortune and a pillar of the Republican Party, had held no diplomatic post of any kind at the time he was nominated Ambassador Extraordinary and Plenipotentiary to the Court of St James. Mr Louis was also one of the largest contributors to the campaign funds of Richard Nixon. When the 1980 campaign came round he was in the top six for Reagan.

It soon became an open secret in Washington that if there were a tough nut to be cracked in Anglo–US relations, or a problem requiring a light and delicate touch, Mr Louis was not the man to confront the British Foreign Secretary. He will be leaving quietly in a month or so.

Until his appointment as America's Secretary of State, George Schultz was President of the Bechtel company. His colleague as Secretary for Defense was the company's legal adviser and another ex-Bechtel man, Ken Davis, was made deputy Secretary for Energy. One-time CIA boss, Richard Helms, is now a Bechtel consultant and John McCone, one-time chairman of the Atomic Energy Commission and CIA director under President Kennedy, was a business partner of Stephen Bechtel Snr. The McCone-Bechtel partnership made a reputed $44 million profit on a $100,000 investment during world war two, building shipyards for the US Navy. Bechtel Snr is now worth some $750 million, his grandson Stephen Bechtel Jnr an estimated $200 million.

The company has built almost half the 75 nuclear plants in the US and is working on a third of the 69 still under construction. As a private company, Bechtel does not need to file profit figures. The top 59 executives own 60 per cent of the company, with six family members holding the other 40 per cent. But all executives must sell their shares back to the company on retirement. Thus Bechtel remains a family affair.

Like all families, it has its secrets and its rituals. The Bohemian Club is the point of contact for many top-level Bechtel

11

connections — Weinberger, Schultz, Ronald Reagan and Vice-President George Bush are all members.

For a three-week summer break, the members take part in a ceremony involving the burning of an effigy named 'Dull Care'. Dressed as priests, torch-bearers and woodland nymphs, they plead with a 40 ft owl god: 'Oh, thou great soul of all mortal wisdom, owl of Bohemia, we do beseech thee, grant us thy counsel.' The giant bird tells them to light the effigy with a flame from the lamp of fellowship, the Bohemians become brothers, and the partying begins.

Bechtel Great Britain employs 1700 people and is building the overland pipeline from St Fergus to the petrochemicals plant at Mossmorran. It is also working for the National Nuclear Corporation on the proposed Pressurised Water Reactor at Sizewell.

Mrs Thatcher quite reasonably extolled yesterday British skill and enterprise in reaping the riches of the sea as she opened the Magnus oilfield. But on the same day we reported that her Government was actively considering dumping 'high-level' (strongly radioactive) nuclear waste in the Atlantic. Conceding that dumping was indeed being looked at (in contrast with its total denial a week earlier), the Department of the Environment insisted that the Government was limiting itself to a feasibility study. But serious consideration of a plan which would bend if not break international law argues a special degree of desperation. (Editorial)

The United States and the Soviet Union yesterday re-launched the propaganda war over nuclear missiles in Europe. President Reagan, in a letter to the Italian Prime Minister released yesterday, said he remained firmly committed to an agreement at the Geneva talks. While President Andropov's latest offer to scrap all but 162 of the SS-20s — the numerical equivalent of the British and French arsenals — contained some positive elements, it showed that Moscow still did not recognise the need for equality between the United States and the Soviet Union, and was not a serious alternative, Mr. Reagan wrote.

Protestors yesterday occupied a nuclear bunker site at Leominster, Herefordshire, to demonstrate against the proposed closure of the town's Priory Hospital. The bunker is being built at a cost of £70,000 for the chief executive and senior officers of Leominster district council.

As Defense Secretary in the Kennedy Administration, Mr

12

McNamara recalled that several nuclear bombs had fallen off the B–52 bomber which crashed in the North Carolina countryside on January 23, 1961. One of the bombs contained a 'permissive action' power system, which came close to detonating. As a result of the crash, five out of the six electronic arming devices contained in the bomb were triggered. The US was just one trigger away from the first accidental nuclear detonation.

The 'fast for life' by 13 people since August 6th in support of nuclear arms freeze is to end today after 40 days. The fasters in Bonn, Paris, and Oakland, California, who took only water and have become dangerously weak, say the action 'has done some good'.

At the outbreak of the Six-Day War in 1967, when he was serving in the Johnson Administration, he received an early morning phone call from the Pentagon's duty officer, who said that the Soviet premier, Mr Kosygin, was on the 'hot-line' and wanted to talk to the President. The message caught Mr McNamara by surprise since he had been in charge of the Pentagon for six years and had never until that moment realised that the hot-line operated through the Defense Department and not the White House. He says he had 'quite a shock' over the difficulty of getting a message to the President.

'Another of those English occasions,' muttered someone as the rain began not long after the start of the 24-hour vigil and readings at which writers and publishers and others in the bookish business raised their voices against the nuclear arms race on the steps of St Martin's-in-the-Fields last week. Well, it was and it wasn't. While I've reported admired political stands taken by Polish or Czech or German writers over the years, I've never seen anything like such a turn-out in a contentious cause by British writers, a breed notorious throughout Europe for so carefully keeping a political low-risk profile.

Naturally there were old CND hands like Adrian Mitchell and Mervyn Jones and other familiar faces from the Left. Dorothy and Edward Thompson shared the midnight watch, and Raymond Williams was there to draw the moral from a violent attack on Sheila Rowbotham by some dossers who weren't interested in nuclear threat while they had nowhere to sleep.

But those who took part, especially in the night watches, say it felt like the beginning of something new in England. We shall hear more from this growing BAND, as they call themselves (Book Action for Nuclear Disarmament). (Reviews page)

NATO plans for the defence of Europe are no longer credible. They ceased being credible when the Soviets achieved nuclear parity with the West. The use of any nuclear weapons by NATO would almost certainly set in motion a chain of events leading to the nuclear destruction of most European cities and the death of most of its people. A nuclear war in Europe would be so catastrophic that no sane leader would deliberately start one. In spite of this, NATO strategy still requires that any attack by Warsaw Pact forces which succeeded in penetrating a significant distance into Western Germany would be countered with nuclear weapons.

The NATO use of nuclear weapons requires, we are told, the permission of the US President. But most commentators believe that the Presidential release of nuclear weapons would take at least 24 hours. The implication is that authority to use battlefield nuclear weapons would have to be given days before a war in Europe began. And given to relatively junior officers at that.

The current US Army Field Manual, F 100–5, clearly envisages the use of battlefield nuclear weapons against 'committed enemy units, reserves, lead elements of second echelon forces, enemy nuclear systems, field artillery, air defense artillery, selected command and control elements, and support forces rearward of the committed elements.'

The manual goes on to say that these weapons would be used in 'packages'; a typical one consisting of two atomic demolition (land) mines (ADMs), 30 rounds of nuclear artillery, 10 surface-to-surface missiles, and five air-delivered bombs. This package of 47 nuclear explosions would, the manual explains, be authorised for use 'in a specified area, within a limited timeframe, to support a tactical contingency.' ('Futures' page)

Federal Europe Likely to Remain just a Vision (headline)

Victim of Berserk Killer Named (headline)

Angry US Left to Pick Up Pieces (headline)

Americans Stay Home (headline)

Could You Save the World before Lunchtime? (advert)

The most disturbing aspect of *Make-Believe* is that Ronnie not only is still the President but could probably be re-elected. Almost as an afterthought, Mr Leamer suddenly reveals, in the last pages of his book, the true Reagan problem which is now a world problem:

What was so extraordinary was Ronnie's apparent psychic

distance from the burden of the presidency. He sat in cabinet meetings doodling. Unless held to a rigid agenda, he would start telling Hollywood stories or talk about football in Dixon. Often in one-on-one conversations Ronnie seemed distracted or with-drawn. 'He has a habit now,' his brother Neil said. 'You might be talking to him, and it's like he's picking his fingernails, but he's not. And you know then that he's talking to himself.'

'If people knew about him living in his own reality, they wouldn't believe it,' said one White House aide. 'There are only ten to fifteen people who know the extent, and until they leave and begin talking, no one will believe it.' (Reviews page)

As the renowned editor of that extraordinary Viennese periodical, *Die Fackel*, once remarked, a year or so before World War One: 'Anyone who could read a morning news-paper, and fully grasp the significance of its content, would go mad.' I appropriate Karl Kraus's remark, because at the moment it is true.

B. S.

Criticism

T. E. Worden: *Critical Paranoia*
reviewed by Frank Maxwall

I once read 50,000 titles in one year. Not books, just the titles.
I was a reviews editor and my job involved a meticulous
monthly scanning of the *Bookseller*, in a frequently futile
attempt to spot forthcoming books the journal should review.
One year of it was quite enough.

Professor Worden's book was perhaps conceived in the
grind of a similar task. His introductory chapter is shaped
round a quotation from William Godwin, writing in 1831 but
looking back to his childhood, when he was apparently prone
to ask himself, in terror and anxiety: 'When I have read
through all the books that have been written, what shall I do
afterwards?' Professor Worden reminds us that in the 1830s
fewer than 2000 new books were published annually in Great
Britain. Godwin could therefore have kept himself permanently amused by restricting his reading to a mere five a day.
By 1900, however, he would have needed to average twenty-
five a day to fulfil his primary ambition. Even if he only relaxed
with three-deckers three times daily it would have taken him
some thirty-six years to consume the 40,000 (or so) works of
fiction published during Her Imperial Majesty's reign. Such
calculations are catching. I have just idled away five minutes by
estimating that the truly conscientious Shakespeare scholar
would need to read a new doctoral dissertation every week for
seventeen years simply to match the manic productivity of
American doctoral candidates during the years 1966 to 1983,
who between them actually managed to start (or finish) a fresh

Shakespeare thesis every week. A certain problem of logistics looms however: surely doctoral candidates are by definition, or regulation, themselves conscientious, so how did any of them ever find enough time free from reading all the others' to write their own? One rather pities the graduate who began work in the dying days of 1983: it would be circa 2000 AD before he or she could put pen to paper.

The first main chapter of *Critical Paranoia* is indeed entitled 'Research Paranoia', but it rather gently skirts the pincer-like directives governing that specific breed of harassed thesis-writers, who are still solemnly assured both that they should have read 'all the relevant material' and that the result should be their 'own work'. Professor Worden's concern is more general, or more personal. He instances his own efforts to write a book on Joyce. Yes, Joyce! He sensibly abandoned it. But only after he had devoted presumably precious research time to concocting a 'computer-aided guesstimate' (Professor Worden is himself, it would seem, the product of an American Graduate School), adding together Joyce's own 'life-time reading-time' and the ditto of Joyce's major critics and commentators, 'allowing for the multiplier-effect of location within the differential generational levels of a dominant commentary-tradition'. Deciphering this quaint idiom, I conclude that he tried to calculate how long it took Joyce to read all the books he read, how long it took the first 'generation' of Joyce critics to read all the books they read, in preparation for their commentaries, then the second (who would have to read the first), and so on. The result, I confess, was of less interest to me (the phrase 'one page-time to the power of eight' merely bemused me) than the stringently suspicious attitude behind the inquiry. I already agree with Professor Worden's saddened conclusion that there is too much Joyce scholarship for any sane man to read — but the sane conclusion is that any sane man simply doesn't, however much he has to take on trust.

Oddly, however, Professor Worden's complaint seems to be that there was too *little* Joyce scholarship available for him to read. I detect traces of some long-unforgotten and unforgiven institutional injury behind his specification of this lament:

that the library resources, research grants and faculty travelling expenses were 'wholly inadequate' to enable him to gain access to all the 'relevant material'. I deeply sympathise. My own polytechnic can afford a book-purchasing expenditure of only £5 per annum per student, and I too — if I desired them — would have to pay for the 63-volume *Joyce Archives* out of my own meagre pocket (at $6000 a set this is not a bargain I contemplate).

I also respond, perhaps less merely masochistically, to the Professor's next reason ('excuse' would be over-harsh) for abandoning his Joyce book: that the published texts are unreliable. I well remember, as an eager first-year, stumbling across an awesomely eminent Joyce critic on the steps of the Martello Tower; I blushingly acknowledged that, yes, I was just setting my first tentative foot on the North Face of *Finnegans Wake*: 'Take Care,' said he, 'there are at least 700 misprints in the current Random printing.' I humbly confess to not having discovered a single one to this day. But his lofty remark (securely roped as he was to the Manuscripts) rather spoilt my relish even for a harmlessly pleasing sentence in *Araby*: 'I felt the house in bad humour and walked slowly towards the school' (current Penguin printing) — perhaps it wasn't, after all, a gentle Joycean joke but just a genuine misprint. Professor Worden's own mean-minded contribution to spoiling my enjoyment of Joyce is to inform me that my favourite copy of *Ulysses* contains some 4000 misprints. After such knowledge, it is difficult to forgive him for quoting a phrase from *Ulysses* as the epigraph to this very chapter:

Reading two pages apiece of seven books every night, eh?

Am I *meant* to detect some minute misprint, or am I to be allowed to relax into the rhythmically reverent alliterative echoes of proverbial wisdom?

If there truly is some tiny departure from the best manuscripts here, I can reassure Professor Worden that it escapes me. Apparently he needs such reassurance, since he sums up his chapter with what is surely a *sotto voce* appeal for clemency:

The inescapable professional dilemma of the academic researcher arises from the inexorable requirement of productivity combined with the advance recognition of inevitable vulnerability. The paranoid reaction to one's own publication is that, always, somebody out there knows more than I do, and knew it before I did, and that precisely that somebody will be — my reviewer.

Well, he doesn't, Professor Worden.

The second chapter also sports an epigraph from *Ulysses*, the second sentence of 'Proteus':

Signatures of all things I am here to read, seaspawn and seawrack, the nearing tide, that rusty boot.

The chapter is entitled 'Significance Paranoia'. (I would myself have preferred 'That Rusty Boot' — but that is *not* a criticism, Professor Worden.) The aspect of paranoia prominent here is not the projection of hostility but the super-sensitive response to every casual gesture as indicative of vast conspiracies: the paranoid sees significance in *everything*. So does the modern literary critic, according to Professor Worden. Or more strictly perhaps, the post-Modernist (literary) critic. The coincidence of the professionalisation of academic criticism with the highpoint of Modernism reinforced the notion (endemic to criticism) that texts *need* 'interpretation', down to the last comma, faced with the saturated, polymathic, polysemic, encyclopaedic productions of Joyce, Pound, Eliot, Jones, McDiarmid, Zukovsky and so on, the ordinary easy-going reader had to be transfigured into Super-Reader, knowing that whatever didn't make sense really did and whatever did made more of it than you thought. Watsons were re-trained as Holmeses. Professor Worden is less concerned with the aetiology of this creature than with its current habits and habitat. He tracks the beast first to Paris, offering his own analysis of the shared significance of Lacan's analysis of Poe's *The Purloined Letter* (including the comma — one notes, incidentally, that Lacan's doctoral dissertation was on: para-noia), Barthes's *S/Z* (including that slash), and Derrida's pinpointing of '*hama*' in Aristotle's *Physics* (including the rough breathing). It is not only the microscopic textual focusing he underlines but also the initial selection of 'insig-nificant' texts and insignificant moments within those texts —

most gloriously exemplified in Derrida's disquisition upon Nietzsche's marginal memorandum: 'I have forgotten my umbrella.'

It is this second facet that he sees as significantly similar to an ostensibly traditional tendency: the ever-accelerating resuscitation of minor, marginal and forgotten authors as PhDs dig deeper into the *DNB* for untouched topics, the maniacal meticulousness of dedicated editorial teams aiming asymptotically for the definitive collected works of everybody (where else did Nietzsche's memo come from?), the proliferation of 'critical editions' with a page of apparatus per line of poem (he reproduces an extract from the *Dunciad* at this point). With a certain maliciousness he assimilates these highly respectable endeavours to the fashionably disreputable manoeuvres of those who read texts 'symptomatically' to disclose precisely what is 'absent' from them, since the root of both procedures he finally locates neither in professionalism nor in post-post-Modernism but in Freud's education of an epoch into seeing even the slip of a pen as requiring and rewarding an entire lovume of commentary.

A brief chapter on 'Epistemological Paranoia' is less successful, less amusing, less sure perhaps of its target. It covers the recent ripples of exultant or despairing scepticism, the 'eclipses' and 'destructions' of reason, the essays 'against' method and 'against' epistemology itself, the deconstructionists and the dadaists. It is not that he is himself sceptical about this scepticism; rather, he argues that since any search for systematic and rigorous knowledge is itself a paranoid ambition, an attempt to connect everything that must finally be delusional, correspondingly the repudiation of system in favour of fragment, of rigid grid for rhetorical gesture, betokens a paranoiac self-defence, an attempt to destroy what is still believed in as threatening. He is mildly more persuasive, I think, when he pinpoints this particular ambivalence in the familiar practice of researchers: the endlessly evasive methodological preliminaries, the continually procrastinated prologemena to a contribution towards a possible model of tentatively partial 'beginnings'. The exact obverse of this supercautious hesitation is, presumably, the gratuitous option of starting one's analysis just anywhere at all: a comma, a fragment, a footnote, a margin, a full stop.

Paradigms

It is in the light of this triple paranoia that Professor Worden next moves to a rather over-caustic examination of what he seizes upon as 'popular paradigms' in recent academic criticism. He surveys marxism, structuralism, psychoanalysis, deconstruction etc., and then asks what they have in common. His basic, even brutal, answer is that an allegiance to any of these currents at least mitigates that aspect of research paranoia to do with library resources. He argues, with some persuasive examples, that in much marxist criticism the chosen text has been 'related' only to a 'history' composed of little more than half-a-dozen references to an approved group of modern marxist historians (he should, of course, have acknowledged the genuine exceptions), while the plethora of Barthesian, Lacanian and Derridean 'readings' he characterises as 'solving' the problem of 'originality' by merely finding a text that no-one else has yet got around to treating in that particular mode. Again, his point (he claims) is not to criticise the quality or to query the validity of such work, but to emphasise — as a form of explanation — its convenient material preconditions: that such work can be done upon the basis of very restricted resources. Few individuals, or even libaries, have large quantities of, say, sixteenth-century song-books, seventeenth-century pamphlets, eighteenth-century periodicals or nineteenth-century popular fiction — the prerequisites of an older fashion for historical criticism — but even a poor polytechnic's grant allows the purchase of the latest theoretical paradigm-texts. One can fruitfully work from one's own desk copies of *Gawain* and, say, Kristeva (any slur upon an existing Kristevan critique of the Green Knight is, one hopes, unintended), just as — within a previous paradigm — all one really needed were the words upon the page and a dog-eared *Revaluation*. The obverse of this development has, however, been a further intensification of 'significance paranoia': *every* word, or comma, upon the page must yield its maximum contribution, to maintain continuous production. (It is an

intriguing implication of this argument that those disgruntled
conservatives who castigate the current vogues should campaign vigorously for an urgent increase in government grants
to college libraries.)

With mild and perhaps forgiveable irony, Professor Worden
concludes this section of his book with a detailed summary of
some recent Joyce criticism founded upon and exemplifying
the notion that the (concept) 'author' is dead — and then
deploys the 63 volumes of the *Joyce Archive* (his salary is
obviously larger than mine) to trace the minutely deliberated
construction by Joyce, in notes, drafts, revisions, amend-
ments, proof-corrections, of every quotation employed in an
influential book premissed upon the dissociation of any
'reading' of Joyce-texts from Joyce's intentions in writing. His
predictable motto for this exercise is Joyce's own remark.

I've put in so many enigmas and puzzles that it will keep the
professors busy for centuries arguing over what I meant.

Yet despite the relish of Professor Worden's critique, one may
still remind him that arguing over 'what *I* meant' is precisely
not what many critics now do. Nor do I see any *a priori*
necessity why they should. Indeed, in his final section the
Professor himself endorses quite other priorities.

Clinical Paranoia

First, however, he steps back from his engagement with recent
critical practices and devotes a long chapter to an examination
of the term he has thus far rather loosely employed: 'paranoia'.
As he recognises, one might be tempted to categorise many of
the phenomena he has listed under the term 'obsessional
neurosis' rather than 'paranoia'. Professor Worden's reply is
twofold: that though individual critics may be justly described
as obsessional neurotics, the 'discipline' of criticism is more
usefully thought of as 'paranoid in structure', and, secondly,
that a neurotic symptom may in any case be the 'nucleus' of a
psychosis. He quotes Freud's 1917 *Introductory Lectures*:

For a symptom of an 'actual' neurosis is often the nucleus and first
stage of a psychoneurotic symptom. A relation of this kind can be

most clearly observed between neurasthenia and the transference neurosis known as 'conversion hysteria', between anxiety neurosis and anxiety hysteria, but also between hypochondria and the forms of disorder which will be mentioned later under the name of paraphrenia (dementia praecox and paranoia).

On this basis, he feels free to utilise Freud's characterisation of obsessional neurosis in order to specify more exactly what he means by 'Critical Paranoia'. For example, he cites a number of passages from the 'Rat Man' case which he offers as paralleling aspects of 'epistemological paranoia':

Another mental need, which is ... shared by obsessional neurotics, ... is the need for *uncertainty* in their life, or for *doubt*.

Their essential characteristic is that they are incapable of coming to a decision ...; they endeavour to postpone every decision ....

In the various forms of obsessional neurosis in which the epistemophilic instinct plays a part, its relation to thought-processes makes it particularly well-adapted to attract the energy which is vainly endeavouring to make its way forward into action, and divert it into the sphere of thought, where there is a possibility of its obtaining pleasurable satisfaction of another sort. ... But procrastination in *action* is soon replaced by lingering over *thoughts* ... in other words, an obsessive or compulsive thought is one whose function it is to represent an act regressively.

Somewhat unkindly in my view, Professor Worden at this point quotes from Derrida (*Marges*, p. 207) on 'undecidability':

There is, then, probably no choice to be made between two lines of thought; our task is rather to reflect on the circularity which makes the one pass into the other indefinitely.

But, as he also explicitly acknowledges, a desire for action (as in Derrida's case) remains at the root of obsessional displacement, and to retain that desire — however unconsciously inhibited or externally blocked — may be preferable to inert acquiescence in inaction. In a very early note (*Draft N* of *Project for a Scientific Psychology*, 1897), Freud had recognised one feature of paranoia as 'pathological distrust of rulers and monarchs', but distrust of rulers may not be pathological.

Freud's later admission that paranoid jealousy may even disclose a certain truth perhaps has its political counterpart:

These attacks [of paranoid jealousy] drew their material from his observation of minute indications, by which his wife's quite unconscious coquetry, unnoticeable to any one else, had betrayed itself to him. ... He was extraordinarily observant of all these manifestations of her unconscious, and always knew how to interpret them correctly, so that he really was in the right about it. ... His abnormality really reduced itself to this, that he watched his wife's unconscious mind much more closely and then regarded it as far more important than anyone else would have thought of doing.

Professor Worden offers in fact his own variation of this suggestion, noting that even Schreber's delusions of world catastrophe have a ring of truth in a nuclear age and that, as in Freud's analysis of Schreber, such a 'delusion ... which we take to be the pathological product, is in reality an attempt at recovery, a process of reconstruction' — or at least may in the case of 'correct' political 'paranoia' be a step *towards* sanity. But such considerations are a sidetrack from his main argument, where he has to confront a major difficulty.

If Professor Worden wants to maintain that the modern discipline of criticism is 'paranoid in structure', that the professional practitioners of criticism (whatever their personal psychic state of health) enter into an endemically paranoid discourse characterised by pro-crastination, obsessional displacement, delusions of persecution, megalomania, undecidability, intrinsic uncertainty, and even pathological jealousy (it's unclear how many of Freud's own sub-categories he would apply), then what is the aetiology of this curious discourse? For Freud, the origins of paranoia are always to be found in 'a secondary narcissism which is a return of the original infantile one' and which takes the form of a repressed libidinal attachment of a passive homosexual character, against which the paranoid is defending him- or herself. Yet though it might be amusing to speculate on the relevance of this insight to the biographies of individual critics, it is hardly intelligible that the character of a 'discipline' might be explained along such lines.

Foreclosure

Professor Worden's solution to this dilemma is to reject Freud's explanation and to rely instead upon Jacques Lacan. Commenting upon Mrs Macalpine's introductory analysis in her edition of Schreber's *Memoirs*, Lacan wrote (with his usual lucidity):

Her critique of the cliché that is confined in the factor of the repression of a homosexual drive, which, in fact, is quite unclear, to explain psychosis, is quite masterly, and she demonstrates this beautifully in the Schreber case itself. Homosexuality, supposedly a determinant of paranoiac psychosis, is really a symptom articulated in its process.

But Lacan is then under an obligation to offer an alternative aetiology of this 'process'. He does so by proposing a general distinction between neurosis and psychosis. Neurosis arises from 'repression' but psychosis from 'repudiation' — respectively *Verdrängung* and *Verwerfung* in Freud's German; the latter term is *'forclusion'* in Lacan's French and can also be translated 'foreclosure'. Professor Worden quotes from a disciple of Lacan to clarify the distinction:

If we imagine experience to be a piece of material made up of criss-crossing threads, we could say that repression would figure in it as a rent or tear which can still be repaired, whereas foreclosure would figure in it as a *béance* [abyss, gap, nothing] due to the weaving itself, in short a primal hole which will never again be able to find its substance, since it has never been anything other than the substance of a hole and can only be filled, and even then imperfectly, by a patch.

Professor Worden tries to elucidate this obscure distinction further, by pursuing the intricacies of Lacan's theory of psychosis and his specifications of the differences between, for example, schizophrenia and delusional paranoia.

I found the details of this exploration both difficult and unnecessary, for the same basic reason: since I am neither analyst nor analysand, I would myself have no assured basis upon which to assess the validity of Lacan's argument. In any case,

Professor Worden is trying to illuminate the character of literary criticism and I have to judge *that* attempt according to whether the analytic distinctions he finally develops, whatever their validity elsewhere, do coherently clarify the state of criticism for me. So I decline to follow him into the less-than-fascinating entrails of *Écrits*. I will, however, single out three further passages he cites, since they provide some of the terms of his later discussion. One is from *The Language of Psychoanalysis* by Laplanche and Pontalis, stating that 'foreclosure'

consists in a primordial expulsion of a fundamental signifier (e.g. the phallus as signifier of the castration complex) from the subject's Symbolic universe. Foreclosure is deemed to be distinct from repression in two senses:

a. Foreclosed signifiers are not integrated into the subject's unconscious;
b. They do not return 'from the inside'; they re-emerge, rather, in 'the Real', particularly through the phenomenon of hallucination.

The other two passages are both from Freud himself, where the concept of foreclosure/repudiation seems to be at work, without the explicit terminology:

There is, however, a much more energetic and successful kind of defence. Here, the ego rejects [*verwirft*] the incompatible idea with its affect and behaves as if the idea had never occurred to the ego at all.

It was incorrect to say that the perception which was suppressed internally is projected outwards; the truth is rather, as we now see, that what was abolished internally returns from without.

The argument returns to literary criticism with a summary of the conclusion of a recent introductory text-book on literary theory. The gist of this is that the adoption of various theoretical approaches to 'literature' has served to dissolve the very notion of 'literature' itself, since those same approaches apply as readily to the *Daily Mirror* as to *Paradise Lost*, and this cuts both ways, denying simultaneously the specific character of any 'literary' object and of any 'literary' method. Therefore:

27

If literary theory presses its own implications too far, then it has argued itself out of existence. ... The final logical move in a process which began by recognising that literature is an illusion is to recognise that literary theory is an illusion too. It is not of course an illusion in the sense that I have invented the various people I have discussed in this book. Northrop Frye really does exist and so did F.R. Leavis.

At this point Professor Worden pounces. Once again he summons up a vivid, even moving, picture of what seems to be his favourite habitat: a library. He invites us to consider those massed stacks of packed shelves in the 'Literature' section, all those works by Joyce and his generations of critics. Are *these* an 'illusion', he asks? They very palpably exist, they surround the weighed-down scholar scratching away in his notebook, they confront him as a material reality, a category of concrete knowledge, a professional challenge and an exemplum. (The professor's style modulates into a pained rhetoric I mitigate.) But what if that scholar has 'repudiated' the very notion of 'literature'? What if the poor researcher never really had a concept of 'literature' in the first place? What if 'literature' were, in short, 'a primal hole which will never again be able to find its substance, since it has never been anything other than the substance of a hole'? One response might be to 'reject' *this* 'incompatible idea with its affect' and to behave 'as if the idea had never occurred ... at all.' But even then, perhaps, 'what was abolished internally returns from without' — in those stacks of 'literature' but also in one's professional identity, qualifications, career, prospects, institutional post — and pub-lications, soon to swell those very stacks.

There seem to be two varieties of this dilemma. The more 'radical' critics are in the most paradoxical position, since 'literature' for them really is acknowledged as a '*béance* due to the weaving itself', despite their daily confrontation with its concrete illusion. But others, and among them the most traditional, seem often to have repudiated 'literature' by other means: in seeking to encompass literature within modes of 'knowledge' that are deliberately constructed as distinct in kind from the object of that 'knowledge', they implicitly refuse the notion they proclaim, that literature might be itself

a mode of 'knowledge'; in endlessly producing non-'literature'
themselves they pay homage to a distinction of status which
their very act of supplementation subverts; in writing criticism rather than poems they repudiate the priorities they
uphold while implying that the poets should really have
provided the necessary criticism in place of the dependent
poems; in asserting their own necessity they remove the
rationale for their very existence.

Now, speaking personally, I quite enjoyed the passion of
Professor Worden's attack in this section, which I have humbly tried to reproduce, in a somewhat briefer compass. Perhaps
there is even a faint touch of paranoia in his own (self-)
hostility, but I agree that the dilemma he gestures at can
indeed be real: one's attachment to literature can at times seem
asymptotically structured, a repeated search for that which is
always elsewhere than the actual object of one's probing
critical attention, a daily discrimination against a norm which
itself dissolves under that discrimination. Yet I take a certain
comfort from two comments, one of which I have shamelessly
cribbed from Professor Worden himself — his earlier quotation from Derrida:

There is, then, probably no choice to be made between two lines of
thought; our task is rather to reflect on the circularity which makes
the one pass into the other indefinitely.

The other is from a *Guardian* review by Raymond Williams of
Anna Karenina and other essays by that same F. R. Leavis who
was no illusion:

I have indeed found myself thinking of Leavis's critical work as a kind
of novel, in which the main events are certain novels and plays, and
most of the characters are from fiction and drama . . . but in which the
central consciousness and the central attention is on what he calls in
this book 'the lived question': an exploration, a dramatisation, an
inward finding and realisation of values through this composed and
apparently objective medium.

Oddly, Professor Worden might endorse at least the spirit
of Williams' remarks, since he clearly wants to salvage a notion

of 'literature' as precisely a distinctive mode, not of 'knowledge', but of attention, even of realisation of values. The pressure for this salvage operation seems to come from two sources, or considerations. First, and perhaps unconsciously, he clearly doesn't really *want* to read all that Joyce criticism, nor add more of the same: his own procrastination (computer-aided guesstimates indeed!) and his rapid abandonment of the book proclaim it. Second, he nevertheless respects, enjoys and admires Joyce's work. That some criticism might increase or modify such respect and enjoyment he probably wouldn't deny. So how does he himself escape the paranoid trajectory of 'criticism'? One option would be silence. Another, to become Samuel Beckett — and it is surely significant that his epigraph for this section comes from Beckett's *The Unnamable*:

What have you done with your material? We have left it behind. But commanded to say whether yes or no they filled up the holes, have you filled up the holes yes or no, they will say yes and no, or some yes, others no, at the same time, not knowing what answer the master wants, to his question. But both are defendable.

But the third option, it seems, is to repudiate the notion of literature as a mode of knowledge or even as an object of knowledge, thus rejecting the paranoid urge after knowledge —while retaining a notion of literature as a mode of persuasion and as a means of persuasion.

Triangles and Lines

In the final section of his book Professor Worden elaborates this distinction in terms of an opposition between what he calls 'the critical line' and 'the critical triangle'. The critical triangle is the basic shape of much academic criticism, and it takes two forms. In the first, the triangle is formed between author, text and reader, with the critic standing 'outside' the triangle. The critic's job from this position is to explicate or explain the text to the reader and to evaluate it for the reader and sometimes for the author too. If he evaluates it for the author (legislative criticism, reviewing) the critic 'knows' more than the author; if for the reader, then more than the reader. If the critic explicates the text for the reader (elucidates its obscurities) then the critic and probably the author know more than the reader (the critic may appeal here to his knowledge of the author's knowledge). If the critic explains the text (by relating it to its generic tradition, historical context, etc.) the critic knows more than the reader and perhaps more than the author. In each case the relations are those of degrees of knowledge, though the contents of that knowledge will vary. In the second form of academic criticism, the triangle is composed between the text and two readers, and the critic is within the triangle as one (or both) of the readers. Here the essential task, shared by both readers, is to 'know' the text more completely (again, the contents of that knowledge will vary), which may involve various detours into the first kind of critical triangle. There have been different attempts to modify these modes of academic criticism, by substituting or redefining the terms: for example, in contestations over the canon of texts, or the concept of author, or the objects of knowledge. Professor Worden, while responsive to many of these efforts, sees them as basically retaining the triangular shape.

By contrast, his notion of a 'critical line' offers a linear model in which the critic stands in a line with a reader, beyond both of whom the line extends to an *issue*. The task of the critic is to persuade the reader to take an attitude, a direction, towards that issue. But that is also, for Professor Worden, the essential task of a 'literary' text, and also of its author. The text is a means of persuading a reader to take an attitude towards an issue. Author, text and critic (and reader) may be in agreement concerning the issue and the attitude, or they may not. The critic may use the text, or parts of it, to persuade the reader, perhaps using knowledge about the author, or the author's attitude, to reinforce that persuasion; the attitude of the author or of the text may be contrary to the critic's, but that may itself be used to persuade the reader to take up an attitude against the text's on the issue in question. But always for Professor Worden what is at stake as the final object of attention in criticism is not the text or the author but, first, an issue (whether one 'acknowledged' by the text or not) and, secondly, an interlocutor, another reader. In that sense, the text is potentially redundant, as indeed are the roles of author, critic and reader: if two people agree about an issue they have no need to discuss 'literature' in relation to that issue. It is perhaps because people often do not agree, about either what is to count as an issue or what attitude to take, that we have found a need for a mode of writing which offers not knowledge but a means of persuasion, and why some modes of writing which did once offer knowledge now survive as literature.

I have tried to be fair to this account, though necessarily simplifying it, and I agree with Professor Worden to this extent, that his notion of a 'critical line' does indeed reflect the way in which we frequently 'use' literature, whether in convenient quotations, urgent recommendations, or dramatic adaptations; moreover, the majority of 'literary texts' may well have been written for purposes of persuasion: to celebrate a victory, support a monarch, seduce a beloved, ridicule an enemy, instil an ideology. But it nevertheless mildly amazes me that, after the recent flurries of impressive theoretical paradigms, a modern Professor of English at a modern university should explicitly propose as the task of criticism what is really a variation upon a long-discredited 'moralism'. Personally, I partly applaud, especially since I suspect most subsequently fashionable modes of in fact operating as disguised moralisms. But I do have one absolute reservation. That great exemplar of a defiantly moralist criticism, Dr Leavis, did indeed want to 'use' (though neither he nor I would endorse that verb) literature to persuade his readers, and pupils, to take up an attitude, and he believed that serious literature shared that aim — but, quite crucially, it was an attitude towards *life* not towards 'issues'. That seems to me a wholly necessary distinction, and one that — if I may so put it — the authorities at Professor Worden's university should bear carefully in mind.

In sum, then, I sympathise to a considerable extent with the dilemma explored and the proposal offered in *Critical Paranoia*, though I remain unconvinced by the precise analysis of that dilemma and I would firmly dissociate myself from some implications of the proposal. Yet in the light of the book's own argument a final question remains. One rather wonders why Professor Worden wrote it, rather than telling us what issue should concern us in reading *Finnegans Wake.*

Frank Maxwall

John Joseph Andrews: *Literary Conversions: studies in the religious ideologic of literature*
reviewed by Lawrence Fielding

Dr Andrews has written an intriguing rather than wholly convincing work, though by the logic of his own curious argument this unsatisfactory result should perhaps count as success more than as failure. His theme is conversion but for him conversion is a suspect process, to be analysed with a wary scepticism. His own work correspondingly appears not quite to wish to convert its reader to Dr Andrews' own way of thinking. This reader at least can report its considerable success in that respect.

There are four main chapters, each with an appendage of fairly brief excurses, somewhat in the manner of the once influential but now neglected *Revaluation* of Dr F. R. Leavis. The main body of each chapter offers a diligently, even tediously, 'close' reading of a single text, while each excursus outlines a more general but associated thesis, whether historical, psychoanalytical or literary-critical.

The overall aim is to examine ways in which certain literary texts are so structured as to entice or trap their readers into a change of mind, a reformation of view, a 'conversion', and Dr Andrews presents these essays as contributions to a larger, twofold inquiry; into what he calls the 'ideo-logic' of literary texts and into the 'transposition' of certain social practices into 'textual strategies'. Though I found some of the individual analyses worth serious consideration, these larger ambitions strike me as extremely dubious. Since, however, they also seem to me very secondary to the substance of the book, I will in fact forgo any treatment of them here.

The first essay — which I will consider in some detail — worries away at a short poem by George Herbert that I have always regarded as pleasing and harmless; it is entitled 'Prayer (I)' in Hutchinson's sadly superseded edition:

Prayer the Churches banquet, Angels age,
  Gods breath in man returning to his birth,
  The soul in paraphrase, heart in pilgrimage,
The Christian plummet sounding heav'n and earth;
Engine against th'Almightie, sinners towre,
  Reversèd thunder, Christ-side-piercing spear,
  The six-daies world transposing in an houre,
A kinde of tune, which all things heare and fear;
Softnesse, and peace, and joy, and love, and blisse,
  Exalted Manna, gladnesse of the best,
  Heaven in ordinarie, man well drest,
The milkie way, the bird of Paradise,
  Church-bels beyond the starres heard, the souls bloud,
  The land of spices; something understood.

For Dr Andrews there lurks in that last phrase, 'something understood', a deep and devious device, the import of which is that the poem itself is something *not* understood. Not at first glance, mind; it is only after devoted critical attention that the poem ceases to be understood. (A sad paradigm perhaps of fashionable critical practices?) As Dr Andrews takes us through the poem in detail (twice), those apparently lucid analogues dissolve into grammatical ambiguities (line 2: 'his' birth as man's or as 'its'?), directional uncertainties (line 4: do plummets go down or up?), and metaphysical conundra (line 1: how old are angels?). Even more drastically, prayer becomes a kind of blasphemy (a siege-engine assaulting God, a new Babel, a Jovian thunderbolt hurled back to heaven, a jab into the dead Saviour's side) — though some of these disrespectful suggestions can be theologically redeemed by appropriate exegetical effort (the spear in John XIX releases sacramental succour in eucharistic blood and baptismal water) or by appeal to seventeenth-century emblem books (where prayers are already arrows shot into the very eye of God). Other lines are revealed as quivering with multiple associations ('Heaven in ordinarie' yields at least five distinct senses), or as too bafflingly simple to delineate any properly illuminating 'definition' of prayer (line 9 suffers from this); while still others defeat our best attempts at clarity (line 7) or at appropriate interpretation (the phrase 'and fear' in line 8 proves intractable). Penultimately, we are taken into a mysteriously impermeable, even mystical, region of meaning as we try to attach some specific sense to prayer 'as' the milky way, bird of paradise or land of spices; even with the footnoted help of seventeenth-century astronomers, ornithologists and cartographers, Dr Andrews confesses, gladly, to a definite impenetrability in these closing images — which he then claims as reinforcing his insistence that the closing phrase 'something understood' is an even more bafflingly opaque conclusion.

His point is, perversely, that in attempting to 'understand' these preceding images the reader is brought to an awareness of the weirdness, the slippery difficulty, the peculiar oddness of that very process we call 'understanding': are we *sure* that we have 'understood' even one of these phrases fully, adequately, appropriately? Even more, do we know (and if so *how* do we know?) that we have 'understood' what is constituted by this total combination of compact images? At the end of our analysis do we any better 'understand' what 'prayer' *is*? At this point Dr Andrews' analytical screw tightens: to understand the poem fully we would finally have to understand the final phrase 'something understood' and to do that we would have to understand what understanding is. And, as Dr Andrews legitimately, but a shade maliciously, reminds us in an extended footnote to this chapter, *that* task preoccupied and, arguably, defeated seventeenth-century philosophers from Descartes — whose *Discourse on Method* was published only four years after Herbert's *Temple* — to Locke, whose *Essay on Human Understanding* closed the century on a note of common sense and therefore uncertain optimism.

So far, I find this critical exercise rather enchanting, though to some extent derivative, but Dr Andrews then takes a sharp step further, into the more rarified air of linguistic (or is it logical?) philosophy and offers us an exhausting analysis of the logical (or is it linguistic?) paradoxes of the term 'under-

36

standing'. I can only grope after him here, but he seems to conclude, first, that since *complete* understanding of anything involves understanding *everything*, only God (if s/he exists) could claim that 'something' was, for her/him, 'understood', so only God could be said truly to pray (an odd but also biblical conclusion: consider Romans VIII: 26); and secondly, or conversely, that if prayer *is* 'something understood' then to understand this poem would be to pray it, to read it 'as' a prayer. In my admittedly amateur response to this logico-linguistic disquisition, I must confess to thinking that Dr Andrews has actually *mis*understood his own conclusion here, as well as playing some rather shifty games with the word 'something' (which one can, in fact, understand quite well in the seventeenth-century sense of 'partial'). Albeit, he concludes that the serious reader of this poem is finally faced with a dilemma (he calls it a 'double-bind', utilising a term from Gregory Bateson): either the reader tries to understand the poem as a *definition* of prayer, but this involves the impossible or paradoxical task of understanding understanding and therefore the reader can never understand what prayer is, even though the poem ostensibly sets out to tell us what prayer is; or, the reader *gives up* trying to understand the poem and therefore, if he continues trying to read the poem at all, opts for trying to read it *'as' a prayer* — even though he has by now acknowledged that he doesn't understand what prayer is, in other words doesn't understand what it is he's attempting to do in 'praying'.

It is here that Dr Andrews finally locates, and pounces upon, what he calls the 'conversion tactic' of the poem. He sees the reader of the poem as having been brought to the point of jettisoning his 'understanding' in favour of a 'belief' (a belief which takes the form, however provisional, of attempting to 'pray'), and that 'belief' is, fundamentally, an acquiescence to an *authority*, the authority of the poem itself. By that he means — to put it over-concisely perhaps — that the title changes its significance for the reader: we took it to indicate that the poem offered a definition of prayer, now we accept it as indicating that this poem *is* itself a prayer; if we accept the title in that latter sense all we can do with the poem is attempt to pray it, not even understanding what it is we are doing but, to pun mildly, simply accepting Herbert's word for it.

Of course, the trap doesn't quite close on us: we needn't read the poem at all, or we could (try to) read it 'simply as a poem'. Rather curiously for a literary critic, the stern Dr Andrews rejects this latter option as a weak-minded 'liberal' position, a gesture typical of twentieth-century indifferentism (he clearly has Dante's antechamber in mind). Instead he urges upon us the 'radical' response of demolishing the poem (he calls it, in a quaintly faded idiom, 'deconstructing'), by analysing the 'ideologic' underpinning the very possibility of prayer in order to conclude (predictably) that 'prayer' (both the poem and the act) *can't* finally be 'understood' at all, since its intelligibility rests upon the ultimately *unintelligible* premise of there being a God to pray (to) in the first place.

This rejection of the so-called 'liberal' literary critic's approach is far too off-hand, in my view, and I will return to it, but at least this first chapter has effected part of its aim: I now admit that Herbert's poem does have a twist in its tail that I hadn't previously been fully alert to, though it may gladden Dr Andrews' rather cold heart to know that I don't fully understand that twist even now. Looking back at the poem again, for example, I recognise that in all my previous readings that marvellous phrase 'Angels age' had been registered by me as an ambiguous paradox, with perhaps three possible meanings — but I am unable to decide which meaning I actually 'understand' *as* I read the poem. In practice, I leave all three hovering, if only because I know that I don't really understand the notion of 'angel', let alone the problem of how angels can have time in their lives — even if praying is, for them, having the time of their lives.

However, let us at this point digress briefly, as the book itself does, and look at the excurses to this chapter. The first is appealingly neat, but spurious. Illustrating further what he means by the 'authority' of a text, Dr Andrews instances the *Oxford English Dictionary* itself. He succinctly recounts its history (its 'ideological context and intended authoritarian function' as he sourly and characteristically puts it), and argues — if that is the word — for the 'unprecedented paeda-

gogical control' exercised over the living growth of the language by this 'exercise in sterilising and halting history' (his
particular *bête noire* here seems to be those teachers who
conscientiously correct spelling mistakes). *Au contraire*, I
would have thought: the *OED* has *given* us a history of word-
use we had no previous access to. His angry demolition of
T.S. Eliot's polemical appeal to the *OED*'s definition of
'definition' in the epigraph to *Notes Towards the Definition of
Culture* is to me merely an unconvincing exercise in adolescent
anti-authoritarianism. As for Dr Andrews' instancing of the
logical *mise-en-abîme* involved in the *OED*'s 'definition' of the
word 'as' as including the phrase 'as in', such unavoidable
hiccups, far from illustrating the 'vicious circularity of ideological closure', indicate no more than that Wittgenstein was
correct in defining meaning as use. It certainly needn't
undermine our use of such phrases as 'as a poem' as Dr
Andrews seems to think. After all, it is not the task of the
OED to teach its readers how to speak the English language in
the first place — it is written *for* such speakers — and an
awareness of how 'as' is used is necessary to competence in
speaking English, though resort to the *OED* might refine and
clarify our grasp of that use. One might, incidentally, apply
these remarks, *pari passu*, to the vocabulary and activity of
'praying'.

His other excurses are more interesting. The second traces
the history of 'interpretation' from biblical exegesis through
literary criticism to the contemporary hermeneutical debate in
theology, philosophy of science and post-Heideggerian philosophy and social theory, in order to clarify the difference
between reading 'Prayer' as a literary critic (concerned only
with textual interpretation) and as a potential convert (one
whose engagement with the text opens up a genuine challenge
to believe or reject belief). The first mode he sees as,
historically, a recent invention, that of the 'complacent and
uncommitted bourgeois spectator-consumer of an inert culture' (his venomous prose really is appalling), while the second
is shown to be 'more thoroughly traditional', linking across
the centuries Talmudic and Patristic commentators, Puritan
autobiographers and German phenomenologists, for all of

whom texts *mattered*, made sense only as demanding application in one's actual or at least mental-spiritual life. (One thinks of the young George Lukàcs passionately arguing about *Crime and Punishment* with his comrades during the Budapest Soviet in 1919, to decide whether they should execute political hostages or not!) This compressed excursus is indeed historically illuminating, even though Dr Andrews' own position seems awkwardly to straddle precisely these two options, since he apparently rejects *en avance* the 'ideologic' he analyses while still getting very angry indeed about it — a surely inconsistent response.

The third excursus is a kind of historical insertion into this overall sketch. He traces the practices of seventeenth-century Puritan and Anglican interpretation of the Bible as personally applicable, and labels this 'textual paranoia' (emphasising thereby the intense *threat* of biblical texts for those who divided mankind into saved and damned). He then links this to the 'political paranoia' of a civil war (in which 'those who are not with me are against me' and indifferentism is excluded). He further binds together these 'subjective' and 'objective' features of the period by means of an adaptation of Jacques Lacan's early theory of aggressivity: that the root mechanism of paranoia is the projection of an ideal-ego which, in the seventeenth century, was articulated as God Himself whose 'aggression' then took the form of pre-destination, which in turn led to textual paranoia, the purpose of which was to discover one's own pre-destined fate in an applied reading of the scriptures. There are some useful sidelights scattered here, concerning the broader context of Herbert's poem (for example, the significance of Puritan objections to Anglican preaching styles, that — in a contemporary phrase — they 'prevented understanding'), and also a suggestive critique of some twentieth-century theories of 'ideal-speech communities' (for example, Habermas's version of Critical Theory) which hold out the illusory possibility of aggression-free 'rational' societies. For the gloomy, materialist and class-conscious Dr Andrews, relying upon Dr Lacan's doctoral thesis, since paranoia is at the root of all knowledge and 'understanding' it is Hobbes rather than Habermas (still less

Hooker), seventeenth-century civil war rather than twentieth-century scientific social theory (still less spiritual enlightenment) that seems to provide the best guide for our political thinking. It's a depressing, perhaps even paranoid, viewpoint.

A lengthy fourth excursus entitled 'Milton's Options' situates Milton as a defeated revolutionary poet in the context of 'Restoration Literature'. The three options Dr Andrews proposes to examine are correlated with the three major poems, *Paradise Lost*, *Paradise Regained* and *Samson Agonistes*. The first he sees as an attempt to 'understand' the eventual defeat of 'God's party', and the thesis he advances is that Milton came to see that defeat — the Restoration — as *necessary*. His argument hinges on the traditional theological problem of the very possibility of Adam's ever 'falling' at all. The familiar formulation is: how could a non-fallen individual ever commit a sin without this implying some 'evil' (i.e. some degree of fallen-ness) 'prior' to the act of sin? Recognising that such a formulation is open to various traditional reformulations which dissolve the problem away. Andrews argues that even allowing these established qualifications and re-definitions, the paradox of the possibility of the fall still remains (he interestingly compares it to the paradox involved in the notion of consciously observing oneself through the moment of falling asleep). He prefers to credit Milton with a radically untraditional answer to the problem. He suggests that Milton presents Adam as 'falling' not because of some prelapsarian evil or sinfulness in him, but precisely because of what is most (humanly) praiseworthy and good in him: his love for Eve. In itself, this is a fairly familiar reading of this moment in the poem, but for Andrews its significance is far-reaching. For him, what must characterise genuine human love is the willingness to *risk* the loss of something for the loved one — but in the world of Eden the *only* thing that could be risked was Eden itself. But to risk Eden knowing that Eden would not in fact be sacrificed, because God would ignore or forgive Adam's choice to follow Eve in tasting the forbidden fruit, would not be a genuine risk at all, an act of real love. The only real risk open to Adam was to risk the loss of Eden, for the sake of his love of Eve, while *knowing* in advance that the loss

41

of Eden was definite — and he could know that because of the very nature of the God whose command he had disobeyed: such a God does not make empty threats. The element of risk, of uncertainty, lay in what was to happen after — and *that* was unknown. Now, it seems to me that Dr Andrews has not only ignored the distinction advanced in *Paradise Lost* itself between love and mere passion but has manipulated the notion of 'risk' to fit a dubious general thesis. He proposes that what makes the 'true revolutionary' is always 'a commitment to a revolutionary action even if that action is bound to be defeated.' He instances James Connolly going out to die in the Dublin Easter rising of 1916, Che Guevara embarking on a doomed *foco* strategy in Bolivia in 1966–7, even Lenin and Trotsky quoting Engels to each other on the night of the storming of the Winter Palace — to the effect that they had already lost. Applied to John Milton after 1660 there is perhaps a germ of psychological plausibility to Dr Andrews' suggestion. Milton had to reconcile two notions: not only that God was on the side of the Puritans but that God knew 'in advance' that they would be defeated. In personal terms this problem of God's paradoxical Pro-vidence meant that Milton himself, even knowing *post eventum* that the Revoluion had indeed been defeated, still would not retrospectively repudiate his commitment to that revolution. Milton's post-Restoration position had to be that even if he had *known* in 1640 that the Restoration would happen in 1660 he would still have fought as he did, still have served as Cromwell's Latin Secretary, still have written his highly risky pamphlets, even on the eve of the Restoration itself. For Dr Andrews, *Paradise Lost* represents Milton's attempt to understand the most basic grounds for holding to that paradoxical or apparently point-less position.

That Milton continued to hold to his pre-1660 commit-ments is clear, so Dr Andrews argues, from both *Paradise Regained* and *Samson Agonistes*. The focusing of *Paradise Regained* upon the Temptations of Christ is Milton's response to the temptation of succumbing to the Restoration, of switching allegiance and settling for a compromised life; that such a temptation was as unappealing (or impossible) for

Milton as Satan's were for Christ is what makes the poem so relatively flat. In a scornful survey of Restoration culture and entertainment, Dr Andrews offers us the speculative vision of John Milton writing a comedy of manners or turning out epilogues to Dryden's plays, perhaps composing drinking songs or Grub Street satires. Yes, that option *is* inconceivable. But if Milton after 1660 refused either to repudiate the revolution or to accept a position within the Restoration, what remaining options as a poet did he have — apart from silence? According to Dr Andrews, Milton had somehow to create a work which could neither be suppressed (as an outright opposition work would be) nor appropriated, a work that precisely by affirming both Milton's own greatness as a poet and his deliberate self-distancing from the ethos of Restoration culture, would serve notice upon the world of the political unacceptability and cultural poverty of the counter-revolution. All three works can be seen as, in part, having this aim, but Dr Andrews emphasises how particularly *Samson Agonistes* matches this option: a work which combines classical Greek tragedy with an Old Testament theme and forges a unique artistic unity from those two sources of Christian civilisation, a work it would be impossible to fault artistically or to suppress politically (despite the clear possibility of localised political interpretation), yet equally a work it would be impossible to present upon the Restoration stage. Again, there is a certain psychological plausibility to this account of what Milton *might* have been intending in writing *Samson Agonistes* (though there are more persuasive accounts available!) but it is certainly implausible to claim that he succeeded!

In one respect, Dr Andrews recognises that, even on his own argument, this 'option' failed, since *Samson Agonistes* was indeed appropriated and tamed to a safe place in counter-revolutionary culture, in the form of Handel's oratorio. More broadly, however, he argues that Milton's entire work after the Restoration was finally rendered harmless and acceptable to the 'reactionary cultural regime' (a regime he actually sees as lasting unbroken to the present!) — precisely by being treated as 'Literature'. At last, the putative relevance of this long excursus becomes apparent. In the attempt to assimilate Milton, recognising the towering stature of his work yet refusing its political challenge, the Restoration had to (re-) invent the very notion of 'Literature' as distinct from other forms of writing, 'endowing "Literature" with such exalted sublimity that it became quotidianly irrelevant and with such profundity that it became practically meaningless' — a process that was soon, and irremediably, to infect and engulf even the 'Classics' themselves. Addison's treatment of *Paradise Lost* in the *Spectator* encapsulates the successful consolidation of this attempt, simultaneously dissolving Milton's political meanings and establishing his 'literary' supremacy. But, Dr Andrews goes on — in an oddly sour way — to argue, Milton had already been responsible for creating a 'radical' concept of 'Literature' in writing the unperformable *Samson Agonistes*, but the significance of that sublime distancing from the everyday to be found in the 'preface' was in fact disdainful political critique of the culture not complacent critical appreciation of the work. In concluding this long excursus Dr Andrews suggests two figures for us to compare with Milton. One is Alexander Blok, whose *The Twelve* remains both the greatest and the most politically enigmatic of all responses in 'literature' to the 1917 Revolution, appropriable neither for nor against the revolution. The second is Arnold Schoenberg, whose uncompromisingly 'difficult' music Dr Andrews — following Adorno — sees as exemplifying a radical distancing from possible appropriation by the 'bourgeois culture industry' which Andrews regards as in continuity with, and even originating from, Addison's efforts.

There is at least a minor difficulty with Dr Andrews' argument in this excursus: that if the concept of 'Literature' is a post-Restoration notion, what on earth were all those pre-Restoration authors writing? He has the grace to acknowledge this troubling question in an aside in his next excursus — the fifth and final one to this first chapter of the book — where he recognises that George Herbert's *The Temple* has 'often, but mistakenly, been taken to be a work of Literature'. But if *The Temple* is not a work of Literature, what are we to read it as? As a spiritual diary, a set of meditations, a book of prayers, a collection of poems? He first surveys the various critical positions concerning the ordering or structure of the work, arguing that none of the usual candidates (architectural, moral, liturgical, autobiographical) actually matches the real diversity of conjunctions and dissociations of subject-matter confronting the consecutive reader of the work, and then probes those poems which themselves discuss the practice of writing (*Jordan I* and *II*, *The Quidditie*, etc.) to conclude that no criteria derived from these poems can be consistently applied to the whole text. He then, however, offers his own candidate and set of criteria. He singles out *The Holy Scriptures I* and *II* as providing the reader with both explicit model and implicit instructions for reading *The Temple*. For example, the lines

> O Book! infinite sweetnesse! let my heart
> Suck ev'ry letter, and a hony gain

are taken as alerting us to that unexpected phrase within the poem

> thou art Heav'ns Lidger here

where the capitalised 'L' and the odd 'i' (where one might expect 'e') require us to ponder the various senses of 'ambassador', 'commissioner', 'ledger', 'register'. More generally, such poems as *Paradise* only yield their specific theological sense if we do indeed 'suck every letter'. *Holy Scriptures II* formulates the very problem posed by the apparent lack of structure in *The Temple*:

> Oh that I knew how all thy lights combine
> And the configurations of their glorie!
> Seeing not onely how each verse doth shine,
> But all the constellations of the storie.

But then, for Dr Andrews, the poem goes on in the next verse to provide a kind of solution:

> This verse marks that, and both do make a motion
> Unto a third, that ten leaves off doth lie:
> Then as dispersed herbs do watch a potion,
> These three make up some Christians destinie.

Just as the Bible itself (*the* model of 'the Book') offers not a single 'order' but an infinite variety of possible readings, since each reader will find therein (guided by God) precisely its personal message to that individual reader — the paranoid reader of the second excursus finding that three widely scattered verses add up to a shatteringly specific revelation — so the only 'structure' *The Temple* has is a deliberately kaleidescopic one (Herbert trusts to God's chance), leaving the particular concatenation appropriate for any individual reader to be arrived at by that reader:

> Such are thy secrets, which my life makes good,
>   And comments on thee: for in ev'ry thing
>   Thy words do finde me out, & parallels bring,
> And in another make me understood.

Somewhat like a paranoid reader himself, Dr Andrews of course fixes upon that word 'understood', and argues that, in the light of this poem, together with *Prayer* ('something understood') and the claim in *The Dedication* that reading the (divinely-inspired) *Temple* will modify the fate of those who read it, we have to see *The Temple* as insisting that any attempt to 'understand' it involves 'understanding' oneself and that the only adequate form of self-understanding is *'metanoia'* — the New Testament term for 'conversion'. A change of mind can only be a change of heart. But if understanding involves conversion, conversion involves a change in the basis upon which we understand, a change which then validates the understanding that led to conversion. Dr Andrews concludes this excursus, and his chapter, by remarking that *metanoia* is, in that respect, akin to *paranoia* : once you think you're being persecuted, everything that happens shows that you are — i.e. the premises of the argument become the conclusion, and vice-versa.

*   *   *   *

The second chapter of *Literary Conversions* moves on to the eighteenth century, with a detailed reading of Samuel Richardson's novel, *Pamela*. Fortunately, the 'close reading' analysis is confined to Volume I only. Dr Andrews begins with a nicely chosen comment on *Pamela*, from the heroine of Henry Brooke's novel of 1774, *Juliet Grenville*:

I think, madam, that the author has much of nature in him; and touches the passions, at times, with a tender and happy effect: but then, I blush at the manner in which he undresses our sex. Indeed his ideas are much too frequently and unnecessarily wanton. Neither can I wholly approve the title of the book: can virtue be rewarded, by being united to vice? Her master was a ravisher, a tyrant, a dissolute, a barbarian in manners and principle. I admit it, the author may say; but then he was superior in riches and station. Indeed, Mr Richardson never fails in due respect to such matters; he always gives the full value to title and fortune.

The problem Dr Andrews extricates from this double-barrelled onslaught is that enshrined in the sub-title of Richardson's novel, *Virtue Rewarded*: how can Mr B. be or become a 'reward' for Pamela's virtue when he begins the novel as a would-be rapist? Richardson's basic strategy for resolving this problem, according to Dr Andrews, is to have Mr B. read through Pamela's letters and journals; Mr B.'s reading, in effect, converts him to a true and respectable love. But — and here Dr Andrews' scalpel begins to quiver with analytical anticipation — the *reader* of *Pamela* has also read precisely those *same* letters and journals, so should not the effect of that reading, also, be a 'conversion' of the reader?

Of course, this 'textual strategy' and its 'logic' — though undeniably, as other critics have perhaps noticed, there — isn't quite that simple, and accordingly Dr Andrews takes his tweezers to the text. He dissects at length the various local varieties and variations of 'reading' by which the reader is enticed, from the first Letter in which Mr B. reads Pamela's writings in her presence (a foretaste of the future), through the often quite complicated embeddings of other letters within Pamela's (those from Mr B. to Pamela, to her parents, to Mrs Jewkes, or from Reverend Williams to Pamela, John's note, the false warning from Lady D., etc., etc.) to the culminating phase of the novel when we find ourselves reading Pamela's speculations about Mr B.'s reactions to her previous journal entries which he is supposedly reading even 'while' we read her further instalments about his reading. This detailed unpacking of the superimposed layerings of readings and writings within the text leads Dr Andrews to insist that Pamela is not (as is often claimed) 'writing to the minute' but rather is writing retrospectively in a double sense: she is almost always definitely if only slightly in advance (diegetically) of the events she recounts (the morning after the night before, as it were) and she is also looking back upon *all* the events as already concluded: the letters are presented to us by the long-married Pamela even though written by the once-persecuted Pamela, since it is only the eventually happy conclusion which allows us to read those letters; Pamela has pre-read them for publication herself, just as, indeed, Mr B. has, prior to our ever opening the book. The logic of the various temporalities at work in *Pamela* is, therefore, that the conclusion is indeed foregone; without it the letters would have no function and therefore no public existence. (It's surprising to realise how close Richardson can seem to Sterne in the light of this reading!)

Dr Andrews insists upon this dimension because he sees an 'internal parallel' to it within the text; Pamela's constant appeals to 'Providence', he reminds us, bring into play the quite literal 'fore-knowledge' of the Divine Omniscience, yet that foreknowledge is also (in that peculiar temporal mode so typical of the Divine) simultaneously retrospective: for Providence, everything that is to happen has already happened; it is only God who is always 'up to the minute', perfectly on time. But to some extent at least Pamela the presenter (whose presence is of course a silent one) similarly is retrospectively fore-knowing about the fate of Pamela the writer. At this point Dr Andrews back-tracks to his question about the reader: if Mr B. is 'converted' by reading Pamela's letters, should not the reader of the novel also be converted? One might of course reply that the 'good' reader needs no conversion anyway — but Dr Andrews slyly punctures that response by asking why a (morally) good reader should have continued reading this novel in the first place, a tale of seduction, near rape and 'Scenes of Immodesty, painted in Images of Virtue' (Charles Povey's opinion in 1741); the moral reader might well 'blush at the manner in which he undresses our sex', but then turns the page quickly to see the next petticoat fall. So we all, as interested readers, are shadowed by the need for purification of our desires — but how is this effected? The twist in the tale is neatly engineered by Richardson: *we* have *already* read Pamela's letters and journals by the (diegetical) time Mr B. reads them: we are already committed to the story, and if the subsequent trajectory of the tale is to remain credible we have to accept that reading these writings can indeed 'change' Mr B. — and therefore ought (we recognise, retrospectively) to have already changed us. To claim immunity is either to admit that we are *more* incorrigible than Mr B. (and therefore even more in need of conversion) or to reject the rest of the novel as based upon an unbelievable premise: that reading these letters could convert anyone, since they haven't converted us. The pincer-trap could be formulated as: either be converted or stop believing this novel. (Once Mr B. has been converted, the *un*regenerate reader is likely to lose interest in the novel anyway, anticipating that the rest will be far less titillating!) But this trap is sprung not only by Richardson but also, it would seem, by God Himself. If part of what we are invited to find credible by the novel is that God foreknows all and that all events are held within the overarching control of God's Providence, then God already knows, 'outside' the novel, which readers will be suitably 'converted' by reading *Pamela*, and which won't. As Pamela herself says, in her struggle against the temptation to suicide (precisely that passage which will most affect Mr B. in his reading): 'God can touch the heart in an instant' — yet if that is true of Mr B. it is also presumably true of the reader: conversion may be set before us (or set up for us) by Richardson's construction of the text but it will always be God's work if it occurs, even though, as so often in Richardson, we have to trust both to Providence *and* to our own best endeavours, at least as sympathetic readers.

This is a fairly attractive, if tortuous argument, and I think Dr Andrews has genuinely uncovered one of the deeper structures of the architecture of *Pamela*. He has clarified one precise way in which the text might be claimed to have a palpable design upon us (one remembers Richardson's own claims). But I fear that Dr Andrews has orchestrated that device a little more coherently in his account than the text itself actually does. He has succumbed to the temptation of many critics: to create a text that only really exists in his imagination, an ideal work; the real text is far less neatly logical in its operations. Dr Andrews seems, in fact, to have overlooked part of his own analysis: that Mr B. actually reads Pamela's correspondence in three separate batches, and that the first — purloined — sequence of letters seems to have no effect upon him; only the second batch lend themselves to Dr Andrews' argument. Moreover, it is to love of Pamela, not to love of God, that Mr B. is brought (though much later Lady D. will remark, it is true, 'My brother turned Puritan!'); I have yet to meet a reader who fell in love with Pamela from reading *Pamela*. And that indicates an even larger hole in this elegantly hollow argument: there is no recognition in Dr Andrews' analysis of the fact that readers are differently *gendered* — yet this surely needs to be integrated into his assertions about the differential responses of the good and bad reader.

Nevertheless, this interesting chapter at least prompted me to reconsider my own responses to *Pamela*. I must report, however, that I still consider Richardson to be adapting not a tactic of Christian conversion but a classically Aristotelian strategy: the fusion of *anagnorisis* (Recognition) with *peripeteia* (Reversal) at the same dramatic high-point (Mr B's reading is both a recognition of Pamela and a reversal of her fortunes). To adapt this tragic formula to the epistolary novel was achievement enough, to my mind.

I actually find the excurses to this chapter more interesting and suggestive than the main body of the text. The first assembles a great deal of material on — of all things — eighteenth-century card games and quite persuasively argues for a parallel between the processes of playing Whist (the craze for which began in 1743, three years after the publication of *Pamela*) and the operations involved in following the moves in an epistolary novel: each letter regarded as a card played, but with the opponent's full hand as yet unrevealed. (On this analogue Mr B. is a complete cad as well as a would-be rapist: he peers over his opponent's shoulder at her hand.) Not only does Dr Andrews reinforce this suggestion by contemporary allusions to the parallel (he even, rather dubiously, instances the allegorical card game in *Pamela* itself), but he further connects the eighteenth-century mania for both novel-reading and card games to the underlying economic structure of eighteenth-century English society. His link is the emergence of the Stock Exchange, in an as-yet not-fully-successful attempt to rationalise and ritualise the random chances and risks of commercial speculation. For Dr Andrews there is a common pattern underpinning these various activities: card games, gambling, South Sea Bubble speculation, and the emergence of novel-reading: an element of playing with risk and with anticipated probabilities within a 'system' of rules that is never fully predictable and never finally systematic. He then tries further to assimilate seventeenth- and eighteenth-century theological notions of Providence and of belief to this pattern: Pascal's famous wager on faith (a kind of two-way bet) offers him a happy peg on which to begin to build his case, while Adam Smith's sadly discredited economic 'guiding hand' provides him with an apposite end-term for his analysis; *en route* he even makes some sense of the significance of Soame Jenyns, and reminds us of the contribution of Pope's friend John Arbuthnot to the development of probability theory. On this account, reading an eighteenth-century novel was almost a practical exercise in probability theory.

The second excursus takes a different tack. He interprets his own reading of *Pamela* as showing that Richardson is here foisting onto the reader a problem (that of believing or not believing in Providence) which is ostensibly only 'internal' to the text (Pamela's trust in Providence) yet which, as a problem for the author, crucially shapes the construction and manipulation of the text. He then suggests that this basic device of foisting one's own problems onto the reader comes to assume a central role in the later development of the novel, offering *Mary Barton* and *Daniel Deronda* as prime instances. (He might, I suppose, have made a more convincing case by beginning from *Robinson Crusoe*'s problems with Providence — or even by linking back to Milton.) In *Mary Barton*, he claims, Mrs Gaskell negotiates her own problem — of how to intervene in liberal sympathy with the industrial classes — *by* writing a novel, the reading of which then leaves the *reader* with Mrs Gaskell's original problem: what to *do* in terms of concretely intervening in the kind of industrial conflict to which the novel has alerted us. Unless the reader is to take Mrs Gaskell's own solution and simply write yet another novel, the reader has been manipulated into trying to solve Mrs Gaskell's original problem *in her place*. Mrs Gaskell's strategy, in other words, is to 'convert' her readers into making an active contribution she herself can avoid having to make, precisely by opting to convert others.

Dr Andrews sees this as evincing the characteristic 'bad faith' of the concerned liberal and locates its eighteenth-century roots in the fundamental writing convention of *The Spectator*: the very title indicates its concerned but merely observational stance *vis-à-vis* all social problems. (He might, one can add, have included those sad figures one sees outside factory gates forlornly selling unwanted left-wing newspapers — but perhaps that would be to approach too near his own problems?) George Eliot's case is even more desperately 'liberal': her Daniel Deronda rightly sees the utter vacuity of the English social system so magisterially depicted in the 'Gwendolen Harleth' sections of the novel, but s/he then 'exports' his critique into quasi-Zionist utopianism instead of turning that critique back upon English society itself. For Dr Andrews, Deronda should presumably have become a Chartist or a Fraternal Democrat and the novel should, formally, have curved back upon its opening and critically demolished it rather than ending upon an open future elsewhere. George Eliot has, for Dr Andrews, taken Mrs Gaskell's device of deflection a stage further: the reader is now encouraged towards a purely imaginary outcome, a displacement of any active response into a world that exists only in the novel itself.

This step is made even more visible in Tolstoy's early short story 'A Landlord's Morning' (1856) where the would-be reforming landlord returns from a morning's preliminary survey of what needs to be done on his estate and simply transposes his reactions into an extempore composition at the piano. For the relentless Dr Andrews, Tolstoy's own story does exactly the same: Tolstoy sees what needs to be done but instead of doing it constructs a short story which encourages his readers to rest content with appreciating the irony of the story rather than actually reforming anything. From that aesthetic 'internalisation' of authorial problems it is a short step to such tales as Henry James's *Turn of the Screw* in which the reader's 'choice' between different causal explanations for what is happening within the narrative remains purely interpretative, changing nothing and solving nothing, since the story is so constructed as to allow radically different readings to lead to the same ambiguous conclusion without even a comma of the text needing to be modified, let alone anything in the real world outside the novel. The final phase in this underlying development of a novelistic strategy is located by Dr Andrews in the matchstick game in Resnais and Robbe-Grillet's film *Last Year in Marienbad*, which he reads as an 'internal model' of the reader's role: whatever 'decisions' or 'interpretations' the reader chooses (whichever matchstick the challenger begins from) makes no difference at all: the system is so rigged that the game always ends the same way — and always remains merely a game (one recalls card games). The hidden rule is, simply, that the novelist — like God's Providence — can choose in advance who will win; all the reader, by this stage in a long process, need be concerned with is the elegance and style of play; real problems have long since been aestheticised out of existence, turned into a pure language-game. On this account, both reading and writing novels are collusive exercises in Bad Faith.

The third excursus reminds us that both eighteenth-century card games and the Stock Exchange were concerned with 'making' (actually, redistributing) money and Dr Andrews then counterposes Adam Smith's Providential economics to Karl Marx's analysis of capitalism in *Das Kapital* — only to find a variation of Richardson's tactic in *Das Kapital* itself. In a tantalisingly brief excursus he analyses Marx's use of the term 'presupposition' in the *Grundrisse* and in *Kapital*, pinpointing that term as the hinge around which the 'logical' and the 'historical' exposition of these texts turn. If we take 'presupposition' in a logical sense we have a formally coherent theory in which all factors mutually support each other: each becomes, in turn, a presupposition of the others. If we take the term in its temporal sense (*pre*-supposition) we have an historical account which rests upon a finally accidental process: without these presuppositions (preconditions) 'capitalism' could not have emerged yet capitalism cannot retrospectively guarantee the emergence of its own 'presuppositions' any more than mere pre-suppositions can guarantee the development of an economic *system* which presupposes them. Though formulated rather confusingly, Dr Andrews' point seems to be that in *reading* Marx's argument in *Das Kapital* the reader is enticed into accepting its own logical structure (its expositional arrangement as a text in which certain sections 'presuppose' preceding ones) as exemplifying a logical structure in an historically existing economic 'system': we find *as we read* that we have to *retrospectively* reinterpret certain *logical* uses of the term 'presupposition' as *historical-temporal* uses of the term in order to make coherent sense of the overall argument. Like most effective 'conversions', it seems, any conversion to marxism is curiously retrospective: it has *already* happened to us before we are prepared to acknowledge it — and the very structure of *Das Kapital* enacts this movement. On this account, reading Marx is like reading a very good novelist. However, while I accept that the role of these excurses is to sketch rather than to demonstrate a case, I suspect that Dr Andrews in this final excursus has not adequately done his homework on Hegel's *Logic*. Still, neither have I, so while it is refreshing to see *Das Kapital* treated as sharing some of its organisational devices with a 'literary' text like *Pamela*, I must register an intrigued but basically sceptical response to Dr Andrews' outline of his approach here.

*   *   *   *

The next two chapters of the book can be dealt with more summarily. Chapter 3 focuses on chapter XIII of Coleridge's *Biographia Literaria* and analyses how Coleridge uses the device of the sudden 'letter from a friend' (which he inserts at this point *instead of* the promised *theory* of the 'imagination') in order, in effect, to create a 'blank space' at the centre of his work which the reader then has to fill for himself. By a series of promises, postponements, digressions and interludes Coleridge has, in the first part of *Biographia*, built up not only an expectation but almost a *need* for the 'theory' Coleridge claims to be able to provide; then, at the last moment, we are deprived of that very theory, at the apparent behest of a 'friend' who writes to Coleridge advising him to omit the chapter. This 'friend' was, as Coleridge once acknowledged in one of his own letters, Coleridge himself.

Clearly, for Dr Andrews, *Biographia Literaria* is another instance of a text foisting onto its reader the author's own unsolved problem, but Coleridge's tactic is shown to be more complex and multi-layered than, say, Mrs Gaskell's — and also more praiseworthy, since inescapable. Dr Andrews traces, through Coleridge's letters and notebooks, the emergence of *Biographia Literaria* as an intended 'Preface' to or even preliminary version of the long-projected *Logosophia*, the '*organum vere organum*', the always elusive *magnum opus* on the *omne scibile* ('everything understood'?) which Coleridge so often planned and never actually wrote. Central to the whole project was, increasingly, the notion of autobiography (itself a relatively new *concept* in the early nineteenth century: the term itself had emerged in the ambience of German Idealist philosophy only in the 1780s), since at the core of Coleridge's ontological and epistemological position was the insistence on identity as constituted by the self-reflexive consciousness of a 'continuousness' of consciousness, in which 'subject' and 'object' are 'co-adunated' in the great 'I AM' which is the primary affirmation of both the Divine and the human individual. Much of this basic strand in Coleridge's thinking is encapsulated in the ten 'Theses' to be found in *Biographia* chapter XII, but they are still offered there as preliminary to the promised treatment of the Imagination in chapter XIII; that treatment is then *not* given. The effect, argues Dr Andrews, is curious: as we read chapter XII, and indeed chapters IV to XI, we give *provisional* assent to Coleridge's outlined positions because we *anticipate* that they will soon be clarified and fully justified *retrospectively* once the theory of Imagination is completely formulated in chapter XIII; but when that theory is, in fact, withheld we then find ourselves endeavouring to *construct* it for ourselves on the *basis* of those previously only provisionally accepted positions. As an account of a reader's possible reaction, I find this very plausible and I also think that Dr Andrews is correct when he goes on to argue that Coleridge's very notion of 'Understanding' requires that this *must* be the kind of process the reader has to undergo. One can put it thus: to understand what the 'Imagination' *is* the reader has to *exercise* his 'Imagination'; a theory of Imagination cannot be simply 'given' to the reader, it has to be co-created (co-adunated?) by an *act* of Imagination. Coleridge's footnote, in chapter XII, on the etymology of the word 'understanding' is relevant here:

The force of the Greek *sunienai* is imperfectly expressed by 'understanding'; our own idiomatic phrase 'to go along with me' comes nearest to it.

In *Biographia Literaria* we are brought to 'go along with' Coleridge in his tracing of his own intellectual history (a history that, of course, involves much more than 'intellect'). As we imaginatively re-create for ourselves and 'enter into' (think of Coleridge on Shakespeare) that personal trajectory we too are brought to the position where we can 'understand' what the 'Imagination' is — though, precisely like Coleridge himself, we cannot fully formulate our understanding. That same footnote continues with a deliberately 'corrected' quotation from the *Enneads* which Coleridge translates as:

'What then are we to understand?' That whatever is produced is an intuition, I silent.

Coleridge's own 'silence' in chapter XIII is intended to generate in us an 'intuition' — but an intuition that has to be worked for. The 'friend's' letter itself directs us to another footnote (in chapter IV) which both indicates the kind of effort required of us and also suggests (in the example offered) the basic process of 'change' we have to undergo:

In opinions of long continuance, and in which we had never before been molested by a single doubt, to be suddenly convinced of an error is almost like being convicted of a fault. There is a state of mind which is the direct antithesis of that, which takes place when we *make a bull*. The bull namely consists in bringing together two incompatible thoughts, with the sensation, but without the sense, of their connection. The psychological condition, or that which constitutes the possibility of this state, being such disproportionate vividness of two distant thoughts, as extinguishes or obscures the consciousness of the intermediate images or conceptions, or wholly abstracts the attention from them. Thus in the well-known bull, 'I was a fine child, but they changed me'; the first conception expressed in the word 'I', is that of personal identity — *Ego contemplans*: the second expressed in the word 'me', is the visual image or object by which the mind represents to itself its past condition, or rather, its personal identity under the form in which it imagined itself previously to have existed, — *Ego contemplatus*. Now the change of one visual image for another involves in itself no absurdity, and becomes absurd only by its immediate juxtaposition with the first thought, which is rendered possible by the whole attention being successively absorbed in each singly, so as not to notice the interjacent notion, 'changed', which by its incongruity with the first thought, 'I', constitutes the bull. Add only, that this process is facilitated by the circumstances of the words 'I' and 'me', being sometimes equivalent, and sometimes having a distinct meaning; sometimes, namely, signifying the act of self-consciousness, sometimes the external image in and by which the mind represents that act to itself, the result and symbol of its individuality. Now suppose the direct contrary state, and you will have a distinct sense of the connection between two conceptions, without that sensation of such connection which is supplied by habit. The man feels as if he were standing on his head, though he cannot but see that he is truly standing on his feet. This, as a painful sensation, will of course have a tendency to associate itself with the person who occasions it; even as persons, who have been by painful means restored from derangement, are known to feel an involuntary dislike towards their physician.

As Coleridge formulates it later (chapter XII, Thesis X): 'intelligence is a self-development, not a quality supervening to a substance.' It is only by this 'self-development' that we are able to grasp that 'realizing intuition which exists by and in the act that affirms its existence' (chapter XII), that very act which allows us to 'go along with' the 'Imagination'.

Now, Dr Andrews quite clearly regards this whole Coleridgean process as so much self-delusion rather than as self-comprehension, as merely another variation on the 'conversion double-binds' he has set out to trace, analyse and reject. For him, Coleridge's bland references back to chapter XIII in subsequent chapters of *Biographia Literaria* (e.g. 'My own conclusions on the nature of poetry, in the strictest use of the word, have been in part anticipated in the preceding disquisition on the fancy and imagination', chapter XIV) are merely sleight-of-mind: the reader is persuaded, even covertly flattered, into believing *retrospectively* that he has already achieved a genuine insight, whereas in fact only a blank space remains in the mind as we think back to what seemed, at the time, an elusive but almost enlightening moment. In a sardonic survey of the immense secondary literature on Coleridge's 'theory', Dr Andrews endeavours to demonstrate that Coleridge's tactic has been 'comically successful', as critic after critic has filled in the 'holes' in *Biographia* with 'word-spinning discriminations and revaluations', all of them the product of 'scholarly fancy'. I find this exercise in malicious carping extremely distasteful, but there are clearly fundamental disagreements at issue here concerning the very nature of literary scholarship, which will have to await another occasion for debate.

The excurses to this chapter on Coleridge are fairly predictable. In the first we are taken on a whistle-stop tour of Hegel, Kierkegaard and Blake, the former two being castigated for similar tactical sleight-of-mind (the victimised texts are the 1820s' *Aesthetics Lectures* and Kierkegaard's *Repetition*), while Blake's *Songs of Innocence and Experience* are lauded, by contrast, as an instance of a 'concrete dialectic' in which each set of songs (to adapt Coleridge's own phrasing in chapter XII, Thesis VI) 'pre-suppose each other, and can exist only as antitheses'. Blake's 'concrete dialectic' — a matter of provoking a *reading* experience which realises the *need* for, yet the actual destruction of, a transcendent criterion of judgement — is favourably compared with Marx's 'abstract' dialectic in *Das Kapital*, a matter merely of the tactics of expository writing. In the second excursus, Dr Andrews takes up some remarks by Coleridge on the effects of the 'theoretical' *Preface* to the

Lyrical Ballads upon readers' 'practice' in evaluating the actual poems (chapter IV), and argues that Coleridge was finally willing to allow a divorce between 'theory' and 'practice' which his own practice partly repudiates. He again analyses the overall structure of *Biographia Literaria*, this time to show that chapters I to XII are a 'preparation' for the 'theory' of chapter XIII, and that that 'theory' then undergirds the 'practice' of the criticism of Wordsworth in chapters XIV onwards; but by omitting the actual 'theory' Coleridge leaves only a spurious continuity in his text: chapters I to XII are *not*, for Dr Andrews, in fact a preparation for the practice of Volume II, despite Coleridge's inconsistent attempt to make them appear so. Dr Andrews then draws a parallel between this textual organisation of *Biographia* and what he sees as a characteristic flaw in the endeavours of 'romantic radical intellectuals': they spend long years 'preparing' an adequate 'theory' (which they never finally produce) and then persuade themselves that such intellectual 'preparation' was really a preparation for *practical* politics. His particular targets here are periodicals, from Coleridge's own *The Friend* (which sought to 'aid in the formation of fixed principles in politics, morals and religion') to such extreme twentieth-century examples as *Theoretical Practice* (an English Althusserian journal of the early 1970s), and he characterises their implicit 'strategy' as fundamentally one of 'the Kierkegaardian leap applied to revolution'. Surprisingly perhaps, he then seeks to salvage his own (Coleridgean?) version of 'Imagination in politics' by citing Coleridge on Kant (chapter IX): 'An idea, in the highest sense of that word, cannot be conveyed but by a symbol; and, except in geometry, all symbols of necessity involve an apparent contradiction.' For Dr Andrews, apparently, 'revolution' is precisely such an 'idea' and therefore, *a fortiori*, all 'theories' of 'revolution' *must* themselves contain 'apparent contradictions'. One can only murmur in response that 'All Power to the Imagination' was therefore presumably a bankrupt slogan even in the moment of its coinage.

*   *   *   *

The final, and in some ways most attractive, chapter of

Literary Conversions begins from the end of T.S. Eliot's *Four Quartets*:

> We shall not cease from exploration
> And the end of all our exploring
> Will be to arrive where we started
> And know the place for the first time.
> Through the unknown, remembered gate
> When the last of earth left to discover
> Is that which was the beginning;
> At the source of the longest river
> The voice of the hidden waterfall
> And the children in the apple-tree
> Not known, because not looked for
> But heard, half-heard, in the stillness
> Between two waves of the sea.
> Quick now, here, now, always —
> A condition of complete simplicity
> (Costing not less than everything)
> And all shall be well and
> All manner of thing shall be well
> When the tongues of flame are in-folded
> Into the crowned knot of fire
> And the fire and the rose are one.

In an impressive and engaging commentary on this passage Dr Andrews delicately evokes the multitude of echoes and resonances that hover round each line, each phrase, in this close. It is an attractive display of perceptive critical powers one had not suspected him capable of (though the close reading of *Prayer* manifested similar virtues at times). Reading his vivid commentary we are brought to recall literally hundreds of previous passages and phrases within *Four Quartets* itself and in the wealth of literary texts those passages themselves allude to. I shall not attempt to summarise this reading: it convincingly demonstrates that the passage acts as an intensely charged summing-up of all that has gone before in these uniquely evocative poems. By the end of Dr Andrews' many, many pages of analysis scarcely a line in the whole of *Four Quartets* has not been brought into play. (I suspect that his copyright fees to Faber & Faber must have been considerable.) But then

Dr Andrews turns the tables upon his reader. He invites us, at the end of his analysis, to re-read the whole quoted passage again, 'bearing in mind' his entire analysis. His experiment succeeded in the case of this reader at least: I found myself quite simply defeated by the demand. I managed to read as far as

> Not known, because not looked for
> But heard, half-heard, in the stillness

before I gave up, acknowledging that my memory, my ears, could no longer hold onto all the associations at once: either I would have to slow down my reading to an infinitesimally meditative pace or I would have to read on in a radically selective way, no longer 'looking for' but only, at best, 'half-hearing' the words, quotations, phrases, allusions, that should have been 'echoing, thus, in my mind' while the music lasted. I then returned to Dr Andrews' merciless argument: he now invited me to re-read the *whole* of *Four Quartets* with a similar degree of intense attention, to return (as the closing passage implicitly invites us to) to

> where we started
> And know the place for the first time.

I dutifully began at

> Time present and time past

but knew the task to be hopeless from the start. By the time (and what 'time' is that?) I would have arrived at

> And the fire and the rose are one

I knew that my mind would long since have faltered, allowed its attention to lapse from the full and total engagement demanded. In a sense, I had always, in practice, known this to be true of my reading of *Four Quartets*; after many re-readings, I have become acutely aware of my own incapacity to 'hold' this poem; I take it, in practice, in short passages. Dr Andrews was now inviting me to reflect upon that process, to realise that the essential strategy of the poem is precisely this: to exhaust the critical responses of the reader by a kind of excessive, impossible over-loading of those very responses. The effect is to make the poem, 'as a poem', as a single consecutive reading experience, literally un-judgeable. No reader could claim to have adequately *read* this poem, from its beginning to its end, and therefore no reader could claim to be in a position to 'judge' it. To 'analyse' it, as we all can, in short passages, or even *in toto*, is not the same as to 'read' it, and the more we analyse it the more literally unreadable we have to recognise it to be. But how then, asks Dr Andrews, are we to arrive at an *assessment* of the religious *claims* the poem advances? He cites the passage which many take to be the doctrinal 'centre' of the poem:

> For most of us, there is only the unattended
> Moment, the moment in and out of time,
> The distraction fit, lost in a shaft of sunlight,
> The wild thyme unseen, or the winter lightning
> Or the waterfall, or music heard so deeply
> That it is not heard at all, but you are the music
> While the music lasts. These are only hints and guesses,
> Hints followed by guesses; and the rest
> Is prayer, observance, discipline, thought and action.
> The hint half guessed, the gift half understood, is Incarnation.

But, he asks, if our actual reading of *Four Quartets* shows us that even in the experience of 'being' 'the music while the music lasts', the poem while the reading lasts, we are mainly, much of the time, in a distraction 'fit', if all our best efforts at 'full and complete possession of the poem' (in Dr Leavis's famous phrase) amount to little more than an 'unattended moment', an intermittence of our total attention, and if *these* experiences are — as the passage asserts — at best 'only hints and guesses', how can we possibly even 'half understand' the line:

> The hint half guessed, the gift half understood, is Incarnation.

We are caught in a trap of our own making. (Though George Herbert, we recall, perhaps first 'set' it.) Can we simply dismiss this line, this claim — in which case must we be claiming to have adequately understood it, which would involve (at least) a total, a full comprehension and possession of the whole poem? Or do we continue to suspend our judgement until we have completed our reading of the whole poem — only to find that we cannot complete that reading without, many times, wavering in our full attention to the poem, a wavering which must, in honesty, lead us to 'try again' before delivering our final judgement? Our only option seems to be to join the ranks of those

> Who are only undefeated
> Because we have gone on trying.

But that must leave us in a 'suspension of disbelief' more radical than anything even Coleridge (chapter XIV) or, in a different context, Milton, envisaged.

The crux of the problem, as Dr Andrews clearly sees, is the *poetic* 'authority' of *Four Quartets*, indeed of T.S. Eliot, in our time. Once we accept that *Four Quartets* is a major literary achievement we must be brought, inescapably, to a personal negotiation of its demands upon us as a *reader* (not just as a more or less detached 'teacher', analytical 'critic' or learned commentator), but as readers of the poem we are defeated by it: we can never fully read it. We are thereby left, if not quite in a state of 'conversion' to its implicit and explicit doctrinal demands, at least in a dilemma of agnosticism concerning its religious 'hints and guesses'; such suspended assent is a characteristic twentieth-century stance in religious matters and it is only a shade away from (provisional) acquiescence.

Dr Andrews, since he views this very possibility with alarm and ideological horror, is determined to demolish the 'authority' of *Four Quartets*. To do so, he seems to think it sufficient to demonstrate the 'trick' (his cheap word) it works upon us. He analyses Eliot's whole *oeuvre* as a gradual refinement and perfecting of this 'trick', from *The Waste Land*'s self-cancelling 'message' (concisely: if this poem is successful it shows us that the unity of European culture has been so shattered as to make it impossible for this to be a successful poem) to the moment at the end of *Murder in the Cathedral* when the audience is impaled on a hermeneutical hook (either you interpret Becket's actions in a secular mode, in which case you must reject the *Te Deum* that follows the Knights' secular explanations, or you accept the *Te Deum* purely as an 'aesthetic' closure, in which case you must shrug off the direct challenge of the Knights' addresses — or you must 'believe', deliberately joining in the singing of *Te Deum as* an affirmation). Dr Andrews sees Eliot as trying throughout his career to fix his readers in double-binds (none of which *quite* work) until in *Four Quartets* he came so close to it that he could regard himself as having succeeded. After that, the essential impetus of his poetic writing was exhausted. I doubt if this will do as a guiding thread for interpreting Eliot's career, and I fail to see why Dr Andrews should regard his analysis as diminishing Eliot's authority and achievement: all great writers are great precisely *because* they exploit the 'tricks' of the language to the utmost. But at least I will concede to Dr Andrews that, in the light of this chapter, I am more prepared to tolerate his earlier rejection of 'liberal' literary criticism: Eliot's work does indeed, for our age, demand of us a response that can shape our lives, not merely a scholarly dissertation. Personally, I am very aware of a pressure upon me, at the end of a good performance of *Murder in the Cathedral*, to join in the singing of the *Te Deum*; though it may slightly reassure Dr Andrews to know that I cannot finally do so — I happen to have no ear for music.

The final two excurses in the book are very different in character from each other. The first is a comparison of two texts, Robert M. Pirsig's *Zen and the Art of Motorcycle Maintenance: an inquiry into values* (1974) and Douglas R. Hofstadter's *Gödel, Escher, Bach: an Eternal Golden Braid* (1979), in each of which Dr Andrews sees an attempt to take the reader 'beyond logic', but the first he sees as operating by a deceitful sleight-of-text, in which basic logical errors masquerade as introducing us to a new mode of thought. He locates the crucial mistaken move in a passage towards the end of chapter 19 of *Zen*:

I don't know how much thought passed before he arrived at this, but eventually he saw that Quality couldn't be independently related with either the subject or the object but could be found *only in the relationship of the two with each other*. It is the point at which subject and object meet.

That sounded warm.

Quality is not a *thing*. It is an *event*.

Warmer.

It is the event at which the subject becomes aware of the object.

And because without objects there can be no subject — because the objects create the subject's awareness of himself — Quality is the event at which awareness of both subjects and objects is made possible.

Hot.

Now he knew it was coming.

This means Quality is not just the *result* of a collision between subject and object. The very *existence* of subject and object themselves is *deduced* from the Quality event. The Quality event is the *cause* of the subjects and objects, which are then mistakenly presumed to be the cause of the Quality!

Now he had that whole damned evil dilemma by the throat. . . . And at that point, . . . he knew he had reached some kind of culmination of thought he had been unconsciously striving for over a long period of time.

This passage constitutes both the climactic moment of insight for 'Phaedrus' and the point of 'conversion' for the reader — but it is as spurious and self-deluding, for Dr Andrews, as all the other 'conversion double-binds' he has traced. In fact, it is even worse, since the logical error here is that of a first-year student: that x is logically *deducible* from y in no way implies that x is the ontological *cause* of y; Pirsig has merely provided yet another variation on the elusively attractive 'ontological proof' of St Anselm. Nevertheless, Dr Andrews concedes that *Zen and the Art of Motorcycle Maintenance* is brilliantly constructed as a literary double-bind upon the reader: it combines Coleridge's device of a 'blank space' with Richardson's tactic of a 'retrospective' enforcement of the central premise of the credibility of the text (both are achieved through the loss of memory of the schizophrenic autobiographical protagonist), but the whole work leads us towards what is, for Dr Andrews, the dangerously irrational post-metaphysical philosophy of Martin Heidegger — Pirsig's re-discovery of the pre-Socratics is merely Americanised

Heidegger. Hofstadter's book, on the other hand, Dr Andrews sees as exposing its own double-bind tactics in its explanation of, as well as utilisation of, Gödel's 'Theorem': *Gödel, Escher, Bach* instructs us in the limitations of logic, in the ultimate self-contradictions of any fully rigorous theory, while also exemplifying our capacity to construct a coherence of a different order: it is Hofstadter rather than Eliot who has outlined the intellectual music of our time, and that music is to be heard in the complex codes that govern both our intelligences and our genes, in the basic languages of computers and in the symmetrical patterns of the DNA double-helix; provided we pursue our real possibilities of self-understanding today, in the light of these disparate scientific advances (which, *as* scientific, are always only provisional), we can indeed hope to arrive at that 'Theory of Life' which so eluded Coleridge — and it will be a fully materialist, not an idealist, understanding. Clearly, Dr Andrews prefers the latter — though it seems to me not only that he is perhaps here guilty of an elementary logical error of his own but also that one implication of this particular excursus seems to be that the textual devices he has been so remorselessly criticising might also have, even in his own terms, positive as well as dubious applications.

The last excursus of all returns to the theme of authority, but, unlike the rest of the book, it is a quite passionately polemical piece of directly political writing. Dr Andrews counterposes the patient pedagogical lucidity of Hofstadter's expositions of such apparently abstruse topics as computer processes and microbiological experiments with the constant recourse of politicians to a contemptuous manipulation of 'public opinion'. By orchestrating a witheringly sarcastic, Kraus-like series of quotations, he surveys the 'public relations' output of government departments and parliamentary spokesmen from all the major political parties in England, and demonstrates how — on a range of issues from nuclear power to defence strategy, from public expenditure to phone-tapping, from Foreign Office diplomacy to transport policy — the 'official' version of events at the time has been deliberately at variance with what was then known to the propagators of those versions but only subsequently and with immense difficulty (if at all) discovered to be the case by concerned citizens. The paradox he pinpoints at the end of this angry marshalling of newspaper reports, Hansard speeches and politicians' memoirs is that the basic 'authority' to which appeal is now made, is that of 'democracy', yet it is in the name of 'democracy' that we are denied access to a full knowledge of the political decisions taken in our name.

The basic device by which this effective disenfranchisement is achieved is an insistence, by the 'professional' politicians and their hand-picked experts, that the issues are too 'complex', too sophisticated, too 'technical' for 'us' to 'understand' — and, faced with what seems an enormous over-load of data, the individual citizen is only too inclined to agree. Even if we make the effort to understand, say, the intricacies of defence expenditure, we soon find ourselves entangled in an over-whelming barrage of 'technical' considerations. At this point, the temptation is to accept our 'ignorance', our 'incapacity', and to acquiesce in whatever decisions 'they' take for us. *This*, concludes Dr Andrews, is the contemporary form of *religious belief*: a trust in a 'Providence' every bit as enigmatic and opaque (and perhaps ultimately as destructive) as that in which Pamela believed, and an agnosticism which is, in practice, simply a 'willing suspension' of our critical responses. But, he argues, there is another process also at work: the perennial *dis*trust in which politicians are held is now intensifying, he thinks, into a latent *paranoia*, on both sides; as the secrecy and impenetrability of 'official' decision-making deepens, so a latent aggression towards this 'ideal-ego' of the political subject is growing; as the credibility of successive government administrations is retrospectively demolished in a rapidly accelerating process of post-mortem demystification (not least by politicians themselves), so the 'authority' of each current government is increasingly eroded, and soon all forms of official statement will be instantly reinterpreted — and even offered — as mere moves in a professional game of political cards. (Already we are being told *in advance* by media commentators how Ministers are expected to manipulate future media coverage of this or that coming issue.) Dr

Andrews clearly sees ahead of us a period of 'political paranoia' (signalled from one side in recent increases in surveillance technology) but since he has already rejected the possibility of a 'rational, critical community' (cf. the excursus to Chapter 1), he can only hold out to us the prospect of a social and political crisis of 'authority' as deep as that in the seventeenth century from which his book began.

On this note his book ends, abruptly. His only concession to a lighter shade of black is a concluding quotation from *Four Quartets*. It sits rather oddly as a final, isolated, line in his text and defies any further commentary from me:

> The end is where we start from.

* * * * *

Postscript

Re-reading this review at proof stage I notice, wryly, a certain inconsistency between my initially declared intentions and my actual performance. On first reading the book, I was inclined to treat at length chapters 1 and 2, while the other chapters and all the excurses seemed of slighter substance. The actual writing of the review has, apparently, persuaded me otherwise. In retrospect, I realise that chapters 1 and 2 have received relatively short shrift, and that, in fact, the later chapters illuminate the earlier while the chapters themselves — tracing a 'logical' development of the 'conversion tactic' in literary texts — now seem mere excuses for the far more intriguing excurses analysing different kinds of 'authority'. Perhaps, after all, Dr Andrews has succeeded in converting me — if not quite as he intended. So the final, retrospective advice of this postscript (too late, of course) is to read my review as well as the book itself in reverse order — starting from the end in order to arrive at 'something understood'.

Lawrence Fielding

Editions du CEAL: *Raisons des textes* reviewed by Robert Laneham

This latest collective and anonymous product of the now notorious *Cercle d'École Abnormale des Lettres* is a strange, even unnerving work, yet despite its pecularities and its undermining effect upon the reader it seems to offer, in an intricate and labyrinthine way, an argument that carries a certain conviction. Not that the argument is pellucid or even easily apparent. Far from it. I was reminded, as I persevered with its elliptical organisation and opaque style, of an occasion shortly after the second world war, when a group of Anglo-American philosophers arranged a conference with what they foolishly took to be their Parisian counterparts, in the hope of exchanging enlightenment on that tricky but topical term 'Freedom'. The opening paper, boldly but simply entitled 'La Liberté' was given, I believe, by Gabriel Marcel. An hour of passionately earnest French from Marcel was followed by a series of wholly uncomprehending questions from the Anglo-Saxons. Communication clearly had not been achieved. Finally, in a desperate response to one bewildered probe from an Oxford don who had yet again requested a lucid definition of 'Liberty', Marcel threw up his hands and exclaimed: 'If I had a piano I could *play* it!' The Anglo-Saxons remained nonplussed.

This book is, I suspect, the score for some unplayable piece on an unimaginable variation of Marcel's piano. Its themes intertwine with such almost uncontrolled complexity that I doubt if I have deciphered more than a minimum of its melodies. But let me attempt my own faltering rendition.

One key lurks in the title. As I hear it, *Raisons des textes* echoes *'raison d'état'* and this is certainly a work concerned with politics. But if we try a translation as, say, 'Textual

Reasons', we are alerted to the predominant procedure of the book: the analysis of how texts deploy or embed particular modes of reasoning. Prominent among the texts chosen are various forms of 'detective' narrative, in a section sub-titled *'Raisons detectifs'*. But the opening part of the book seems to concentrate on two other usages of *'raison'*, the notion of reaching *'l'age de raison'* ('years of discretion') and what in English we would call 'taking the law into one's own hands' (*'se faire raison à soi-même'*).

The actual text begins abruptly, bafflingly:

Does not the true character of each epoch come alive in its children? A child has much to learn before it can pretend. Full citizenship belongs to men both of whose parents were citizens, and they are inscribed on the list with their fellow demesmen when they are eighteen years old. When they are being registered, the members of the deme vote under oath first on whether they appear to have reached the legal age, and if they do not, they are returned to the status of children, and secondly on whether a man is free and born as the laws prescribe. If they decide that he is not free, he appeals to the *dikasterion*, while the demesmen select five of their number as accusers; if it is decided that he has no right to be registered as a citizen, the city sells him into slavery.

From the third sentence on, it is easy to recognise that we are faced with a quotation from Aristotle's *Athenian Constitution* (XLII). But the initial two sentences might puzzle us. The first is, however, another quotation, part of Karl Marx's embarrassingly naif response to the problem he formulates in the *Grundrisse*:

the difficulty lies not in understanding that the Greek arts and epic are bound up with certain forms of social development. The difficulty is that they still afford us artistic pleasure and that in a certain respect they count as a norm and as an unattainable model.

The second sentence comes, I'm told, from Wittgenstein, but its source is perhaps less important than its placing here, suggesting that, somehow, it links Marx's problem with Aristotle's account of the constitution of Athens. But how? The next paragraph offers some definite clues. Again, the

whole paragraph is made up of quotations, rather bewilder-
ingly interlacing Aristotle's *Rhetoric* and *Poetics* with the
closing pages of Wittgenstein's *Philosophical Investigations*.
The text itself disdains to identify the quotations beyond
marking transitions with a slash, thus:

The Emotions are all those feelings that so change men as to affect
their judgements. Such are anger, pity, fear. / Imitation is natural to
man from childhood; he is the most imitative creature in the world,
and learns at first by imitation. / Take for instance the emotion of
anger: here we must discover what the state of mind of angry people
is, who the people are with whom they usually get angry, and on what
grounds they get angry with them. Unless we know all three, we shall
be unable to arouse anger in any one. / Is there such a thing as 'expert
judgement' about the genuineness of expressions of feeling? Even
here there are those whose judgement is 'better' and those whose
judgement is 'worse'. / Can one learn this knowledge? Yes; some can.
Can someone else be a man's teacher in this? Certainly. What one
acquires here is not a technique; one learns correct judgement. / Ask
yourself: how does a man learn to get a 'nose' for something? And
how can this nose be used? / He who feels the emotions to be
described will be the most convincing; distress and anger, for
instance, are portrayed most truthfully by one who is feeling them at
the moment. / It is not right to pervert the judge by moving him to
anger, envy, pity — one might as well warp a carpenter's rule before
using it. / Tragedy is an imitation not only of a complete action, but
also of incidents arousing pity and fear. Such incidents have the very
greatest effect on the mind when they occur unexpectedly and at the
same time in consequence of one another. / Fear sets us thinking
what can be done. Consequently, when it is advisable that the
audience should be frightened, the orator must make them feel that
they really are in danger of something, pointing out that it has
happened to others who were stronger than they are, and is
happening, or has happened to people like themselves, at the hands
of unexpected people, in an unexpected form, and at an unexpected
time. / All terrible things are more terrible if they give us no chance of
retrieving a blunder. / There might actually occur a case where we
should say: 'This man *believes* he is pretending.' / Rhetoric is an
offshoot of dialectic and also of ethical studies. Ethical studies may
fairly be called political; and for this reason rhetoric pretends to be
political science. / The older poets make their protagonists discourse
like statesmen, and the moderns like rhetoricians. / When children

71

play at trains their game is connected with their knowledge of trains. It would nevertheless be possible for the children of a tribe unacquainted with trains to learn this game from others, and to play it without knowing that it was copied from anything. One might say that the game did not make the same *sense* to them as to us.

I'm not convinced that these jittery transitions achieve anything other than compression, but the task of disentangling the juxtapositions does force one to *think*, to come to one's own conclusions as to what line of argument is being implied, while at the same time driving one back to the quoted texts themselves, disengaging those texts from the uses made of them. The irritation this causes is at least accompanied by a certain freshness, a relief from the tedious familiarity of unresolvable arguments about the relation between the *Rhetoric* and the *Poetics*. Moreover, that placing together of, for example, *Rhetoric* 1356a, *Poetics* 1450b and Wittgenstein's laconic remarks reminds us that not only our own reactions to 'Greek tragedy' but also Aristotle's are situated within a moving history, as Marx had recognised; furthermore, in awarding undifferentiated textual status to quotations from all three thinkers, *Raisons des textes* relativises the authority of each epoch against the others.

Clearly, however, the main insinuation of these opening paragraphs is that Greek tragedy is somehow linked to the assumption and exercise of adult citizenship in Athenian society, as perhaps the familiar pastimes of children in our society are associated with their eventual achievement of adult status. Pretence and imitation, performance and judgement, are being elliptically correlated for us. Though the precise reason for the enigmatic inclusion of the last entry in *Philosophical Investigations* II, xi, next to that famous use of *hamartia* ('retrieving a blunder') eludes me, unless 'believing that one is pretending' is somehow the most terrible mistake of all, *the* tragic error.

It is judgement that provides the next main thread. We are given two parallel columns, dividing the page. The left-hand quotes, in full, chapters LXIII to LXV of the *Constitution of Athens*, detailing the elaborately complicated process by which the *dikastoi* ('jurors') were allocated to particular law-courts each day. The right-hand column contains a selection of the meagre textual evidence that survives concerning the judging process at the dramatic festivals. What emerges from this implied comparison is that in both courts of justice and dramatic contest the judging was entrusted to citizens assigned to their role, as far as possible, by lot; the Athenians even devised an elaborate 'randomiser' in the form of an 'allotment machine' (a diagram of which enlivens the text here) to distribute jurors between courts and cases.

These parallel passages are suddenly succeeded by a single quotation in English:

The sheriffs, instead of suffering the Jury to be struck at the places where the book of the Freeholders is kept, and by the officers to whom that care ordinarily falls, sent for the books from the office and took the task upon themselves ... It is very obvious to every person who casts his eye over the lists, that it consists of a most extraordinary assemblage, king's tradesmen, contractors, and persons labouring under every kind of bias and influence.

I myself had to wait until I was much further into the book before I was confidently able to identify the source here: William Godwin's *Cursory Strictures on the Charge Delivered by Lord Chief Justice Eyre* — an article published in *The Morning Chronicle*, 21 October 1794, criticising the 'charge' to the deliberately 'packed' Grand Jury in the trial for 'High Treason' of the radicals Thomas Hardy, Horne Tooke, John Thelwall, and Thomas Holcroft.

The next of these abruptly juxtaposed quotations was easier to trace:

6. *The uneven development of material production relative to, e.g. artistic development.* In general, the concept of progress not to be conceived in the usual abstractness. Modern art, etc. This disproportion not as important or so difficult to grasp as within practical – social relations themselves. E.g. the relation of education ... But the really difficult point to discuss here is how the relations of production develop unevenly as legal relations.
7. *The point of departure obviously from the natural characteristic;* subjectively and objectively. Tribes, races, etc.

These jottings are of 'points to be mentioned here and not forgotten' at the end of Marx's *Notebook 17* (the 'Introduction' to the *Grundrisse*). They immediately precede the notorious passage on Greek art. The authors of *Raisons des textes* obviously think the jottings are intimately related to that passage. Their own link, however, is made more immediately with the final two words 'Tribes, races', for they follow the Marx quotation with a series of fragmentary extracts from a range of sources, all describing the 'reforms' of Cleisthenes in 508 BC; for example:

The people had taken control of affairs, and Cleisthenes was their leader and champion of the people . . . He first divided all the citizens into ten tribes instead of the earlier four, with the aim of mixing them together so that more might share control of the State . . . He divided Attica into thirty sections, using the demes as the basic unit; ten of the sections were in the City area, ten around the coast, and ten inland. He called these sections *trittues*, and placed three into each tribe by lot, one from each geographical area. He made fellow demesmen of those living in each deme so that they would not reveal the new citizens by using a man's father's name, but would use his deme in addressing him. Hence the Athenians use their demes as part of their names . . . These changes made the constitution much more democratic than it had been under Solon.

One could add, of course, that Cleisthenes' reshaping of Athenian social identity made things a great deal more complicated as well! I suspect that any Parliamentary Boundaries Commission faced with a proposal along Cleisthenes' lines would promptly ignore it as impractical. Yet there is a genuine simplicity underlying this surface complexity: tribal, kinship and even regional interest-groups were replaced by constituencies whose only real definition was one of electoral equality. Even the apparent basis of the 'demes' (wards) in geographical neighbourhoods had little effective weight, since a change of residential location did not modify one's deme-membership As one distinguished historian has commented:

If a man still belonged to his deme, no matter where he lived, the neighbourhood principle was no longer in full force, but neither had it been replaced by new bonds of kinship. If anything now counted beside the local principle, it was the individual citizen whose political activity had sometimes few ties left with any larger groups.

In other words, what we can see in the reforms of Cleisthenes is the creation of that curious (even etymologically paradoxical) unit: the political individual. *Raisons des texts* concludes this selection of extracts on the 508 reforms with a single Greek word: *isonomia* — which is perhaps not quite translatable. It indicates not only 'equality at law' or equal access to law, but also equal rights over the law, an equal say in determining what 'the law' is. In a sense which escapes even the literal meaning of our colloquialism, each Athenian citizen 'took the law into his own hands'.

In the kind of textual gesture one is now prepared for, that single glowing word *isonomia* is immediately followed by a news item from *Le Monde*, concerning the activities of the Communist Mayor of a small town in France who personally led an illegal attack on an immigrant workers' hostel. No doubt different French readers will draw their own conclusions from this particular juxtaposition!

The same could be said of the next abrupt switch from classical to contemporary sources. Two brief extracts, from Aristotle and Plutarch, offer interestingly divergent summaries of Solon's reforms (c. 594 BC):

The following seem to be the three most popular features of Solon's constitution: first and most important, that nobody might borrow money on the security of anyone's freedom; secondly, that anyone might seek redress on behalf of those who were wronged; thirdly, the feature which is said to have contributed most to the strength of the democracy, the right of appeal to the *dikasterion*, for when the people have the right to vote in the courts they control the constitution ... Some think that Solon made his laws obscure deliberately to give the people the power of decision. This is not likely; the obscurity arises rather from the impossibility of including the best solution for every instance in a general provision.

The rest of the citizen body were known as *Thetes*; they were not entitled to hold office and their only political function consisted in sitting in the Assembly or on a jury. This latter privilege appeared at first to be worth very little, but later became extremely important, because the majority of disputes were finally settled before a jury. Even in those cases which Solon placed under the jurisdiction of the magistrates, he also allowed the right of appeal to the popular court. He is said also to have framed the laws in obscure and contradictory terms and to have done this deliberately so as to increase the power of the popular courts. In consequence, since the parties to a dispute were unable to settle it according to the letter of the law, they were constantly obliged to resort to the juries and lay every disagreement before them, so that in a sense the jurors became the arbiters of the laws.

These two quotations are followed, quite impishly, by a chart showing the social origins, educational background, and estimated average earnings of the legal profession in France. In the spirit of this procedure, but with a slightly different point in mind, I would myself have also included an extract from, say, the small print in a deed of conveyance.

Here the text of *Raisons* again divides, and in parallel columns we are offered: (a) accounts of the various formal stages in a Greek trial; and (b) an extremely truncated version of Aeschylus, *Eumenides*, lines 408 – 753. Readers familiar with, for example, A. J. Podlecki's *The Political Background of Aeschylean Tragedy* will need no reminding that this confront-ation between Athena and the Furies at Orestes' trial does indeed follow, in broad terms, the actual processes of a Greek court. What the authors of *Raisons* make insufficiently clear by their method of simple parallelism is that Greek legal procedures differed considerably, depending on the nature of the case and of the court to which it was referred. The procedure in a homicide case before the Areopagus court would not have been identical to, say, a theft case heard before an ordinary *dikasterion*. In addition, our sources for recon-structing Greek legal modes make it clear that, as one would expect, practices current in the early fifth century cannot be assimilated to those obtaining in the late fourth. For example, even the passage from Aristotle concerning Solon's reforms clearly reads later developments back into Solon's time — and it is even worth reminding ourselves here, incidentally, that Plutarch was writing some 600 years after the events re-counted.

However, within the context of what I see as the emerging argument of the book, the point is appropriately and adequate-ly, though not exactly, made: that Aeschylus embeds within his play a formal process of trial which, as it were, recapitulates the process which the whole audience is also following, on two levels: they too are passing judgement both on Orestes and on the play itself, and of course — as George Thomson argued long ago — the whole Oresteian trilogy deals with the trans-ition from modes of justice associated with kinship (ven-geance, vendetta) to judicial forms of law developed in the city-state democracy, the *polis*; in passing judgement upon this trilogy the assembled audience is judging a dramatic represent-ation of part of the development whereby they came to be 'judges' themselves.

One can see how some at least of the themes in this book are harmonizing at this point. But a perhaps unexpected variation intervenes here. Three words, in Greek, spread themselves across the page:

> *Choephoroi*   *Electra*   *Electra*

The point of so emphatically isolating the titles of the three dramatisations of the avenging of Agamemnon's murder — by Aeschylus, Sophocles and Euripides (though omitting Eurip-ides' further version in the *Orestes*) — is indicated in the quotation from the *Poetics* that follows:

Tragedy is an imitation not of persons but of actions and of life, of happiness and misery. All human happiness or misery takes the form of action; the end for which we live is a certain kind of activity, not a quality. Character gives us qualities, but it is actions that are happy or the reverse. In a play accordingly they do not act in order to portray the characters; they include the characters for the sake of the action. So that it is the action and the shape of the action that is the end and purpose of tragedy; and the end is, as always, the chief thing. Besides, a tragedy is impossible without an action, but there may be one without characters. The tragedies of most of the moderns are characterless — a defect common among poets of all kinds.

The fuller implications of placing these titles and this passage here is signalled rather startlingly by what immediately follows: a full-page reproduction of a photograph of a young child who is obviously near to death from starvation. Across the photograph is a headline, 'Famine in Somalia', and printed at the foot of the picture is the address of a voluntary aid agency. The photograph is taken from a popular French magazine, and is the equivalent of our familiar Oxfam posters.

Faced with this, it is clearly intended that the reader should pause.

* * * *

Let me do so, in order to make some general comments, prompted by this particular concatenation, concerning the overall 'argument' of the book thus far — as I reconstruct it.

Aristotle, in the *Poetics*, emphasises that once a dramatist has chosen his 'story' he should reduce it to the essential elements of its *structure*, its *dramatic shape*. After that he can fill up the necessary 'positions' in the 'plot' with suitable 'characters'. But the 'tragedy' resides in the structure of events, the chain of episodes, the diagram of forces, not in the characterisation of the agents in the action. For example, we can see Sophocles solving some of the technical dramatic problems he had inherited from Aeschylus (and, probably, Euripides) in his introduction of a sister for Electra into his re-working of the Electra situation: the 'personality' he attributes to Crysothemis is subordinate to, is subject to, the considerations of plotting and sequence of 'effects' which constitute the core of his *Electra*. It is the tragic situation that demands our response, not the secondary feature that it is Electra's situation. But the very fact that Sophocles calls his play *Electra* indicates a certain tilting of an ancient balance: *a* 'character' is always essential for a 'situation' (an Oedipal complex requires *someone* to be Oedipus) but with Sophocles and even more with Euripides we feel that the character, the personality, looms larger than it did in Aeschylus, begins even to loom larger than the *persona*, the mask. Here we might note that a post-Romantic sensibility — i.e. anyone attuned to the presuppositions of the Romantic lyric or realist novel — has great difficulty in grasping the basic movement of, say, *The Libation Bearers (Choephoroi)* where 'character' is assumed with function in the process of the curse: 'Orestes' summons up and is in part 'replaced by' the 'character' of the dead Agamemnon — the great (transfiguration) scene at the tomb which gives the play its first focus and title. One might say that after Wordsworth's 'Preface' to the *Lyrical Ballads* (a title which itself indicates the threshold of a new outlook), we have sought the situation in literature for the sake of the emotion, rather than grasped through the nature of the emotion the nature of the situation. An instance of the kind of problem a Wordsworthian approach generates might be our response to Thomas Hardy's poems of 1912-13: we tend to read 'through' them to the autobiographical situation which prompted them, rather than grasp in the reading of the poems themselves the x-ray Hardy offers us of a *kind of situation*, a *type* of a whole relationship. Some audiences have a similar difficulty with Beckett's plays, for example *Footfalls* or *That Time*.

It's fairly clear, however, from Aristotle's *Poetics*, that the kind of response familiar to a Greek audience was balanced the other way: it is the dramatist's ability to reveal to us the basic pattern of a situation that constitutes his value. And that value is fundamentally *political*, since it is the 'political situation' that we are summoned to grasp, to understand, to appreciate: the situation of the *polis*. But given this balance between situation and character, between dramatic structure and its agents, it can be suggested that a certain capacity for 'emotional' reaction was available to an Athenian assembly or audience in a way we characteristically find it hard to summon up today. Faced with a real 'tragic' situation which does not involve those known personally to us, those near to us or those of our own 'kin', we can remain unmoved, whatever the scale of the 'tragedy'. Reading our morning papers about yet another famine or flood disaster, massacre or 'outrage', we tend to *need* the stimulus of personalised presentation — the hollow cheeks of the starving child on the Oxfam leaflet — before we react with what we feel to be the appropriate feelings. Yet 'pity' or even 'anger' may be deeply *in*appropriate for any effective *action*: feelings diminish fast, the basic situation remains. It is not merely, or only, particularly sharply vivid *events* that demand our political judgement and verdict, but rather that *structure of relations* which shapes and generates those events. Those relations are not 'personal' relations in the first instance, though it may be *through* recognising the sufferings of individuals that we are brought to recognise the shape of the whole. Recognition is not, however, enough. At the dramatic centre of a Greek tragedy is a moment of *anagnorisis* — of re-cognition, of seeing-as, of the acquisition of *knowledge*, but a peculiar and unwelcome kind of self-knowledge. When that moment was *also* constituted as a moment of *peripeteia* — of a reversal of direction, a pivot of *action* — the lesson of the drama was most valued: the aim, the end, of the dramatist was to show *process* changing into *praxis*.

Now, to return to *Raisons des textes*, the point that the authors from C.E.A.L. seem to be suggesting is that the essential function of Greek drama was precisely to provide a *political education* for the citizens of democratic Athens, a form of public training in the nature of decision-making, a representation of what is involved in correct and incorrect judgement both within and about certain kinds of critical political situation. By selecting passages from the sources which present Athenian citizens as 'judges', as members of the courts which (according to Plutarch) became the crucial decision-making centres in the internal life of the *polis*, we are reminded that each citizen had the responsibility for deciding the laws by which he was governed (*isonomia*). Yet this needs, I think, qualification.

The collective 'judges' of the courts comprised very large numbers of the citizen body: each 'jury' was probably 200 or more, and up to 6000 citizens could be involved in deciding an important case. But one could only sit in the courts after reaching the age of thirty, though one could attend the Assembly, and vote, from the age of eighteen. In other words, from eighteen to thirty the Athenian citizen was still an apprentice 'politician', still learning to qualify as a fully responsible member of the *polis* — and one (perhaps *the*) crucial element in that qualifying process is to be located in the attendance (compulsory for some categories) at the dramas, which were themselves (so it is implied by the passages from Aristotle) concerned with exploring and presenting the various ways in which 'emotions' could sway and warp correct judgement. What the plays essentially present are situations, within which someone — normally in authority — makes an incorrect judgement, while the audience is prompted not so much to make a correct judgement themselves as to see why

80

the 'character's' judgement was *in*correct, what it led to and why. In that sense, the plays offer a negative training. And this is certainly consonant with that interesting feature of the legal procedures which is highlighted in the extracts we are offered: the interchangeability of all (adult, qualified) citizens, implied and secured in the apportioning of jurors by *lot*. It is not the 'individual' characters or qualities of the jurors that are important, nor are the merits of the individual in each case to be judged; it is the case itself that has to be judged, impartially, without the jurors being affected by 'inappropriate' emotions. There is, of course, considerable difficulty even in formulating this requirement, since 'emotions' and the individual charac-teristics of the litigants would, obviously, play a role in any specific actual situation. But just as each citizen is inter-changeable, so each law-making decision has to be applicable to every citizen, in principle. What is ultimately at stake in the Athenian courts is a decision as to what is 'correct' or 'incorrect' for the *polis*, i.e. for the citizens as a whole. It is this which is the fundamental meaning of *isonomia*. But such collective decision-making requires a very considerable degree of *individual responsibility*: each juror decides the law in deciding each case (existing 'laws' were regarded as only part of the 'evidence' in a case, not as determining rules) — and the jurors were not even allowed to discuss the case together before voting on a verdict.

An argument along these lines is, I think, apparent in the particular selection of quotations that *Raisons des textes* offers. There are problems to which I want to return, but an important point needs to be made here concerning the relation between this 'argument' and the mode in which it is presented by the C.E.A.L. authors. From 378 BC all 'evidence' in an Athenian court had to be presented in a *written* form; it was then read out during the hearing by the 'clerk of the court' (to use the English term). A sharp formal differentiation was thereby made between the *evidence* and what was said *about* that evidence by the interested parties — a distinction echoed in Aristotle's differentiation between persuasion which can be produced by the art of the orator and persuasion which cannot (1355b 35). What the authors of *Raisons* have apparently

attempted to do is simply to provide 'evidence' while eschew-
ing the 'art of the orator' entirely. By selecting, arranging and
juxtaposing quotations from various sources they are, of
course, using a mode of 'persuasion', but they have deliberately refrained from arguing about that evidence and from
making explicit any conclusions they themselves might draw
from it.

But this procedure itself has further implications. Presumably, for example, they are aware that Aristotle himself
maintains — in the very *Rhetoric* from which they quote so
often — that:

Persuasion is achieved by the speaker's personal character when the
speech is so spoken as to make us think him credible. We believe
good men more readily than others ...It is not true ... that the
personal goodness revealed by the speaker contributes nothing to his
power of persuasion; on the contrary, his character may almost be
called the most effective means of persuasion he possesses.

But in *not* citing this passage, in ignoring its relevance to what
seems to be their general case, are they implying that their
'evidence' is *deliberately* 'slanted', or that they are — perhaps
more legitimately — constructing an 'ideal' case which may
not have actually obtained, or at least no longer obtained by
the time Aristotle wrote? Perhaps, however, one has to
acknowledge an even more drastic implication. Anyone even
reasonably familiar with the sources they extract from will
recognise that a quite different selection could have been
made — and therefore rather different conclusions could be
drawn, suggested. But in fact *they* draw no conclusions at all!
At most, they prompt the reader to see connections; in
particular, by their sudden inclusion of such passages as those
from Wittgenstein, Godwin and *Le Monde* they invite an
application of this body of material to issues and concerns
which are not, in any direct sense, 'relevant' to a discussion of
fifth-century BC legal or dramatic practice at all! It is, in any
case, the *reader* who draws any 'conclusions' or 'parallels' —
and in doing so either does or does not connect this material
with the current concerns of the reader. An instance of this
would be my own response to that particular juxtaposition of

three titles of Greek plays, a passage from the *Poetics*, and the photo of a starving child: the argument I outlined earlier is my responsibility, not theirs. But then, in a rather curious way, aren't I 'answering' Marx's question concerning the continuing relevance of Greek art and drama — the problem implied in the very first quotation in *Raisons des textes*?

There is a further turn to this spiral the text sets up, but for the moment let me return to the text itself. If I have coherently grasped the overall direction of the implied argument so far, it is clear that a problem now looms. Is there any 'evidence' within the plays themselves that they could have operated as modes of 'political education' in the way *Raisons* (or, more strictly, I myself!) has implied — and, more intriguingly, how could *Raisons* present any such case without itself finally resorting to some form of critical commentary, or oratorical persuasion?

* * * *

The C.E.A.L. authors 'solve' this dilemma with a certain impudent neatness. They simply print a number of Greek plays — but not in full! By a skilful process of cutting and editorial stitching they present us with extremely condensed versions of selected plays, which not only retain the movement and shape of the originals but are actually composed entirely of authentic lines and phrases; yet the resulting texts are only between 150 and 250 lines long. (In addition, they italicise words or phrases — a *sotto voce* rhetoric?) Because, however, the reader already knows the originals, the effect is almost as powerful as reading the whole: as we read we simply 'supply' what is missing. I remember once seeing a performance of a fifteen-minute 'version' of *King Lear*: the impact was quite overwhelming, as if the whole of the play had actually been compressed and intensified into that brief time. The impact of these cut-down versions of the Greek dramas is somewhat similar. In a sense, Aristotle's advice to prospective playwrights has been reversed: starting from the whole text of the play, the authors have here 'reduced' it back to what it might have been in an earlier stage of its composition, the 'essential shape of its action' according to Aristotle's notions. At the same time, their procedure reminds us that, in many respects, contemporary critical writing does, in effect, do the same: a critical essay on a novel, for example, often deploys quotations precisely in such a way as to create an 'edited version' of the whole novel, a selective reading of linked passages which then substitute for the whole. And, of course, the selection or editing is made in the light of a (prior) critical 'case' — just as the editing process which produces any actual performance-text today results from the interpretative decisions of the director and producer. The composite production of *The Greeks* by the Royal Shakespeare Company some time ago is a case in point.

In all, seven Greek plays are presented in this way in *Raisons*, arranged in two groups: Aeschylus, *The Suppliants*, Sophocles, *Antigone* and *Oedipus Tyrannos*, Euripides, *Bacchae*, in one group, and three plays by Euripides in another: *Women of Troy*, *Helen* and *Ion*. The first group are obviously related to the general theme of law. In *The Suppliants* we are given a drama about the relations and conflicts between laws based on kinship (parental authority in particular), laws decided by the citizen body (the norms of behaviour which the Suppliants apparently agree to accept in seeking sanctuary), and laws derived from the gods. *Raisons*' version of the *Antigone* emphasises not the Hegelian contrast of two 'absolutes' but rather the conflict between Creon's imposition of his own authority, as political leader, and the final appeal — which the broken Creon eventually has to make — to the decisions of the whole citizenry, represented by the Chorus. In this version it is Creon's line at 1099 which becomes the pivotal moment of *peripeteia* and *anagnorisis*:

What must I do? Speak, and I shall obey.

Creon has finally to accept the 'counsel' of the citizens (which is in favour of releasing Antigone, too late, and also endorses the laws of the 'gods'), and the most basic 'political error' in the play is presented as the *rejection* of good advice from the democratic citizens' assembly (lines 1242–3). The *Bacchae*, in *Raisons*' condensed version, becomes an exploration of the inadequacy of behaviour based either on political force or on

84

unthinking pleasure. But it is the treatment of *Oedipus Tyrannos* that most intrigues me. From being a drama concerned with the discovery of incest and parricide, the play is almost turned into an intellectual detective story! By rapid juxtaposition of apparently unrelated lines, what emerges is a play predominantly concerned with a single question: the relation between the One and the Many (to use a formulation more familiar from pre-Socratic philosophy), the individual and collective identity and responsibility. An example can illustrate this. The whole prologue of *Oedipus* (lines 1 – 150) is compressed into some 15 lines (the italicisations are those of *Raisons*):

Oedipus:	*Children*, what do you *fear* or want?
	I would be hard not to *pity* suppliants like these.
Priest:	A pestilence is upon *our city*.
Oedipus:	I *pity* you, *children*. Your *several* sorrows each have *single* scope, but my spirit groans for the *city and myself* and *all of you* at once.
Creon:	I have good news though hard to bear.
Oedipus:	What you say leaves me uncertain whether to *trust* or *fear*. Speak your news to *all*.
Creon:	Apollo says it is the guilt of murder that pollutes the *city*. The murder of King Laius.
Oedipus:	Can no one tell us what happened?
Creon:	*All* Laius's servants were killed save *one*. He said the robbers they encountered were *many*; it was no man's *single* power.
Oedipus:	Come, *Children*, call the *assembly*, and let it meet on the understanding that *I'll do everything*.

Even in this elliptical form, a number of themes are obviously at work: the relation between kinship, autocracy and democracy; the role of pity and fear and trust; the various possible equations between one and many. The play, in this version, is made to hinge on the moments when these themes are most plainly operative, but the most important turning-points are at line 845, where Oedipus fends off the truth concerning his murder of Laius by insisting that 'One man cannot be the same as many', and the exchange between Oedipus and the messenger

85

from Corinth, at lines 1014-20, which is retained almost in full:

Messenger: Do you know that all your *fears* are empty?
Oedipus: How is that, if they are father and mother and I their son?
Messenger: Polybus was *no kin* to you.
Oedipus: Was not Polybus my father?
Messenger: *No more than I but just so much.*
Oedipus: How can my father be my father as much as *one that's nothing to me?*
Messenger: Neither he nor I begat you.

Once we connect this exchange to the theme of one being identical with many it is clear that *Oedipus Tyrannos* is, for the authors of *Raisons*, essentially an inquiry into the nature of 'democratic' relations (i.e. those *not* based on kinship or territory) in which each citizen is equally related to every other. While it may be the inappropriate 'fear' of Jocasta (1076) or the perhaps misapplied 'pity' of the shepherd (1178) which has brought about the opening situation, it is primarily Oedipus's angry refusal to recognise that he is *only* one among many that leads to his attempted repudiation of both truth and purification. In other words, the deepest 'error' presented in this play is the refusal to understand and accept the very nature of a 'democratic city'.

But what *is* the 'very nature of a democratic city'? How are we to think that? *Raisons* at this point gives us another Greek word and another quotation, in transliterated Greek, from Aristotle's *Nicomathean Ethics* Book I, 13, 1102a:

eudaimonia

estin hē eudaimonia psykes energeia tis kat'aretēn teleian

This is followed by a standard translation:

happiness: happiness is the activity of the soul in accordance with the highest virtue.

but then by various entries from a Greek dictionary:

eudaimon(os): prosperous, happy, fortunate; well-fated by the gods.
daimon: a minor god.

daimoōn (daemōn):	skilled in something.
en-ergos:	busy, working; on active service (soldier); productive (land).
energazomonai:	to make, create; pursue a calling; labour; work for hire.
ergōn:	a man's business, his work.
ergō:	to work, accomplish.
aretē:	skill, excellence in workmanship (v. *teknē*).
teleios:	full, complete, fulfilled, perfectly done.
teleios anēr:	full-grown, man with full rule and authority.

and finally by another quotation, in Greek, from Aristotle's *Politics*:

Man is a political animal.

Clearly, we are meant to attempt our own translation, our own definition of the terms 'happiness' and 'politics'. Something along these various lines might emerge:

Working well as a human being means being busy at doing or making something which demands a great deal of skill when you're good at it.

Having a good time with your life means being able to do something well worth doing that demands and repays a lot of skilful effort.

Happiness is an activity that demands and generates energy by putting the most complex skills and techniques we have to work on something.

Being happy in one's work involves the most complete skill, the most demanding technique, and the better the technique the more productive and enjoyable the work will be.

I've no idea if these are the kind of 'translations' *Raisons* is encouraging by its dictionary entries. Certainly they are far removed from any traditional reading of Aristotle! On the one hand, that may not matter very much to the C.E.A.L. authors; on the other, it's possible to recognise an affinity between such translations and the implications of that laconic remark by Aristotle that 'in a tyranny only the tyrant can be happy.' If, for Aristotle, it is the *ergon*, the job, the point, the defining characteristic, the peculiar 'end', of a human being to 'make cities', to be 'political', then in a tyranny only the tyrant can fulfil that definition, has that job, so the rest of us can't be 'happy': we are prevented from exercising our most complete skills and energies, those involved in 'making' the 'city'.

Given our contemporary understanding of — or respective reaction to — the terms 'happiness' and 'politics', this line of argument, or suggestion, seems sufficiently bizarre to make one suspect a joke. I wonder if the members of the *Cercle Abnormale* have ever spent a futile, depressing, frustrating, wearying evening attending a meeting of their local Labour Party Management Committee, or its equivalent? One advantage of their procedure of declining to comment on the material they present is that they can avoid tackling such awkward thoughts. Another is apparent from what immediately follows this section on *eudaimonia*.

A single page is headed 'A Short History of Happiness', and consists of just four quotations! The first is:

true and perfect happiness is that which makes a man self-sufficient, powerful, worthy of reverence and renown, and joyful.
Question: Do you imagine that there is any mortal and frail thing which can bring about a condition of this kind?
Answer: No.

The only identifying information they give us is:

Boethius, b. 480, Consul 510, Master of the King's Offices, 520, imprisoned 525, wrote *The Consolation of Philosophy*, c. 530.

Pondering that skeletal career, perhaps no further comment is actually needed. The second quotation is a composite passage from St Thomas Aquinas, *Summa Theologiae*, Ia 2ae, q. 1, art. 6, q. 3, art. 2, art. 5:

Is everything a man wills on account of an ultimate end?
Is it an activity?
Of the theoretical or practical reason?
Response: The activity happiness is in the theoretical rather than the practical intelligence. Given that happiness is an activity, then it ought to be a man's best activity, that is to say when his highest power is engaged with its highest object. Man's mind is his highest power, and its highest object is divine good, an object for its seeing, not for its doing something in practice. Hence the activity of

contemplating God is principal in happiness. And since, as Aristotle puts it, that strikes each man as himself which is best in him, such is the activity most proper and congenial to man.

The third is from Friedrich Schiller's *Letters on the Aesthetic Education of Man* (1793–5):

To declare it once and for all, Man plays only when he is in the full sense of the word a man, and *he is only wholly Man when he is playing.* We enjoy the pleasures of the senses simply as individuals, and the race which lives within us has no share in them; hence we cannot extend our sensuous pleasures into being universal, because we cannot make our own individuality universal. We enjoy the pleasures of knowledge simply as race, and by carefully removing every trace of individuality from our judgement; hence we cannot make our intellectual pleasures universal, because we cannot exclude the traces of individuality from the judgement of others as we do from our own. It is only the Beautiful that we enjoy at the same time as individual and race, that is, as *representatives* of the race. Sensuous good can make only *one* man happy, since it is based on appropriation, which always implies exclusion; it can also make this one man only partially happy, because the personality does not share in it. Absolute good can bring happiness only under conditions which are not to be universally assumed; for truth is only the reward of renunciation, and only a pure heart believes in the pure will. Beauty alone makes all the world happy, and every being forgets its limitations as long as it experiences her enchantment.

The final quotation is from Chapter V of John Stuart Mill's *Autobiography* (1873, posthumously):

It was in the autumn of 1826. I was in a dull state of nerves, such as everybody is occasionally liable to; unsusceptible to enjoyment or pleasurable excitement; one of those moods when what is pleasure at other times, becomes insipid or indifferent; the state, I should think, in which converts to Methodism usually are, when smitten by their first 'conviction of sin'. In this frame of mind it occurred to me to put the question directly to myself: 'Suppose that all your objects in life were realised; that all the changes in institutions and opinions which you are looking forward to, could be completely effected at this very instant: would this be a great joy and happiness to you?' And an irrepressible self-consciousness distinctly answered, 'No!' At this my heart sank within me: the whole foundation on which my life was constructed fell down. All my happiness was to have been found in the continual pursuit of this end. The end had ceased to charm, and how could there ever again be any interest in the means? I seemed to have nothing left to live for.

The only biographical information on Mill given in *Raisons* is — quite bizarrely — that he was MP for Westminster from 1865-8, and they refer us to, of all things, his 'Speech to the Electors of Westminster' and a letter to the *Daily News*, 23 March 1865!

This is, one might think, a remarkably meagre cull even for a 'short' history of happiness! At the very least, I would want to add a passage from Karl Marx's *Economic and Philosophical Manuscripts* (1844) on 'the relationship of man to woman' as the index to 'the entire level of development of mankind', in demonstrating 'the extent to which the *other*, as human being, has become a need for man, the extent to which in his most individual existence he is at the same time a communal being.' Though perhaps I would then have to add some near-contemporary remarks from Kierkegaard's *Either/Or* (1843) on 'The Unhappiest Man' and 'The Aesthetic Validity of Marriage' — and possibly complement these two with an extract from their common intellectual ancestor, Hegel's essay 'On Love' in his early theological fragments. As soon, in fact, as one thinks of further passages one recognises the advantage of *Raisons'* austere procedure: the trajectory they indicate, from 'politics' through philosophy and theology and aesthetics back to the atheist Mill's Benthamite dilemma, does probably encapsulate an essential movement — though one might recall that Mill at least found solace in Wordsworth, and this 'history' could be read simply as a repertoire of permanent possible options.

The next quotation in *Raisons'* idiosyncratic organisation could only come from a history of unhappiness — though no indication is given that we have actually switched 'histories'. It comes from Diodorus of Sicily (1st century AD):

On the borders of Egypt and in the adjacent districts of Arabia and Ethiopia, there are many large gold mines worked intensively at great expense of misery and money. The rock is black with rifts and veins of marble so dazzling white that it outshines everything. This is where the gold is prepared by the overseers of the mines with a multitude of labourers. To these mines the Egyptian kings send condemned criminals, prisoners of war, also those who have fallen victim to false accusations or been imprisoned for incurring the royal displeasure, sometimes with all their kinfolk — both for the punishment of the guilty and for the profits which accrue from their labour. There they throng, all in chains, all kept at work continuously day and night. There is no relaxation, no means of escape; for, since they speak a variety of languages, their guards cannot be corrupted by friendly conversation or casual acts of kindness. Where the gold-bearing rock is very hard, it is first burned with fire, and, when it has been softened sufficiently to yield to their efforts, thousands upon thousands of these unfortunate wretches are set to work on it with iron stone-cutters under the direction of the craftsman who examines the stone and instructs them where to begin. The strongest of those assigned to this luckless labour hew the marble with iron picks. There is no skill in it, only force. The shafts are not cut in a straight line but follow the veins of the shining stone. Where the daylight is shut out by the twists and turns of the quarry, they wear lamps tied to their foreheads, and there, contorting their bodies to fit the contours of the rock, they throw the quarried fragments to the ground, toiling on and on without intermission under the pitiless overseer's lash. Young children descend the shafts into the bowels of the earth laboriously gathering the stones as they are thrown down, and carrying them into the open air at the shaft-head, where they are taken from them by men over thirty years, each receiving a prescribed amount, which they break on stone mortars with iron pestles into pieces as small as a vetch. Then they are handed on to women and older men, who lay them on rows of grindstones, and standing in groups of two and three they pound them to powder as fine as the best wheaten flour. No one could look on the squalor of these wretches, without even a rag to cover their loins, and not feel compassion for their plight. They may be sick, or maimed, or aged, or weakly women, but there is no indulgence, no respite. All alike are kept at their labour by the lash, until, overcome by hardships, they die in their torments [*en taîs anánkais*]. Their misery is so great that they dread what is to come even more than the present, the punishments are so severe, and death is welcomed as a thing more desirable than life.

This sobering passage is undoubtedly familiar, if only from George Thomson's *The First Philosophers*, where he points out that this 'is the only example in classical literature of a writer who had the intellectual and moral courage to discover for himself and describe the mass of human misery on which his civilisation rested.' Thomson continues, incidentally:

These, then, are the realities that first inspired the imagery that underlies so many Orphic parables of this life and the next — the Platonic Cave, in which men are chained from childhood hand and foot, and have never seen the daylight, and the topography of Tartarus, with its subterranean channels of water, mud, fire and brimstone; or the upper regions, under a clear sky, where the souls of the righteous are at rest ....

— enjoying the consolations of contemplative philosophy, no doubt.

As the next abrupt quotation might indirectly remind us, however, philosophy too could have its drawbacks. The passage is again taken from Aristotle's *Constitution* (XXXIV):

The people shortly overthrew the Five Thousand. In the seventh year after the overthrow of the Four Hundred, the battle at Arginusae was fought. Thereafter, first the ten *strategoi* who won the battle were all condemned by a single vote, although some had not been present at the battle and others had been rescued by other ships; the people had been misled by those who were enraged by what had happened.

The incident happened in 406 BC, during the Peloponnesian war: though the sea-battle was won, a storm destroyed the returning fleet and the generals were held responsible for the ensuing deaths. Aristotle's account is both inaccurate and incomplete, but it does point to the problem which haunts Greek democracy — that the Assembly could indeed make 'tragic mistakes' when it was swayed by emotion, perhaps rage and pity in this case. On this occasion the Assembly was also inquorate and broke its own standing orders. Two other aspects of the incident are worth noting: that the slaves who took part in the battle were enfranchised, and that the President of the Assembly on the day of the condemnation of the generals was the philosopher Socrates, who refused, unavailingly, to ratify the improper verdict. Seven years later Socrates himself was also condemned to death, for his endless questioning. The year 406 was also, incidentally, the year in which both Sophocles and Euripides died, bringing the great period of Greek tragedy to a close almost at the same moment as — on Aristotle's account — Athenian democracy entered its period of degeneration.

What connection we are meant to make between Diodorus's description of slavery and Aristotle's brief mention of Arginusae is perhaps made clearer by what immediately follows: the compressed versions of three of Euripides' plays mentioned earlier, *Women of Troy*, *Helen* and *Ion*. As with the previous 'versions' of Aeschylus and Sophocles, the tactic is, in effect, to re-write the plays in order to point up their connections with each other and with, it would seem, the problem of democracy. In *Raisons'* versions of the Euripides plays the emphasis is upon women, slaves and children.

Women of Troy is reduced to a series of confrontations between attempts to impose 'predefinitions' and attempts to refuse or avoid those predefinitions. Thus, Helen's refusal to accept her assigned role as guilty, as unfaithful, as responsible for the Trojan war, is contrasted with Hecuba's final acquiescence in her demotion from Queen to captive slave (after her foiled attempt at suicide, a last desperate assertion of her previous royal status). The play, of course, locates these women precisely *between* definitions: their old roles and status in Troy and the new lives that await them after the suspended moment of the play is over. But the centre, the pivot, of the play in this compressed version is the death of Astyanax, the infant son of Hector — killed not for anything the child has done but because he is defined in advance as avenger. The whole issue of fate and destiny is focused in this murder, an attempt to avert destiny; but as both the opening of the play (the old, old prophecies) and the ending (the gathering storm that will destroy the homeward fleet) remind us, destiny is still dominant in the story as a whole. The *Helen*, on the other hand, hilariously undermines the entire 'story' of the Trojan war: Menelaus, shipwrecked in Egypt, finds that Helen never went to Troy at all and has been living in Egypt during the whole ten-year conflict, while a mere mirage of her had been foisted by the gods upon the deluded armies at Troy. The version offered in *Raisons* brings out the sheer arbitrariness of the relation between events, descriptions and 'definitions', from the opening words, establishing that 'this' (the arena of the theatre itself) is 'Egypt', to the closing reminder to the Athenians (during the war between Athens and Sparta) that the very name of 'Greeks' (Hellenes) derives from a Spartan: national identities are, in the end, only a matter of how we name ourselves and others. This lesson is instantiated in the play by the inefficacy of Menelaus's use of his own 'great name' in a country outside his sphere of power, and by the dispute between himself and his slave as to the meaning of both 'slave' and 'king'. Finally, the uncertain status of names and identity is pointed up as central to the *Ion*, where the boy who is eventually to be called Ion has to decide between apparently irreconcilable accounts of his paternity and the future possible lives that would be determined by his 'choice' of father. (English readers may be more familiar with Eliot's reworking of the *Ion* in his *The Confidential Clerk*.) With this version of *Ion* we seem to have come full circle, back to the very first quotation from Aristotle in *Raisons des textes*, concerning the requirement that citizens be born of parents both of whom were citizens themselves. It is time to step back.

* * * *

Pondering this sequence of quotations and compressed plays presented thus far in *Raisons* — Marx, Wittgenstein, Aristotle's *Rhetoric*, *Poetics*, and *Athenian Constitution*, *The Suppliants*, *Antigone*, *Oedipus Tyrannos*, happiness, slavery, Arginusae, *Women of Troy*, *Helen*, *Ion* — we can move in various directions. One central point is presumably obvious: that what we call 'democracy' in fifth-century Athens was organised in an extraordinarily elaborate and rational way, but it was also very strictly curtailed (excluding women and slaves) and was ultimately based upon two decidedly *non*-rational premises: the initial accident of birth and the final sanction of death. Full participation in the 'democracy' depended on the accident of being born the male child of Athenian citizens, while the entire structure of democratic government rested upon a horrendous edifice of slave-labour, specifically in the silver-mines which underpinned the Athenian economy and imperial power. One could also pick out from the *mélange* of texts quoted the importance of the jury system and allocation by *lot*, as a crucial a-rational and deliberately 'accidental' mechanism of democracy. Or one might emphasise the implied relation between the processes of democracy and the various functions of drama within Athenian society.

But there is a frustrating sense in which any such 'conclusions' are neither indicated by nor even drawn from the texts presented in *Raisons*. In order to arrive at those conclusions and certainly in order to think through their implications for Athenian democracy, the reader of *Raisons* *already* has to know, to some extent at least, the significance, the point, of those texts. But that surely requires a degree of specialist knowledge and expertise, and in that respect certainly not all readers of the book are 'equal'. One is, in fact, acutely conscious of a paradox within the form of *Raisons des textes*: that while the argument one can elicit is concerned with radical democracy, the evidence (if that is what it is) they appeal to derives from that branch of learning which has peculiarly characterised the ruling élite of modern European societies: a 'classical education'. But if the reader has been excluded from or denied such an education, how is one meant to assess the worth of the evidence offered? Indeed, how is one to assess the 'argument', since mere juxtapositions provide the only 'links'? It simply isn't clear whether we are being presented with an argument about history (the composite form of the first paragraph suggests otherwise) or perhaps merely with textual gestures, passages extracted from any historical context, for us to think about. But why should we regard such passages as worth thinking about — and *how* should we think about them? Are we simply to endorse those that in some way 'appeal to' us, or are we to judge them, somehow, 'rationally'? After all, it is the claim that all human beings are rational that has sometimes been offered as the basis of and justification for 'democracy'.

*   *   *   *

With these questions in mind we can now turn to Part II of the volume. Here we are first confronted with a section entitled 'A

Short History of Reason', which consists of not even four
passages but just four phrases!

> *akribeia*
> Sic et Non
> *cogito*
> Age of Reason

Perhaps indeed that is all that needs to be said on the topic!
But how are we to take this sequence (or typology)? Is
Aristotle's justified insistence, that in any inquiry one should
(and can) only aim for that degree of precision (*akribeia*)
appropriate to the object of inquiry, meant to be taken as
contradicted by or ratified by the notorious work of Abelard
(the capitalisation, of course, suggesting, anachronistically,
Abelard's famous title), opposing disproofs from reason and
proofs from revelation, and vice versa, concerning the same
item of doctrine? Or are we to see Abelard's maintained
tension (Sic *et* Non) as inevitably collapsing into the radical
doubt and axiomatic rationalism of Descartes? Is the 'Age of
Reason' (the English in the original alerts us to Paine rather
than Sartre), that moment of revolutionary optimism in which
Reason herself was enthroned as a goddess, to be seen as the
final abandonment of the Aristotelian precept (one thinks of
Burke's strictures) or as the triumphal (disastrous?) political
application of the Cartesian scepticism and search for a new
starting-point? Should one rather read this short history as
suggesting a recovery of Aristotelian emphasis upon the
objective and necessarily social character of inquiry, after the
long reign of personal self-questioning? One could undoubtedly envisage different trajectories through these four 'moments', and one is inevitably prompted to query the selection
and at least to question its historical limits. Are pre-Socratic
modes of thought also pre-rational? Is Kant to be assimilated
to the 'age of reason'? Has the post-Revolutionary era seen the
implementation of 'reason' in human affairs (surely not!) or
rather its demise: after 1789 is the history of reason a blank?
Yet C.E.A.L.'s own text is entitled *Raisons des textes*. Is there
then a mode of 'literary' reason?
    The bulk of Part II, headed '*Raisons detectifs*' (are other

modes perhaps '*raisons defectifs*'?), is certainly concerned with literary texts, though the implied criterion of 'literary' is perhaps peculiar. Here the authors almost reverse their procedure in Part I: instead of highly selective quotations eclectically mingled from a variety of sources, they offer us just one long quotation from each of four works, followed by a commentary which requires us to bear in mind the rest of the relevant text. The texts themselves, however, are an odd mixture: Conan Doyle's first Sherlock Holmes short story, *A Scandal in Bohemia* (1891), Freud's first classic case history, *Dora* (written 1901, published 1905), Arthur Koestler's novel, *Darkness at Noon* (1938-40) and Bertolt Brecht's play *Caucasian Chalk Circle* (c.1944).

The Conan Doyle quotation is actually the very first paragraph of the story:

To Sherlock Holmes she is always *the* woman. I have seldom heard him mention her under any other name. In his eyes she eclipses and predominates the whole of her sex. It was not that he felt any emotion akin to love for Irene Adler. All emotions, and that one particularly, were abhorrent to his cold, precise but admirably balanced mind. He was, I take it, the most perfect reasoning and observing machine that the world has seen, but as a lover he would have placed himself in a false position. He never spoke of the softer passions, save with a gibe and a sneer. They were admirable things for the observer — excellent for drawing the veil from men's motives and actions. But for the trained reasoner to admit such intrusions into his own delicate and finely adjusted temperament was to introduce a distracting factor which might throw doubt upon all his mental results. Grit in a sensitive instrument, or a crack in one of his high-power lenses, would not be more disturbing than a strong emotion in a nature such as his. And yet there was but one woman to him, and that woman was the late Irene Adler, of dubious and questionable memory.

The commentary has a compact style:

Wedlock suits Watson, but not the bohemian soul of Holmes which responds rather to the pretty problem of the King of Bohemia: a dishonourable liaison to be disowned before legitimate marriage by the dispossession of a photograph, through theft, deception, force, and gold.

This is harsh, but arguably accurate. Holmes-lovers may, however, repudiate the implications of this curt description: 'the hired secret agent of an unscrupulous foreign state'. Indeed, as Holmes' role is here described, it becomes indistinguishable from that of a more recent brand of agent:

If it is important that justice should not only not be done, but also not even seen not to be done, authority funds an agency to work outside the law, swearing to absolute secrecy and operating in disguise. The rationale for such a hidden hierarchy of law-breaking law-enforcement agencies is the need to prevent crime. A comprehensive data-bank on all potential criminals — i.e. a paragraph on everyone — will help prevent any truths emerging that might cast doubt on the conduct of those who authorise, condone, finance theft and violence in their own interest.

One has to search the text rather unsympathetically hard to justify that exegesis! At this point, the CEAL authors promptly step outside the text to inform us that records of all reported crimes were initiated in England in the 1870s and that by the late 1970s an estimated 36,325,000 current names were available on the Hendon Police National Computer Unit, including 6.7 million 'criminal names' and some 3 million Special Branch files. They cite similar figures for most countries in Europe, then switch back to the Holmes story to focus upon Watson's 'moment of compunction and shame' before he chooses to 'release the rocket' rather than commit 'the blackest treachery' to Holmes, and the King. Watson, on their reading, becomes potentially the moral centre of the tale, precisely because he allows, however momentarily, the 'softer passions' to 'remove the veil from Holmes' motives and actions'; in doing so he operates as 'latent grit in the finely adjusted machine, a crack in the most high-powered surveillance system the world has seen'. One purpose of that surveillance machine is, literally, 'repression' — of '*the* woman, of sexuality, of Irene'. After so much Greek in Part I, we are presumably expected to recognise the etymology of that name: *eirene*, 'peace'. And it is a kind of peace that Irene makes — by getting married herself, to a lawyer. In doing so, moreover, she even brings Holmes out of the shadows and

98

endows him briefly with a quite different status as 'observer':
as 'witness' to her wedding. But while witnessing a marriage
ceremony is indeed a form of seeing, it is not one which can be
assimilated to deduction (cf. Holmes's arrogant 'I see it, I
deduce it'); at the end of the tale Holmes is left merely with an
image of Irene, from which he is unable to deduce anything at
all.

One is tempted after reading this commentary (of which
there is more, concerned mainly with the 'spuriousness and
irrelevance' of Holmes' 'powers of reason', and with the
various reversals of expectations, roles and levels in the tale) to
complain, with Watson: 'at each successive instance of your
reasoning I am baffled', though with the CEAL authors one
cannot even add 'until you explain your process', for we seem
to be drawn by this book into a process without any attempt at
'explanation'.

*　*　*　*

Some links between *A Scandal in Bohemia* and Freud's *Dora*
might be guessed at in advance: Freud, like Holmes, prides
himself on successfully interpreting slight clues of behaviour
and speech that others overlook; both operate on a mistaken
assumption as to the actual love-object of the woman; both
seem to succumb to an only half-admitted attraction; and it is
the woman in each case who finds a way to 'close' it
'prematurely'. Yet *Raisons des textes* does not draw attention
to these parallels. The passage chosen for quotation and
commentary is Dora's 'second dream', though they modify
Freud's own text to include, within square brackets, the
'addenda' and alternatives in Dora's later renditions of the
dream, which Freud himself relegates to footnotes:

I was walking about in a town which I did not know. I saw streets and
squares which were strange to me. [I saw a monument in one of the
squares.] Then I came into a house where I lived, went to my room,
and found a letter from Mother lying there. She wrote saying that as I
had left home without my parents' knowledge she had not wished to
write to me that Father was ill. 'Now he is dead and if you like [There
was a question-mark after this word, thus: 'like?'] you can come.' I
then went to the station and asked about a hundred times: 'Where is

the station?' I always got the answer: 'Five minutes.' I then saw a thick wood before me which I went into and there I asked a man whom I met. He said to me: 'Two and a half hours more' [alternative: 'Two hours']. He offered to accompany me. But I refused and went alone. I saw the station in front of me and could not reach it. At the same time I had the usual feeling of anxiety that one has in dreams when one cannot move forward. Then I was at home. I must have been travelling in the meantime, but I know nothing about that. I walked into the porter's lodge, and enquired for our flat. The maidservant opened the door to me and replied that Mother and the others were already at the Cemetery. [I saw myself particularly distinctly going up the stairs.] [After she had answered I went to my room, but not the least sadly, and began reading a big book that lay on my writing-table.]

The 'commentary' begins with a summary of Freud's own interpretation of this dream, arranged in a quite extraordinary fashion: as a musical composition, perhaps an opera score. Phrases from the dream form the libretto or vocal line, while the complex over-determinations Freud instances are arranged on successive staves, like the instrumental parts for an orchestra, so distributed as to indicate the chordal character of their interaction. It's an effective mode of illustration, but they perhaps stretch their point by then referring to Freud's mode of thinking and analysis as 'polyphonic'. Something of what they intend by this is made clearer by some parallels they then draw with the 'musical' structure and 'thematic' arrangement of various Modernist literary works: *Ulysses*, the *Cantos*, *A la recherche* and *Four Quartets*. Their suggestion seems to be that to 'read' these works or to respond to a dream-interpretation is closely akin to reading a score or listening to music: an alert but also shifting attention to simultaneous 'levels' of interacting notes, images, themes, sounds. The 'unconscious' would, on this model, be more like those sequences within a musical composition which escape our conscious attention yet which form a necessary part of its structure, its very intelligibility.

The application of this suggestion to our reading of Dora's dream is not immediately apparent, however, since we are next given two sets of dates, thus:

| Dora's analysis: Oct.–Dec. 1899 | *Interpretation of Dreams*: Nov. 1899 |
| *Interpretation of Dreams*: 1900 | Dora's analysis: Oct.–Dec. 1900 |

The second set is historically accurate, but the first is that actually given in Freud's own account: Chapter 1 of the case-study opens 'In my *Interpretation of Dreams*, published in 1900' (the prefatory remarks also, incidentally, opens with dates of Freud's works) and consistently in later life and in later textual additions to the case-study Freud 'misremembered' the date of Dora's analysis as 1899 instead of 1900. Indirectly at least, the CEAL authors imply an explanation for Freud's uncharacteristic memory-lapse. They invite us to suppose that Dora *read* the *Interpretation of Dreams*, probably in the last stages of her analysis. Given what we know of the actual 'Dora', this is indeed plausible. They then quote again the final addendum to her dream, pointing out that Freud himself normally regarded such addenda as crucially significant:

After she had answered I went to my room, but not the least sadly, and began reading a big book that lay on my writing-desk.

Freud referred this dream-book to an encyclopaedia Dora had guiltily read in March 1899, the clue to this interpretation being her familiarity with medical terminology 'known to physicians but not to laymen' which she must have 'derived from books', though her sexual knowledge must also have been supplemented by 'a second and oral source of information'. Freud constantly returns to the question of this 'source' and suggests various possibilities — but consistently (as in other matters) fails to recognise Dora's own mother as a possible, even likely, source. We are then invited to re-read the complete dream-text and to see it as a (perhaps artificially and deliberately constructed) text with two levels of meaning: that given in Freud's own interpretation (which *Raisons* does not dispute) and a second, almost overt, significance: as a narrative of Dora's experience of psychoanalysis! She had entered the strange world revealed by psychoanalysis, partly at the behest of her father but also (once her father's original motivation was sidestepped, by Freud) on her own behalf; after, in effect, asking many times in her life about her own sexuality and always being promised that she would know when she was a little older, she finally meets a man (Freud) who offers to accompany her on her path of self-knowledge — but he too only promises an ever-receding and postponed conclusion. (Slyly, the commentary quotes Freud: that analysing this dream 'had so far occupied two hours'.) She therefore takes a successful short-cut, going it alone but with the help of a 'big book' intended for experts not for laymen, supplemented with what she had already learned from her 'oral source', Freud's own treatment.

There is a certain outrageous humour in the notion that Dora made up her dream to fulfil Freud's wish to analyse her, but also used her knowledge derived from his own book to inform him that she no longer needed him — she opened the third session on the dream by telling Freud, to his surprise and resentment, that she was concluding the analysis. But the suggestion definitely sheds an amusing light on Freud's account of the interpretation process in those final sessions: we read that Dora conveniently provided him with a childhood-related accident that made her 'drag her foot' (almost a translation of the name 'Oedipus'), that 'every difficulty was resolved at a single blow by her prompt reply: Nine months later' (a well-prepared and far from innocent patness?), that Dora offered 'immediate confirmation' of his guesses, 'disputed [his] facts no longer', 'nodded assent, a thing which I had not expected', and in general 'listened to me without any of her usual contradictions'. Surely, we almost say, Dora was finding it difficult not to burst out laughing as she beautifully led him down the path his own book had enabled her to map out for him!

How serious the CEAL authors are it is difficult at times to say, but they do raise a crucial issue for psychoanalysis: not simply the problem of circular feedback from the analysand's own advance knowledge of psychoanalytic procedures and interpretations (Dora having a doubly privileged position of priority in that respect) but the more difficult question of the distinction between 'expert' and 'layperson'. Freud's *Dora* text is littered with appeals to his own experience and extensive knowledge of other cases and to general 'rules' — but, arguably, he misses the main point in Dora's own case (she perhaps even tries to help him, with her significant references to pictures of 'nymphs' and the Madonna). Freud becomes, for Dora, superfluous, and in principle Freud could not argue otherwise, on the evidence of his own *self*-analysis in the *Interpretation of Dreams*. Later, Freud will insist upon the necessity of the trained analyst on the grounds that a negotiation of the 'transference' is essential to analysis — but it is his own blindness to his own transference in the case of Dora that the text reveals.

Raisons des textes offers no conclusion to this commentary — except in the odd, displaced form of an 'Addendum to the History of Reason': the single word *Gedankenfreiheit* followed by the name Adorno. The German word is Freud's term normally translated as 'free association', but is also open to the rendering 'free speech', in the political sense. The reference to Adorno presumably directs us to his meditation on this word in his *Minima Moralia*:

Freedom of thought — The displacement of philosophy by science has led, as we know, to a separation of the two elements whose unity, according to Hegel, constitutes the life of philosophy: reflection and speculation. The land of truth is handed over in disillusion to reflection, and speculation is tolerated ungraciously within it merely for the purpose of formulating hypotheses, which must be conceived outside working hours and yield results as quickly as possible. To believe, however, that the speculative realm has been preserved unscathed in its extra-scientific form, left in peace by the bustle of universal statistics, would be to err grievously. First, severance from reflection costs speculation itself dear enough. It is either degraded to a docile echo of traditional philosophical schemes, or, in its aloofness from blinded facts, perverted to the non-committal chatter of a private *Weltanschauung*. Not satisfied with this, however, science assimilated speculation to its own operations. Among the public functions of psycho-analysis, this is not the least. Its medium is free association. The way into the patient's unconscious is laid open by persuading him to forgo the responsibility of reflection, and the formation of analytic theory follows the same track, whether it allows its findings to be traced by the progress and the falterings of these associations, or whether the analysts — and I mean precisely the most gifted of them, like Groddeck — trust to their own associations. We are presented on the couch with a relaxed performance of what was once enacted, with the utmost exertion of thought, by Schelling and Hegel on the lecturer's podium: the deciphering of the phenomenon. But this drop in tension affects the quality of the thought: the difference is hardly less than that between the philosophy of revelation and the random gossip of a mother-in-law. The same movement of mind which was once to elevate its 'material' to a concept, is itself reduced to mere material for conceptual ordering. The ideas one has are just good enough to allow experts to decide whether their originator is a compulsive character, an oral type, or a hysteric. Thanks to the diminished responsibility that lies in its severance from reflection, from rational control, speculation is itself handed over as an object to science, whose subjectivity is extinguished with it. Thought, in allowing itself to be reminded of its unconscious origins by the administrative structure of analysis, forgets to be thought. From true judgement it becomes neutral stuff. Instead of mastering itself by performing the task of conceptualization, it entrusts itself impotently to processing by the doctor, who in any case knows everything beforehand. Thus speculation is definitively crushed, becoming itself a fact to be included in one of the departments of classification as proof that nothing changes.

A certain pattern, or score of themes, is perhaps emerging: the relations between expert and layman, reason and the 'softer passions', moral responsibility and the possibility of self-knowledge. But also some tentative parallels faintly suggest themselves: the search for self-knowledge recalls the Socratic 'know thyself'; Dora's refusal of definition echoes Helen's role in *Women of Troy*; her presentation of 'another' Dora even evokes the *Helen* play itself. But I confess to a certain bemusement at this stage, an inability to hear whatever polyphony is being composed for me. Yet the peculiar 'reasoning' of this text does seem, somehow, to work on one, perhaps at some other level than hearing. For example, after reading those earlier analyses of the fate of children in *Women of Troy* and *Ion*, I curiously found myself thinking of that strangely disturbing moment, nearly twenty-five centuries later, at the end of Chekhov's *Three Sisters* (1900, the year of Dora's analysis), when the stage-direction specifies the last 'action' of the play:

Andrey enters; he is pushing the pram with Bobik sitting in it.

That moment always makes the theatre go chill for me. Bobik would have been seventeen or so in 1917. Think of that speech of Toozenbach in Act I:

> The time's come: there's a terrific thunder-cloud advancing upon us, a mighty storm that is coming to freshen us up! Yes, it's coming all right, it's quite near already, and it's going to blow away all this idleness and indifference, and prejudice against work, this rot of boredom that our society is suffering from. I'm going to work, and in twenty-five or thirty years' time every man and woman will be working. Every one of us!
>
> Chebutykin: I'm not going to work.

I think forward to Russia, twenty-five, thirty years later. Bobik would have been about thirty-five in 1935. What would the child have become? *That* child. And I *don't know* what I feel about Toozenbach's speech.

*   *   *   *

The authors of *Raisons* cannot, of course, be held responsible for my personal unconscious chords and connections across their text, but even so the very title of the next novel they comment on, *Darkness at Noon*, seemed highly apt at this point. They single out one passage:

We have learnt history more thoroughly than the others. We differ from all others in our logical consistency. We know that virtue does not matter to history, and that crimes remain unpunished; but that every error has its consequences and venges itself unto the seventh generation. Therefore we concentrated all our efforts on preventing error and destroying the very seeds of it. Never in history has so much power over the future of humanity been concentrated in so few hands as in our case. Each wrong idea we follow is a crime committed against future generations. Therefore we have to punish wrong ideas as others punish crimes: with death. We were held for madmen because we followed every thought down to its final consequence and acted accordingly. We were compared to the Inquisition because, like them, we constantly felt in ourselves the whole weight of responsibility for the superindividual life to come. We resembled the great Inquisitors in that we persecuted the seeds of evil not only in men's deeds, but in their thoughts. We admitted no private sphere, not even inside a man's skull. We lived under the compulsion of working things out to their final conclusions. Our minds were so tensely charged that the slightest collision caused a mortal short-circuit. Thus we were fated to mutual destruction.

But how can the present decide what will be judged truth in the future? We are doing the work of prophets without their gift. We replaced vision by logical deduction; but although we all started from the same point of departure, we came to divergent results. Proof disproved proof, and finally we had to recur to faith — to axiomatic faith in the rightness of one's own reasoning. That is the crucial point. We have thrown all ballast overboard; only one anchor holds us: faith in one's self. Geometry is the purest realisation of human reason, but Euclid's axioms cannot be proved. He who does not believe in them sees the whole building crash.

Once reason itself has crashed, all that is left, apparently, is faith and ultimately only faith in oneself. But at this point (the second hearing, the fifth day) in the logic of Rubashov's argument, it is the a-logical, precisely in the form of that enigmatic 'self', that 'grammatical fiction' of the first-person singular, that begins to intrigue and attract him. But the 'self' becomes apparent only as an uneasiness, a curiously palpable silence of response to certain (self-) questionings, in those muted monologues that are really dialogues of a special kind. In that silence, particularly, are to be heard echoes of repressed moral dilemmas and guilts: the sacrifice of other 'I's for which Rubashov has been responsible and which, for many readers, are sufficient to condemn him. Such readers concur with his final self-condemning plea of 'Guilty', but on quite other grounds than his accusers.

That common reading does not, however, satisfy the authors of *Raisons*. It is worth quoting the opening of their commentary on the quoted passage:

This formulation of the argument secretes a paradox which under-mines the strategy of the text. Rubashov's temptation to put himself in his opponent's position, to recognise the potential reversal of roles with Ivan, provides Koestler's governing device. He puts the reader in Rubashov's position, seeing the scene through his eyes, thinking within his premises: a quasi-first-person narration. The final plea convinces us as true to Rubashov's own movement only if we too have become sufficiently inward to Rubashov's own commitment to endorse the justice of that plea according to the logic of that commitment, even though we are also invited to reject its justice in rejecting the premisses of that logic. Yet this double-movement rests on that questionable formal device: in adopting a quasi first-person viewpoint, the novel necessarily endorses in advance the position of the grammatical fiction while precluding the possibility of that historically objective perspective which is both premise and demand of the logic it rejects. Yet it is only through that very inwardness that the ostensible problem of the novel can be posed: only from within that particular personal history with its specific memories and its uncertainties concerning the future that the question of History's judgement can be plausibly rendered as a credible dilemma. Since the logic of the argument within the novel cannot by the novel's own admission be resolved by any logical argument concerning the claims of the grammatical fiction, it is only by this formal option of empathetic narrative that the logic of political commitment is ostensibly discredited. Thus the form doubly begs the questions posed. Only from the perspective of 'I' can a mathematics which adds 'I' to 'I' and makes 2 be considered as *a priori* invalid.

Presumably that last reference is to the various passages in the novel on the 'algebraic' treatment of history. This complicated, even tortuous, commentary can be inadequately summarised as saying that despite the appearance of two positions engaged in a struggle for supremacy within the novel — ruthless determination versus moral judgement — one position has already been endorsed in advance by the very narrative mode of the novel. But this is surely to reject the very possibility of a specifically novelistic treatment of these issues. A novel can only present an issue as experienced and debated by specific individuals in a specific situation, but then at least some aspects of the issue are 'already' settled or taken for granted by those individuals, not least the genuine impossibility for those individuals of an answer to any dilemmas in terms of the actual future judgement of history. It's worth remarking that any search for moral *premises* ignores this simple social fact. One might, of course, argue that a fictional treatment of *this* issue is inappropriate on other grounds: that what is at stake in the 'sacrifice' of an individual must always be an actual individual, one therefore situated in a myriad of ways more complicated than any form of fiction can adequately deal with.

But in fact *Raisons des textes* is not concerned with the problems, or appropriateness, of fiction; its interest is fixed on logic. The commentary continues, with its own compact mode of logic:

Yet if the reader is brought to a recognition of the 'justice' of Rubashov's plea according to the logic of the political position Rubashov continues to maintain, and if one consequence of that position is indeed a legal system by which Rubashov can be condemned not for what he did but for the 'consequent logic' of what he believed (where the distinctions between opposition, assassination and civil war are, rightly, judicial subtleties), then a reader who judges that legal system and its consequences to be unjust is thereby placed in a position parallel to Rubashov's own. Either the reader accepts the consequent logic of his own judgement upon that system and is thereby committed to an opposition which (in any real world) may not stop short of war, or in recoiling from such practical opposition accepts that system, at least for others, thereby conceding to Rubashov a consistency the reader has evaded. Yet the legal system which condemns Rubashov cannot be judged unjust merely against the norm of some other legal system since that too would have to be judged to be the norm; nor by any appeal to history, since that would be to re-embark on Rubashov's own trajectory; and to judge by any form of appeal to one's own infallibility would merely be to re-enter that same trajectory at a later stage. In judging Rubashov's plea we therefore have to judge Rubashov rather than the system which accepts and endorses his plea, yet we can only judge Rubashov by the criteria which we recognise as governing our own self-judgements, and they necessarily derive from our own first-person viewpoint, precluded as we are from attaining an objective perspective or historical judgement upon our own lives. Thus the reader is left by the logic of this novel with no consistent basis for judgement.

Tightly wrought as it is, I have two major objections to this argument. First, that neither the novel nor actual history convinces me that it was a 'consequent logic' of Rubashov's kind of commitment that political opposition should be eradicated by executions. Second, I am unpersuaded that an objective perspective upon one's own life is wholly precluded

— though I recognise the problem of locating the grounds for that objectivity. Oddly, the commentary itself argues that *all* legal systems eventually have recourse to a notion of 'objective guilt', in the crime of 'treason', since what makes an act specifically treasonable is not simply the character of the act or the intention of the agent but the fact of the accused being a citizen of this State rather than of some other. That 'objective' fact is thereby legally presumed to involve a 'consequent logic' of commitment to that political – legal system; conversely, it is suggested, any deliberate rejection of a specific law implicates one in a consequent logic of, if necessary, a rejection of the entire legal, and ultimately political, system of which one is 'objectively' a member. Involved in any self-judgement, then, is a judgement concerning the State one chooses, or would choose, to commit oneself to. Again, one is rather uneasily aware of a distant echo back at this point to the discussions in Part I, of the Athenian constitution, of the relations between juries and law-making, of Socrates, and even perhaps of *Oedipus Tyrannos* — another victim of 'objective guilt' who learned, tragically, that the structure of the State is such that a judgement upon unknown others implicates oneself.

The issues that *Raisons des textes* successively forces upon us seem ferociously entangled with each other. One wishes, even desperately, for disentanglement and elucidation, for a clarity and lucidity of analysis that both the structure and the style of this book seem deliberately to refuse. Certainly the authors have not chosen to write a treatise in political philosophy or a constitutional handbook (though they began by quoting from a combination of both), yet the disparate and mainly literary texts they focus on do seem, for them, to operate in a register akin to those familiar modes of inquiry and analysis. Perhaps by their very obliquity and opacity, they are prompting us to a difficult recognition of the nature of our own, actual, 'political' thinking: which rarely takes the form of professional philosophical analysis, expert constitutional inquiry, or even knowledgeable journalistic commentary (though we may need to call upon these skills) but rather operates 'polyphonically': a disturbingly opaque interplay of passion, logic, rhetoric, commitment, moral judgement, emotion — and, overall, a peculiar form of 'reasoning' in which the conclusions are sometimes only a step towards acknowledging the premises from which we know we should have begun and upon which we feel bound to act.

* * * *

The final commentary in *Raisons* is upon the Epilogue to Brecht's play, *The Caucasian Chalk Circle*, the closing words of the Singer – Narrator:

And after this evening Azdak disappeared and was never seen again.
But the people of Grusinia did not forget him and often remembered
His time of judgement as a brief
Golden Age that was almost just.

But you, who have listened to the story of the Chalk Circle
Take note of the meaning of the ancient song:

That what there is shall belong to those who are good for it, thus:
The children to the maternal, that they thrive;
The carriages to good drivers, that they are driven well;
And the valley to the waterers, that it shall bear fruit.

The commentary initially concentrates on reminding us not only of how, as the epilogue indicates, two stories are intersected in the structure of the play — the tale of Grusha and the child, and the story of Azdak the judge — but also of how, in many of its local details and arrangements, episodes, sub-scenes and gestures echo each other across the texture of the play. That Azdak characteristically hears two cases simultaneously, his unpredictable judgements interweaving apparently disconnected issues, is offered as exemplary of the play's whole organisation. (Here again we can sense the CEAL authors endorsing a peculiarly 'polyphonic' mode.) Yet Azdak's rulings are not wholly unpredictable: they are clearly *class*-based judgements, invariably for the poor against the rich. Yet it is characteristic of the play (some would say a weakness) that these class-preferences are dramatically re-inforced by an appeal to the audience's simpler emotional responses: the rich are presented as arrogant and unpleasant, while the poor in at least some cases (the old widow and the good-hearted bandit) are sentimentally portrayed. The kind of

110

judgement being invited or evoked is certainly class-based but supplemented by what could be variously termed (judged as) 'moral', 'emotional' or 'empathetic' judgement. The *Raisons* commentary opts for 'empathetic', arguing that empathy is the real basis of any actual solidarity or class-feeling between the poor and oppressed — an imaginative identification with others' suffering — rather than the rationalistic basis some-times proposed, of a common recognition of interest or generalised self-interest based on one's own class-position. Their point is that commitments, positions or arguments based on (self-)interest are necessarily modified as soon as one's 'interest' is even marginally differentiated from that of others: any 'solidarity' on that basis is fragile and temporary. Empathy however to some extent can both override and outlast self-interest. They enroll Grusha in their argument, maintaining that it is precisely her empathy with the child that commits her to saving it in the first place:

> For a long time she sat with the child.
> Evening came, night came, dawn came.
> Too long she sat, too long she watched
> The soft breathing, the little fists
> Till towards morning the temptation grew too strong.

It is empathy too which makes her let go of little Michael in the tug-of-war contest with the 'real' mother in the circle ('Am I to tear him to pieces? I can't do it!'). Empathy overrides rational consideration, both of self-interest and the apparent interest of the child (that she should 'prove' herself the mother by *not* letting go).

I remain largely unconvinced by this argument, both in its general claims and in its application to Grusha. Class-empathy seems to me as fragile and as temporary as any other kind of class-identification, and indeed — as I argued earlier in relation to Aristotle's *Poetics* — as any other kind of 'empathy'. And in Grusha's case Brecht's own commentary (which *Raisons* does not cite) deploys quite other terms: maternal instincts, love and even interest. He also uses 'productive' in an odd sense:

Her maternal instincts lay Grusha open to troubles and tribulations

111

which prove very nearly fatal. All she wants of Azdak is permission to go on producing, in other words to pay more. She loves the child; her claim to it is based on the fact that she is willing and able to be productive.

And elsewhere, in a 'dialogue' on the play, we find this:

B: ... the trial scene isn't about the maid's claim to the child but about the child's claim to the better mother. And the maid's suitability for being a mother, her usefulness and reliability are shown precisely by her levelheaded reservations about taking the child on.

R: Even her reservations strike me as beautiful. Friendliness is not unlimited, it is subject to measure. A person has just so much friendliness — no more, no less — and it is furthermore dependent on the situation at the time. It can be exhausted, can be replenished, and so on.

W: I'd call that a realistic view.

B: It's too mechanical for me: unfriendly. Why not look at it this way? Evil times make humane feelings a danger to humanity. Inside the maid Grusha the child's interests and her own are at loggerheads with one another. She must acknowledge both interests and do her best to promote them both. This way of looking at it, I think, must lead to a richer and more flexible portrayal of the Grusha part. It's true.

Only if the *Raisons* notion of 'empathy' can incorporate these more complex considerations could it serve to make the link required by the play between the story of the circle and that other 'second' story which frames the play: the debate between two collective farms in the post-war Soviet Union.

Yet even the relation between the chalk circle verdict and the decision over the disputed valley is less simple than it might appear. In that dispute there is no class difference upon which to base a preference, which crucially distinguishes it (as a political problem) from Azdak's judgements, yet no compelling parallel can really be drawn between the respective positions of Grusha and Abashvili and the fruit-growers and goat-breeders. It is, after all, the *latter* who, like Grusha, base their claim on 'love' and even upon having 'tended' the land. On the other hand, the fruit-growers can claim to have defended the valley against the German 'Ironsides' during the war. *Raisons* quotes an early draft of the epilogue in which the goat-breeders explicitly repudiate the suggested parallel:

how dare you compare us ... with people like that Natalia Abashvili of yours, just because we think twice about giving up our valley.

Yet the final version of the epilogue does seem to make a direct parallel:

The children to the maternal, that they thrive ...
And the valley to the waterers, that it shall bear fruit.

Despite this, I have known audiences who were convinced after a performance that the decision had gone the other way — perhaps swayed by the rather more attractive character-isation of the Old Man who offers the barely-tolerable cheese.

Raisons rather side-steps this problem, and concentrates instead on an analysis of how the decision is actually reached in the Prologue. Returning to a favourite theme, they emphasise the minimal role played by the 'expert' from the capital, while highlighting the mingling of rhetoric, appeals to sentiment, use of humour, arguments about legal rights, etc., which all enter into the discussion and influence the outcome. But they then single out the quotation from Mayakovsky: — 'The home of the Soviet people shall also be the home of Reason' — as signalling the decisive argument, the real turning point: the fact that the detailed plans for the irrigation development are based upon the specific material features of the valley. In a curious way this does seem to be true in Brecht's composition of the scene, yet it is difficult to see why this should be *the* decisive factor. I suspect it is because the very precision of specification (sometimes given little emphasis in production: 'Why is there a fall of 66 feet?', '*This* rock is to be dynamited!' 'They force the water down *here*, that's clever!', etc.) indicates that the project can only happen 'here' (whereas the goat-cheese *can* be produced elsewhere) and that in itself shows a close respect for the particular materiality of the land which is akin to, and part of, that 'love' for the land which is the main claim of the original villagers. Nevertheless, I can imagine a version of this discussion in which the decision did go the other way — and it would be remarkably easy to adapt the epilogue's final line accordingly. Brecht's own comment (again ignored by *Raisons*) is illuminating:

The *Caucasian Chalk Circle* is not a parable. Possibly the prologue may create confusion on this point, since it looks superficially as if the whole story is being told in order to clear up the argument about who owns the valley. On closer inspection however the story is seen to be a true narrative which of itself proves nothing but merely displays a particular kind of wisdom, a potentially model attitude for the argument in question. Seen this way, the prologue becomes a background which situates the practicability and also the evolution of such wisdom in an historic setting.

Brecht's comment might even be adapted to apply to the basic organisation of *Raisons des textes* itself: it certainly 'proves' nothing, but does perhaps display a certain mode of grappling with a problem, a potentially model attitude for a kind of 'reasoning' that would itself be 'democratic'. (Whether it presents a 'narrative' is another matter!) Disappointingly, *Raisons'* own conclusion, not only to their Brecht commentary but to the whole book, is rather less complex than Brecht's. They basically suggest that the necessary components of 'democratic reasoning' — i.e. the mode of political argument and decision-making appropriate to a fully classless society — would be a combination of 'empathy' and 'material knowledge', the first being a capacity for imaginative identification with and recognition of the need of another, and the second a precise grasp of and respect for the material possibilities of the resources available. Yet this is surely only a disguised version of the traditional marxist position, a mere displacement or re-labelling of, respectively, 'class consciousness' and that practical knowledge and skill attributed to those who concretely produce the material necessities of social life. In a way, the ending of the book is not only simple and unsatisfying but actually sentimental: the final page consists of a photograph of a quite delightfully happy and laughing child, flanked on one side by two quotations from Wittgenstein's *On Certainty*:

Children do not learn that books exist, that armchairs exist, etc. etc. — they learn to fetch books, sit in armchairs, etc. etc.

Is it wrong to say: 'A child that has mastered a language-game must know certain things'? If instead of that one said: 'must be *able to do* certain things', that would be a pleonasm, yet this is just what I want to counter the first sentence with.

And, on the other, by the quotations from Wittgenstein and Marx with which the book began:

A child has much to learn before it can pretend.

Does not the true character of each epoch come alive in its children?

Yet even this last gesture of repetition reminds us that this curious text greatly exceeds its unsatisfactory conclusion. Its own polyphonic structure pushes us away from simply seeking a 'conclusion' to a clearly linear argument. The various uncompleted strands, the only half-acknowledged echoes (Michael's fate in *Chalk Circle* is surely another reworking of that of Ion or even Astyanax), refuse to shape into an 'expert' or 'authoritative' statement. Each reader is left to construct from these materials an overall response — an oddly, even infuriatingly, 'democratic' gesture! Yet at the same time the various devices of the text and the texts chosen for compression or commentary seem to imply that what we have generally classed as drama and literature may, in at least some cases, be read primarily as modes of (initiation into) 'political' thought. For example, in trying to grasp the relation between the personal and the structural in those resistantly opaque and often tragic dramas of the Athenian *polis* we are learning, as once the young ephebes did, how to participate appropriately (yet precisely not as 'experts' in a later sense) in the processes of democratic decision and of law-making. *Raisons des textes* certainly shares something of that same opacity, and may even have the overall 'shape' of a tragedy, but — like the audiences at the Athenian festivals — I perhaps have had to learn from responding to the performance itself the grounds upon which I might judge it.

*   *   *   *

Each reader will respond differently. This reader found his mind revolving two main issues. The first is how to organise a genuinely class-less democracy. The usual proposals concentrate on such matters as mandated delegates, single-issue representatives, complex hierarchies of elected committees, or forms of localised 'direct' or 'mass' decision. If a role for 'experts' or 'professionals' is retained it is seen often as that of providing alternative or opposing plans and detailed proposals, between which a choice can be made, with full information publicly accessible. Yet one merely has to skim, say, Harold Wilson's frenetic memoirs of his premiership from 1964 to 1970 to realise not only the ludicrously crowded personal timetables enforced by our present arrangements but also the appalling amount of 'information' that has currently to be assimilated by the political professional. Given the present intricate global interactions, economic, diplomatic, military, it does not seem feasible to envisage any effective forms of direct democracy, of non-hierarchical responsibility structures, or even of public access to and *assimilation* of 'full relevant information'. Nor is it clear that class-less social formations would constitute *less* complexly interrelated elements in a global order. But even beyond these formidable problems of concretely realising democratic participation (rather than occasional electoral transmission of political power), there remains the acutely difficult but quite crucial issue of the *modes of argument and thought* appropriate to a fully democratic political system: how does one (or the many) *think politically*?

It is here perhaps that *Raisons des textes* suggests some possible emphases, though no more than that. A number of themes resonate together: childhood, self-knowledge, self-judgement, active learning, non-'rational' modes of thinking, the relations between 'expert' knowledge and 'lay' insight in certain areas, the ability (in Brecht's words) to think within the flow as well as above the flow. If democratic participation and responsibility is still seriously possible, a crucial precondition is adequate 'political education' before full adulthood, a learning by both practice and 'pretending', and the most appropriate mode of such 'education' would seem — if we acknowledge the Athenian lesson — to be through 'dramatic' and 'aesthetic' experience. This would involve, not only in schools but necessarily there, sustained involvement in 'judging' 'political' plays and fictions, in constructing and performing political dramas, in practising responsibilities in both real and 'pretend' situations, in learning rhetorical and persuasive skills as well as those of rational calculation. The qualifying term 'political' in this context need not indicate a narrow focus upon the immediately topical and controversial, as the treatment in *Raisons* of Greek plays indicates! Indeed, those classical dramas may well be a crucial component of such an educative process, raising as they do problems of self-knowledge, of the relations between State and individual, conflicts between law and moral responsibility — in ways which demand genuinely difficult judgements. If such an educational programme recalls in some of its elements precisely that 'classical education' (Greek, rhetoric, debating) associated with a discredited 'public school' system, that is perhaps not surprising: in certain limited ways — as one would indeed expect — the ruling élite *has* successfully used *its* educational system to train its children in the exercise of political power (over and above the social 'superiority' they were bred to), and the traditional concentration on 'the classics' was by no means mistaken. It is perhaps the very contradiction between the implicitly 'democratic' character of the material studied and the restrictions upon democratic participation sustained by that ruling élite which increasingly condemned 'classical education' to decadence and irrelevance. Perhaps a recovery of the political significance and function of those 'aesthetic' modes which first emerged within Athenian democracy is now possible. But of course the point of such an educational focus would be frustrated if the real exercise of political responsibility were denied in adult life. Here again, there may possibly be lessons available from the Athenian reliance upon allocation to legal, political and administrative positions by *lot*, a principle we retain only in the case of juries. Radically to extend that principle, alongside electoral procedures and 'professional expertise', might indeed be possible at both local and national levels, in the form of a proportional composition of local councils or the 'allotment' of some members of reconstituted 'second chambers' and 'select committees'.

The necessary continuation of 'political education' into adult life might well involve tackling the problem of 'assimilating' 'information' along related lines. Even at present some of the most impressive and memorable work on television, for example, has been in the form of dramatic treatments of political principles, issues and problems. (The work of Trevor Griffiths, from *Occupations* to *Bill Brand*, has been in some respects exemplary.) Informed participation at a public inquiry into, say, a proposed nuclear power station can involve the assimilation of (to cite one recent case) 22,000 pages of documentation. Yet one can envisage competing dramatisations of the issues involved, each controlled by — and partly subject to judgement in terms of — the *aesthetic* demand to present the strongest possible arguments and counter-arguments within the work. Here we can recall Aristotle's remark that 'Persuasion is achieved by the speaker's personal character when the speech is so spoken as to make us think him credible.' That is a controlling consideration not only for the creation of 'characters' but for the overall credibility of a work: the composition of a serious work of art involves a commitment to the fullest possible engagement with, and not evasion of, the issues tackled. That difficult demand upon the 'character' of the artist is different from the demands placed upon either the professional politician or the expert, if only because, in Brecht's words, a 'true narrative' of itself 'proves nothing but merely displays a particular kind of wisdom, a potentially model attitude for the argument in question.' It is partly from those Greek dramas of two millennia ago that we have inherited that crucial criterion of serious art: 'in a certain respect', as Marx remarked, they do indeed 'count as a norm and as an unattainable model' — unattainable, that is, until we recover and go beyond the democratic impulse and forms of social organisation which fostered them and which they helped sustain.

Raisons des textes cannot be judged a successful work, but in trying to respond thoughtfully to its own polyphonic mode of thinking I at least have been brought to confront — with perhaps equal lack of success — a range of formidably difficult problems, including the peculiar and frustrating problem of *how* I am to think about them. For that prompting, I respect — however critically — the impulse behind this curious book.

Robert Laneham

Fiction

'David Blake: a continuing argument'
Derek Lemming

The editor asked me to write an obituary. That doesn't seem right somehow, too formal for David and probably not very illuminating. There isn't much to tell, about David's life, or death. He was once a student; he was caught in a car-bomb; he survived, half-paralysed; and he died this year. You can imagine much of that life, without my talking about it. I would find it difficult anyway. David was a friend, and I miss him.

So what follows is more like the continuation of an argument, one we had every time I read anything he'd written. He wrote incessantly, though he published only three novels. Two of them were, in a way, 'successful' — though not, in my view, either as novels or as the political propaganda he so sincerely wanted them to be. They were, frankly, too badly written and they were politically naive — in my view. But that's what we argued about.

Actually, we more or less agreed about the first one, *Six Weeks in June*. He had to write it, I suppose, to get those events out of his system. Perhaps we all did, then. The reviews were kind, on the whole, but since most of the younger reviewers, in those days, had the same problem it didn't complete surprise us. I remember we giggled helplessly over the judiciously distanced approval of one press reviewer whom we both recalled fleeing for his life in Grosvenor Square:

His central group of characters live out the hopes and expectations of the radicalised students of the late sixties, beginning with the eruption of 'May' (1968) in Paris and ending with the London

121

Dialectics of Liberation Congress in July (1967). By condensing, conflating and interweaving the 'events' of those successive optimistic summers into one imagined month Mr Blake has given us an appropriately packed canvas and a vivid kaleidescope of the utopian gestures of that tumultuous moment ...

And so on. But we were both mildly amazed when the book crept into the best-seller lists, and genuinely staggered when the film rights were snatched up. Perhaps we shouldn't have been. Even by then the sixties were a suitable cinematic myth and the novel's time-trickery lent itself to some irresistible shots: Stokely Carmichael and Allen Ginsberg making impassioned speeches at the Liberation Congress transposed to the liberated Odéon, a goggle-eyed Sartre fumbling for a Gitane as Stokely's pained black voice lashed the crowd: 'What have you *done*? *What* have you done? What have *you* done?' That's the way mythic memories work — though the casting could have been less bizarre.

The only part of the novel I can now re-read is the ending. It has all David's writing faults, but with its echoes of David's own near-death a few years after '68, perhaps it has its aptness here:

He swung round as Peter jerked his arm and pointed to the side-gates.

As he turned and lowered the camera he could see in the viewfinder the absurdly small figures of the advancing militia while fifty feet in front of him those same soldiers, in their camouflaged battledress and black face-shields, seemed alarmingly larger than life-size.

As in an old slow-motion movie, he saw their heavy polished boots lift in unison as they began a controlled charge towards him. In the uproar of the battle and the slogan-chanting behind him, only the directional-microphone's dial registered the pounding of those boots on the roadway.

Peter was yelling something at him but he still stood there, rivetted by the threat and by a sense of distanced unreality.

Almost automatically, he raised the camera again to eye-level and began to film the last few seconds of the charge. Through the lens he glimpsed the out-of-focus shape of a long thick baton and then his right eye seemed to explode inward into his brain.

The sky somersaulted and a brief blackness blinded him.

As he tried to lift his leaden head from the pavement he sensed that the shattered camera lay a foot from him. Through the tears and what he knew was blood he tried to focus his left eye, to locate the camera and if possible reclaim it. The grey paving stone seemed very close, clear, immense, and strangely bright, each speck of dirt large like a pebble.

Then a shadow moved slowly across that huge area and he knew, in some peculiar recess in the empty universe that was the inside of his battered brain, that the front wheel of the leading armoured car had mounted the kerb and was about to crush this strange new light out of the hard cold stone.

In the film this 'final' episode was replaced, of course. The last shot summoned another mythic memory: an isolated line of guitar-playing youngsters sitting across the path of an inexorably oncoming tank. That image was actually elsewhere in the novel, and the tank had both Nato and Soviet insignia on it. The Nato ones disappeared in the film.

Predictably, one might say — and so would begin the argument. Since long before the explosion that physically wrecked him David had been politically opposed to urban guerrilla and armed insurrection strategies in England. That image of the guitar versus the tank remained dominant for him. He wasn't particularly embittered by becoming a victim himself; he knew the arguments, and perhaps that helped. When I saw him in hospital he simply said: 'I always wanted time to write. Now I don't have any excuses.' His motto, the old, familiar one, had been: 'Educate. Organise.' Since he couldn't now 'organise' he would 'educate', and since the same film-producer had an option on his next novel he would take the opportunity to experiment: 'We *have* to *imagine* a revolutionary scenario — otherwise we have no right to think that we know where we're going.' *Just Demands* was his reply to my arguments.

The film of *Just Demands* hasn't been in general distribution for some time now, so it's worth recapping the basic 'plot'. Certainly, he gave the producer, in part, what he wanted: pace, excitement, spectacle — and a 'special ingredient'. That first, terrible, sentence of the novel (which perversely delighted David) signalled the style of the movie:

There was the sound of a royal flush, and the Prince emerged grinning.

The Literary Labyrinth

The film sketches the initial situation rapidly. At some indeterminate but not-too-distant date in the future, the youngest prince of the British Royal Family begins a postgraduate course at the new University of Rochester, an institution specialising in media studies and training (Prince 'E.D.''s diploma is to be in Personal Appearance Presentation). A group of students take him under their wing and we have twenty minutes or so establishing the group's 'characters', with their privileged hobbies (sailing, flying) and more 'typical' student activities: videodrama production training, some 'live' theatre rehearsals (E.D. is persuaded to make a 'personal appearance' in a forthcoming performance), documentary interview field work (filling in the contours of the society and offering some nice cameo parts), even some snippets of lectures, lab-work and libraries, plus the usual ration of quasi-orgiastic all-night parties and occasional political arguments, even a brief demonstration at Chatham Arsenal. Then E.D.'s two brother princes come down to watch his drama début and a wild cast party after the performance is hosted by E.D. on his royal yacht moored in Rochester harbour. The student documentary group are there to film it all — except that their cameras conceal guns. So the three princes are held hostage and the royal yacht commandeered, together with the helicopter that brought the visiting princes. One of the best scenes in the film follows: as dawn breaks, the yacht and the helicopter (now with one hostage prince aboard) set out for the open sea, with a wary cordon of police, navy and air-force hovering in their various boats and planes. But as the yacht and helicopter clear the Medway they turn not towards the Channel but into the Thames itself and an awakening London finds itself watching a bizarre royal progress, as both vessels and their accompanying nervous flotilla make their way slowly upstream. The yacht finally drops anchor in mid-river between the Waterloo and Hungerford bridges, and the initial demands are announced — on Citizens Band wavelength: the exchange of one prince for six named bankers and industrialists, and the penthouse suite at the Savoy (overlooking the river at this point) to be made available to the kidnappers.

124

From then on the film exploits the spectacular aspect of the novel. Once the new hostages have reluctantly but 'loyally' offered to take the place of one released prince, with the remaining two now divided between the moored yacht and the Savoy penthouse, thereby making rescue attempts very risky, the students stage an indication of their grim seriousness. The helicopter takes off from the Savoy and hovers 400 feet above the river near the Houses of Parliament: to the horror of the crowds on the banks, a tied and hooded figure comes tumbling from the helicopter; at 200 feet a parachute opens; but then at 100 feet the figure explodes in a sheet of flame and charred bits scatter over the water. In the shocked silence the demands of the kidnappers are heard from the thousands of transistors tuned to the CB wavelength previously used: that all TV stations should broadcast for the next six nights a series of video-programmes previously made by the kidnappers and that public phone-in facilities be arranged to the group in the Savoy, these also to be broadcast live on radio. In return, one hostage will be released each night; if the broadcasts don't occur, one prince will be publicly executed. These demands are finally met, and the first broadcast goes out that evening, detailing the business and political dealings of the dead industrialist. As the broadcast ends, that 'dead' industrialist is landed ashore from the yacht: the exploded figure had been a dummy.

The film now begins to enjoy itself: each successive release of the hostages becomes a spectacular set-piece staged by the kidnappers, with some precision helicopter flying. A plump and perspiring property speculator is released onto the scaffolding at the top of an unfinished prestige office skyscraper. An industrialist whose criticism of supplementary benefit as 'more than the country can afford' had been quoted in the previous broadcast, is ditched in the Pool of London with a small rubber duck tied to him. A banker with extensive South African interests is deposited in the lion-pit at Regents Park Zoo. The last industrialist is simply lowered straight into the exercise yard of Wormwood Scrubs. For the last banker, suggestions as to his fate are invited over the phone-in: he is finally dumped in the outfall from the main drainage and sewer system at Barking Creek. Each of these set-pieces is bracketted in the film by extracts from the kidnappers' programmes and from the counter-programmes put out by the TV channels — but we get very little of either. What takes their place, interspersing the releases and gradually dominating the film, is the build-up of rescue plans and the assembling of an élite assault team in preparation for the Bond-like ultra-spectacular finale — but we can here leave the film to its own devices.

I loathed the film. So did David, as he knew he would. And our argument continued. His position was simple and deliberate: in the wake of the film (which had a certain success) more people would read the 'book of the film' — and find themselves confronted by a rather different work. That was certainly true, up to a point. The novel includes the texts — or rather scenarios — of the programmes the kidnappers have made, and David didn't do too bad a job of imaginatively presenting a great deal of material. The programme on 'Who Rules?', for example, combines wicked candid-camera footage of some of the students' own families, intercut with data on the companies and organisations they work for and control, which is gradually drawn together to outline a ruling bloc some of those families would be surprised to find they are part of — and the novel shows us their reactions to that self-discovery. The programme on economics is a studio game, a cross between Monopoly and poker, in which one team can change the rules. International relations is treated as a murderous thriller ('The Lie that Comes in with the Gold'). And the novel also gives us the counter-programmes, the phone-in discussions, the field-interviews (later used in the programmes) with shop-stewards' committees, women's groups, anti-racist organisations, disarmament campaigners, etc., etc. All this material not only has the effect of relegating the 'plot' of the film to a mere skeleton, but it makes the novel as a whole a shapeless blockbuster. The pace is slowed down even further by the opening hundred pages, which outline in a detail we only retrospectively appreciate the different activities of the students, all of which do eventually have a role in the subsequent 'action' — but that's a long time coming for the impatient reader. Various sub-plots excised from the film further retard the action: the lecturers too are involved in a variety of undercover political activities, and some of these figure in the novel's own finale. The novel in fact offers three alternative endings: the group retain one prince as (a not unwilling?) hostage until they reach Lisbon, where one sub-plot has indicated a 'revolutionary' government; or they sail to Liverpool, where a 'general strike' and workers' occupations have begun; or they trade their last hostage for a live broadcast in which they declare that they don't know what to do next — and then give themselves up!

Those endings indicate not only what was wrong with *their* 'strategy' but also what was wrong with David's — in my view. In using the film of *Just Demands* (it was actually released as *Hostage!* as a detour to getting people to read the novel, itself only a bait for them to read the political material in it, David did precisely what his fictional kidnappers did: exploited one aspect of the spectacularity of social control to get a foothold into another section. The students, in effect, tried to constitute themselves as an 'alternative' (and temporary) BBC/ITV: a small group of ideologically-motivated pro-gramme-makers who decide on the basis of arbitrary power what is broadcast to the rest of us, and their phone-in apparatus and invitations for 'suggestions' for the next spectacular are merely a sham form of responsiveness. Which is where, for me, their — and David's — notion of 'political education' breaks down, for three main reasons. Though in the novel we see that their own mode of education is active (they themselves learn mainly from production-training, field-work and rehearsals rather than from lectures), what they present as 'education' for others is largely 'passive': an alternative content in a medium that remains unidirectional, a mono-logue. The title of the novel encapsulates another dilemma: the 'demands' may be 'just' but they are also 'just' demands, mere demands addressed outwards, to someone else — but to whom? Thirdly, and directly following on from this, if one claims to 'educate' someone else politically one surely has to be able to get beyond the very familiar kind of critical analysis incorporated in those video-programmes, and indicate *where* one should try to get *to* and *how* — yet the third ending, combined with the sketchiness of the other two endings, recognises that they can't.

David and I came back to this again and again. He argued that my third objection actually cancelled out my first one, since any attempt to 'imagine' a coherent future would have to take the form of a monologue, be the act of an individual or a small group, in the first instance at least. He was more worried by a different problem: that a plausible future and related strategy could only be imagined on the basis of a very particular and concrete present, yet the ever-changing present remorselessly 'dated' all imagined futures and strategies: 'We need to imagine a future that changes with the present.'

His third novel developed from this complaint. Again it was an attempt to imagine a process and strategy of 'revolution', but this time he tried to depict an 'alternative' past, on the basis of a once-imagined future which, in our actual past, we now know did not occur. This third novel was a complete commercial flop, though it certainly contained his most sustained effort of writing. Entitled *Late News* it took as its skeletal plot the chapters in William Morris's *News from Nowhere* (published in 1890) in which Morris tried to imagine 'How the Change Came', a process that Morris had dated as beginning in 1952. David organised his novel according to forty 'moments' from Morris's compressed account of a British socialist revolution and tried in each case to imagine that 'moment' in detail, as it might have occurred in the real England since 1945, using as far as possible real organisations, people and news items from those decades. In following Morris's outline David's novel obviously diverged more and more from what did happen in the 1950s and after, but what was remarkable about much of *Late News* was how real incidents and events over three decades lent themselves to re-description within this 'imagined' process. The chapters of the novel were each headed with consecutive extracts from Morris, which provided the narrative link of *Late News*, but the detailed content of each chapter was relatively self-contained, sometimes almost a documentary account of an actual incident. For example, Morris's effective starting-point was a 'Resolution' of the 'Combined Workers':

Fiction

The Combined Workers watched the situation with mingled hope and anxiety. They had already formulated their general demands; but now by a solemn and universal vote of their federated societies, they insisted on the first step being taken towards carrying out their demands: this step would have led directly to handing over the management of the whole natural resources of the country, together with the machinery for using them, into the power of the Combined Workers, and the reduction of the privileged classes into the position of pensioners obviously dependent on the pleasure of the workers. The 'Resolution', as it was called, which was widely published in the newspapers of the day, was in fact a declaration of war, and was so accepted by the master class. They began henceforward to prepare for a firm stand against the 'brutal and ferocious Communism of the day', as they phrased it.

David 'mapped onto' this an account of the TUC and Labour Party Conferences of 1945–51 and the debates on nationalisation, keeping close to the actual arguments of the time, but culminating his account with the publication of a joint Manifesto rather more intransigent than the actual Labour Party's! The next three 'moments' in Morris concern demonstrations in Trafalgar Square and the escalating response of the police and Government. As his equivalent David describes what are recognisably demonstrations from the 1950s (against rearmament), late 1950s (CND) and late 1960s (Vietnam Solidarity Campaign). This is followed by: 'Several of the popular leaders were arrested', and David briefly recounts what looks like the arrest of the Shrewsbury Seven. Later 'moments' in Morris — the emergence of a 'Committee of Public Safety', a London-wide strike, and the delcaration of a 'state of siege' by the Government — are shadowed by events drawn from Belfast and Londonderry (the Ulster Workers' Defence Council strike, no-go areas, etc.), as are some of the details of the civil war which Morris leads up to. Some moments in Morris barely needed to be given a contemporary parallel:

Yet one ally they (the employers' federation) had, and that was the rapidly approaching breakdown of the whole system founded on the World-Market and its supply . . .

— David simply summarises the British press during the oil-

129

crisis of the early 1970s. For other moments he draws upon the miners' strikes of 1984 and 1974 (Saltley Gates finds a vivid parallel) or the 'winter of discontent' of 1978–9, but where necessary he makes a determined effort simply to imagine parallels to Morris's moments.

The effect of *Late News* is very curious indeed. David's own chapters are not linked as a narrative by recurring characters or personalities, by a shared location or even by very much reference back of episodes to each other, but simply by their positioning within the process maintained across the chapters by the quotations taken, in their original order, from Morris. The reader recognises many of these moments as having 'happened' but not in that order, and is also aware that the process traced by the detailed accounts suggests that a great deal *else* has 'happened' in the fictive world of the novel which is not being described. This interaction between plausible detail taken from 'real' history and overall compressed structure taken from Morris's imagined 'future' tends to create a 'third' layer in one's reading: a constant awareness of the overall development of the actual history of post-war Britain and an acute sense of it as *only* one alternative among many once-possible pasts, presents and futures. In my own view, the novel was a considerable achievement, formally and politically.

David was, however, deeply dissatisfied. The ending had given him a great deal of trouble, for a start! After toying with various formal possibilities, he simply followed the final 'moment' from Morris with a further chapter, in which he quoted from the conclusion to *News from Nowhere* in which Guest returns to the nineteenth century:

Once more without any conscious effort of will I set my face toward the old house by the ford, but as I turned round the corner which led to the remains of the village cross, I came upon a figure strangely contrasting with the joyous, beautiful people I had left behind in the church. It was a man who looked old, but whom I knew from habit, now half-forgotten, was really not much more than fifty. His face was rugged, and grimed rather than dirty; his eyes dull and bleared; his body bent, his calves thin and spindly, his feet dragging and limping. His clothing was a mixture of dirt and rags long over-familiar to me. As I passed him he touched his hat with some real good-will and courtesy, and much servility.

Inexpressibly shocked, I hurried past him and hastened along the road that led to the river and the lower end of the village; but suddenly I saw as it were a black cloud rolling along to meet me, like a nightmare of my childish days; and for a while I was conscious of nothing else than being in the dark, and whether I was walking, or sitting, or lying down, I could not tell.

To this David added an extract from the newspaper for the morning on which he finished the novel, describing the poverty of a single-parent family in Leeds. It was a telling juxtaposition, but, as David himself pointed out to me, that newspaper extract would already be 'late news' for his own readers, the item itself forgotten by the time the novel was published and read, and that was also more or less true of many of the incidents he had used in the bulk of the novel. 'How many readers *will* actually recognise that Saltley Gates, the Shrewsbury Seven or the Ulster Workers' Defence Council were once *real*?' He also felt that Morris's account gave too little attention to international factors, was too sanguine about ruling-class response and about working-class solidarity, and ignored all the sectional groups within society. ... In sum, he felt that he still hadn't solved either the formal or the strategic problems of 'imagining' revolution.

I suppose I made matters worse by adding that Morris himself hadn't really resolved the issue of motivation, with his claim that

the great motive-power of the change was a longing for freedom and equality, akin if you please to the unreasonable passion of the lover; a sickness of heart that rejected with loathing the aimless solitary life of the well-to-do educated man of that time ...

There wasn't much sign of that 'longing' or 'instinct' he talked so confidently about, and David still had to show why people should *want* a 'revolution' rather than personal advancement for themselves and their children. 'Clearly,' he replied, with a grin, 'you haven't read *Just Demands*,' and began to trot out the usual material: that 7 per cent owned 84 per cent of the wealth, that a quarter of the world was starving, that .... But then he stopped and said: 'Yes. I can't give them that longing either. Not unless they already know what "freedom and equality" would actually mean for them as well as for others, and unless they think that it's really possible.' We had a drink and left it there, for another time.

Shortly after *Late News* came out, David's health began to worsen rapidly. He couldn't write very easily, but he was determined to try once more. He bought a word-processor and a small home-computer and tried to write on the word-processor, but as a result his style deteriorated even more than his health. He even devised a programme for the computer, which he christened 'sub-plot', to try to help him in constructing the next novel. That didn't help either. Day after day I would find him in his wheelchair, reduced to watching teletext or playing computer games.

Then one day he seemed suddenly more his old self. 'I've done it!', he said as I came in, and pointed to a small cassette. I looked suitably puzzled. He grinned: 'The do-it-yourself revolutionary history programme.' I asked for a reading, or a demonstration, not sure which was appropriate. 'Bring three friends tonight and I'll show you the basics.'

We assembled that night and he fed the cassette into the computer. In rapid succession on the visual display unit appeared all the teletext news items of the previous week. He then asked us each to act as news-editors, selecting two items from the teletext list and imagining two more 'scoop' items, typing them into the word-processor. We then had to choose eight items each from the resulting 'newsbank' of eight real items and eight imaginary ones, to make up the front page of a Sunday newspaper. The four resulting 'newspapers' were then shown us in succession on the screen, indicating the overlaps and differences of 'coverage'. We were beginning to get interested. David explained: 'Each item gets a news-value rating based on how many of you used it — maximum score 4, minimum 1 — and the total of news-values for your eight published items gives you each a circulation-score.' He punched the keyboard. 'But you also get scoop bonuses and penalties: a bonus of the scoop item's news-value if it was your own scoop, and a penalty of the same value if it wasn't.' Again we saw our respective scores. 'But, of course, you have to pay for news: equivalent to two news-value units for each item. So, how good are you as commercial newspaper editors?' Again he punched the board, and the scores came up:

	A	B	C	D
Circulation	18	20	19	20
Cost	16	16	16	16
Operating a/c	+2	+4	+3	+4
Bonus	+6	+3	+5	+3
Penalty	–3	–9	–11	–12
Overall a/c	+5	–2	–3	–5

'Now,' he said, 'comes the first rule of the game. The circulation figures are public, but the scoop-points are only known to each editor — you can do that by using password-access or separate VDUs. So you each know the circulation figures of your rivals and therefore the operating profit or loss, but you don't know the 'hidden assets' account, or therefore the overall 'profitability' of your rivals. Want to produce the next issue?'

The second rule was that any items used by only one editor in the first issue were erased from the newsbank. We then had to select two items each from the remainder and write a 'follow-up' story (which could be 'real'); to that we each added two more 'scoops' (which again we could imagine or draw from real news). So again sixteen different 'items' went into the newsbank and again we each had to publish eight of them as our front page. One further rule now came into play: the items remaining from the first issue were 'tagged' to their 'owner', whoever had introduced that item into the first newsbank; if an editor wanted to use someone else's item for a follow-up story in issue 2 there was a penalty of –1, and a bonus of +1 to the 'owner'. Again we were given our scores:

	A	B	C	D
Circulation issue 2	20	18	19	21
Cumulative circulation	38	38	38	41
Cost issue 2	16	16	16	16
Operating a/c issue 2	+4	+2	+3	+5
Bonus issue 2	+3	+5	+4	+5
Penalty issue 2	–9	–3	–7	–8
Overall a/c issue 2	–2	+4	0	+2
Cumulative assets (1 & 2)	+3	+2	–3	–3

We had got the general idea, and David let us play for a few issues. By then we were competing to entice each other to publish 'our' versions of events and a fierce circulation war was in progress as well. The game stretched our imaginations, as the scoops veered between the wildly unrealistic (good news-value, but short-lived) and the subtly plausible (longer running-power in follow-ups). Suddenly one of the players asked: 'How do you *win* this game?' 'That depends on your priorities,' said David. He let us think for a moment, and then said: 'You can aim to maximise your circulation, or maximise your cumulative assets, or you can try to maximise your contribution to the newsbank, eventually re-shaping the reported world of your rivals, or you can maximise control over publication — by, if necessary, buying control of the other papers. And you can 'lose' if your circulation figure isn't viable for a number of issues, or if you get taken over. Different players can choose different priorities, and it's easy enough to decide on rules governing those priorities and objectives — but I doubt if they can all 'win'.' He showed us some of the rules he had devised himself: criteria for successful takeover bids, the conditions under which a paper was no longer viable. But I was more interested in another question: 'How does the revolution get into this game?'

David's response was to join us at the console and invite us to play again — but this time he changed the cassette program to include an extra newspaper, his own: 'That version was called *Editor*. This is *Stop Press*. My paper is a small paper,' he explained. 'It can only publish four items each issue, but it can operate on very low circulation figures and has smaller operating costs. It also has the minor advantage that for each issue it can, if it wishes, put four completely new items into the common newsbank. And in the full version of the game, the origin of a particular news-item is known only to its originator. My aim, therefore, is to persuade the rest of you to give my items their news-value by publishing them — but in doing so I can try to re-shape the world you report. As it happens, that may also have the effect of increasing my circulation figures. It may even eventually put me in a position to take some of you over as well — but that's not my priority. Want to play?'

We met every weekend for a month after that, playing the game, refining the rules, modifying the program, devising variations: *Political Parties* and *Serial* (developed from David's original 'sub-plot' program) were the easiest to develop. We could soon operate with a 64-item bank for each issue or with eight players in various roles. We rarely played the revolutionary version, *Stop Press*, but we all became proficient at *Editor*, David himself proving unexpectedly adept at building up large assets concealed by dismal circulation figures.

What pleased him most about the game was that every player had to decide his own priorities, his own sense of what had news value, and his own criteria of plausible news (the cautious kept a close eye on the actual teletext during the week — though we also learned to anticipate news developments). Every weekend we could accommodate real events but they soon interacted with our own current news-stories, as the follow-up rule re-shaped them. One long weekend, when we'd all become totally absorbed and had reached our 50th issue, David called a halt — and pointed out that he had by then quietly managed to get us all to about chapter 15 of *Late News*!

That wasn't his last game, though it was probably the one he enjoyed most. As he slid into the last stages of his illness he used to fantasise about the game being played on secretarial VDUs in offices, then over company-wide networks, in neighbourhoods on DC link-ups — till finally it really did become the basis of a national news medium, but with real news instead of imagined: news from factories, offices, homes, from people rather than to people. 'But you wouldn't be able to trust that news,' I objected. 'No more than now,' he agreed.

He died shortly after. He asked us simply to make the program available to any one who wanted it — 'though anyone can write the actual program for themselves once they get the idea.' By now I don't know how many groups are playing the game — quite a lot, I imagine, though most of them have probably never heard of David.

I suppose that's the kind of 'obituary' he would have wanted.

Derek Lemming

Autobiography

William Armstrong: *Objectivities: a materialist autobiography* reviewed by Anne Arthur

This is an attractive book, based on an interesting, even provocative, idea. Like most autobiographies, it prompts autobiographical reflections on the reader's part but in a specifically deliberate way, which some prefatory autobiographical recollections of my own might illuminate.

An article I once wrote contained the following ambitious sentence:

It is possible to analyse the contradictions of contemporary capitalism starting from the contents of a decent English breakfast.

What I had in mind, clearly enough, was the notion of tracing the connections between a typical breakfast menu and the production of its various items as commodities: the occluded links between the grapefruit and the fruit-pickers, the canning factory, the advertising, the supermarket, the price of tin, the profit of the importer, transporter, wholesaler, retailer, the wages of the till girl, etc. — the complex hierarchies of domination in the agricultural, industrial, transport, retail and commercial branches of economic organisation. As each item was traced back through its routes of production and distribution, different sectors, different countries, different problems would be disclosed and connected. Irish bacon, American or Canadian wheat, British eggs, Kenyan coffee, New Zealand butter, Barbadan sugar, Indian tea — whole histories of English imperialist exploitation are deposited upon our breakfast tables. And different economic, political and military institutions are implicated in their appearance: the EEC, the US–UK 'special relationship', the Commonwealth, NATO, SEATO, etc. A deep history of — in its most literal sense — 'taste' is also imbricated: the cultural and class specifics of food choice, of cooking methods, of culinary preferences; an economy of nutritional disparities lurks in any comparative study of food intake. Sexual divisions of labour also hover — starting from that backward male glance over the shoulder to the kitchen where his wife sizzles a fresh rasher of bacon. As does the distribution of information and ideology: which newspaper flutters over the débris of the toast and marmalade while the radio oozes out the suave morning tones of the BBC?

The model for such a suggested analysis was an anecdote about Lenin: his ability to analyse the problems of Czarist Russia starting from a glass of water on a peasant's table. But a further variation on that Leninist procedure had intervened since I first came across that particular anecdote. A friend had been asked to write a book on Roman Catholicism. A wide commission. We discussed possible formats. I suggested that the structure of the book might be provided by taking a single day in the life of an average English Roman Catholic and by tracing back the deep influences upon the thoughts, emotions, dilemmas, decisions, habits and frustrations of that day, to the immensely complex inheritance of a manifold tradition of morality and doctrine stretching over 2000 years, influences locally and minutely active within a still continuing and globally ramified ideological institution. That book was, not surprisingly, never written, but an echo of it remains in the continuation of the sentence I quoted earlier:

and it would be possible to analyse the depth and intractability of the problem of 'ideology' by starting from a pair of rosary beads in a Provo's pocket.

Clearly, it would be extremely difficult to offer any thorough or adequately systematic analysis of either cornflakes or rosary beads along such lines — if only because the sheer complexity of the connections, and the amount of 'information', that would have to be incorporated would tend to overload the original starting-point. The analysis would be centrifugal in the extreme and its circumference could only be that of the globe itself. A series of essays might approach something of what is gestured towards in these suggestions. For example, I once wrote some brief journalistic pieces on such matters as the connections between buying a postage stamp and the purchase of arms by South Africa (the link was the GPO Pension Fund, then invested on advice from Barclays Bank, which was financing the Cobara Bassa Dam project) or between the price of petrol, the poverty of Eskimos and the strategic importance of Alaska (the oil pipeline eroding the permafrost). But such essays wouldn't add together, in precisely the same way that our comprehension of a breakfast menu doesn't constitute or provoke any synthetic grasp of the whole world we live in. Yet to attempt any such totalising account is to search, apparently futilely, for a 'model' of analysis that advances beyond the limitations of the essay format or the journalistic insight while avoiding the formidable and off-putting rigour of a textbook or treatise in political sociology and economics.

Two such models obviously suggest themselves: the novel and the autobiography. The formal problems of fiction in relation to 'totalisation' are familiar enough and needn't be pursued for the moment, but a slightly new edge has been given to the genre of autobiography in recent years by the emergence of the women's movement. For it is in autobiographical writing that a certain current in the women's movement has found or sought its most appropriate expression: that current which emphasises that the 'personal' *is* 'political'. (Perhaps surprisingly, and certainly rather disappointingly, this mode of writing has not — for reasons I can't explore here — been imitated or paralleled in male writing with the same intention: to demonstrate, or illustrate, the politics of the personal in the lives of men also.) I'm not at all sure that I myself, as a feminist, would want to write an English equivalent of, say, Kate Millett's *Sita*, yet insofar as my own daily experience is in some respects constituted in ways similar to a breakfast menu — a series of apparently discrete items, each with considerable ramifications — an extended analysis of even one day in my own life could lead to the kind of global connections glimpsed in the notion of writing about cornflakes or rosary beads. For a start, I ate a breakfast today, I posted a letter, I travelled on a bus, which used petrol. Etc.

As with writing a novel, however, there is a problem of selection. Any item within my reach at the moment could lead outwards from itself: the pen I write with was manufactured, sold and bought; I acquired it for 'free' (as part of my job) and that very fact opens onto large perspectives within which would be included differential employment 'perks', bureaucratic expenditure, status hierarchies, and eventually — in my own case — the politics and history of the journalistic profession. The packet of cigarettes on the table could be the focus for a study of the conditions of workers on plantations in Latin America or the politics of pressure groups, medical, ecological, commercial, in the UK. With Italo Svevo's *Confessions of Zeno* in mind, I might even embark on a psychoanalytical self-exploration to understand why I still smoke, to find out why I keep having a 'last fag' — an inquiry in which the death principle would not be merely the terminus point.

This tactic of focusing on what is ready-to-hand has itself, of course, respectable antecedents in the familiar practice of philosophers choosing the table on which they write as a topic for ontological or epistemological discussion, or the more exotic practice of distinguishing between what is 'ready-to-hand' and what is 'ready-near-at-hand' that takes up so many pages in Heidegger. Lévi-Strauss's notion of *bricolage* might stimulate a further variation on that academic ploy of assembling an argument from random bits and pieces lying around in one's physical or mental attic or filing cabinet. That habit, or trick, of philosophers tends, however, to stand in for any *principle* of selection: it is precisely the sheer neutrality or mere facticity of the object chosen that makes it suitable for the purpose of probing ontological problems.

In the case of the novel, however, it is precisely the principle of selection in relation to the totality that has provoked considerable debate, particularly in the context of the historical novel — one need only recall Lukàcs on Balzac or Scott.

140

When the period in question is not the past but the actual present, decisions about the 'selection' of the very characters and protagonists of the novel itself become peculiarly acute. For example, if it was once possible to envisage a 'central character' not only as a focal point for the novel's formal organisation but also as 'representative' of major components or facets of the extra-textual world as well — a character upon whom important social strains, contradictions and preoccupations could be seen as converging — it is now very difficult indeed to find a contemporary structural equivalent to, say, the nineteenth-century governess (the Brontës) or eighteenth-century country vicar (Goldsmith), still less the monarchs of Elizabethan and Greek tragedy. Whom, in this late twentieth century, could a novelist take as focusing the contradictions not simply of one culture or nation but of the international globe we so patently inhabit? An executive of a multinational corporation? A United Nations diplomat? An airline stewardess? An 'international' film producer or superstar? An 'international terrorist'? A refugee? One characteristic ploy in early twentieth-century fiction was to take the writer-figure himself (it was rarely *herself*) as the point of intersection and this device, from *Death in Venice* to *Sons and Lovers*, from *A la recherche du temps perdu* to *Ulysses*, has tended to modulate modern(ist) fiction towards the autobiographical mode.

But in autobiography, too, the problem of 'selection' has been a major difficulty: what to 'leave in' from a whole life, often an existence richly full of incident, adventure, people — precisely that complex superfluity of episodes and experiences which is thought to justify writing the autobiography in the first place. The problem here could be formulated as the relation between event and significance: what are the details relevatory of character, the moments meaningful for a career or a life? That problem could be tracked back within the history of the genre and indeed beyond it, to the emergence of biography as a form. In Suetonius, for example, omens tend to act as the focus for selecting incidents which fall outside the *res gestae* of an emperor's public life, while in medieval lives of the saints miracles provide the essential anecdotes. In the various 'Lives' of Charlemagne we can read an overlap between these two modes: Einhard as the Suetonian chronicler, Notker the Stammerer as the religious hagiographer. With Vasari's *Lives* the artist enters the picture and the artist's own works and paintings operate as the anecdotal pegs, but, a century or so after Vasari, Aubrey can only offer us pure anecdotal chaos without pegs or pattern: the anecdotes are the life that matters. The search for pattern — moral, psychological, political — tends to shape or to defeat later biographies, from Johnson's character study of Savage to Freud's psychoanalysis of Leonardo, from Carlyle's abandonment of coherent ordering in his documentary life of Cromwell to Isaac Deutscher's retrospective attribution of ambitions of apotheosis in his life of Stalin: it is in the light of these various superimposed patterns that biographical details are selected. Yet the tendentiousness of pattern and the circularity of 'significance' have been explicitly admitted, and therefore undermined, in recent experiments in autobiography, from André Gorz's exploratory blending of marxist and existentialist/psychoanalytical constructions of his identity in *The Traitor* to André Malraux's swirling, semi-mythological *Anti-Memoirs*; from Jan Myrdal's myriad moments in *Confessions of a Disloyal European* to the disparate lexical items in *Roland Barthes par Roland Barthes* or the disdainfully alphabetical entries in his *Fragments d'un discours amoureux*. In the last two of these, moreover, that fundamental 'selection' of the main protagonist which had seemed the core and foundation of all autobiography, the *a priori* of the very form, has been demoted if not finally deconstructed: the self itself has been decentred, the subject is no longer the focus even of its own 'life'.

Which is where the book under review seeks to locate itself. William Armstrong's *Objectivities* offers us not a central subject but a selection of objects, not a subjectivity with whom we might empathise or identify but an arrangement of material things, most of which we can readily recognise as having their equivalents or parallels among our own possessions. He doesn't in fact make either his reasons for this procedure or his principle of selection explicit — hence, in part, these introductory remarks of mine — but his basic intention would seem to be to present us with what one could call (if Eliot hadn't appropriated the phrase) 'objective correlatives'. His book is constructed of short, separate passages, brief essays, each focused upon a particular object which he possesses: as he writes about each object he explores 'backwards', as it were, into the memories associated for him with that object and in each case he uncovers a political dimension in those memories which he then pursues 'forward', to account not only for his present possession of that object but also for some important facet or defining aspect of his present life, life-style, way of living. The objects are thus treated almost as 'fetishes' around which 'free association' occurs and that process of association then discloses the basic structures and contradictions of his present 'identity'. Crucially, however, in displacing attention away from any direct *self*-analysis, in taking these objects as the nodal points of his text, he suggests and promotes the possibility of the *reader* performing a similar operation upon his or her own particular possessions. It is not primarily William Armstrong's own memories and associations that we are being invited to share or respond to but rather the constitutive function of familiar, taken-for-granted objects in our own lives. As we read, we find our attention being caught by the things around *us* — the furniture, the bric-à-brac, the utensils in our own home — and we perhaps find ourselves following, almost automatically, Armstrong's own procedure: our own peculiar and particular memories and associations come flooding back unbidden and we begin to question their political as well as their personal significance for us. It is a curious but seemingly deliberate effect, as if this book were actually written in order to distract us from it — the book thereby de-centres not only its subject but even itself.

In this review, I can most usefully present you with a few examples in full and briefly indicate some of the others which seem to me successful. You may then judge for yourself whether the effect I attribute to the book actually occurs. I will, however, indicate why it seems to me that the project as a whole is built upon presuppositions which finally (and necessarily?) make it unsuccessful.

* * * *

The book opens with a passage where the procedures, and the presuppositions, are plain enough. Given that the reader has just opened, and perhaps has even just bought, the book itself, the opening is appropriately, and effectively, concerned with the author's own books. Each passage has a mildly punning title; this is headed

On the shelf

'After a while, the expected comment comes. The friend, the acquaintance, the stranger, entering my study for the first time, after relaxing and agreeing to a coffee, looks round and asks, "Have you read them all?" Sometimes it's a genuine question. Usually it's an ironic or mocking alternative to something sharper, more direct and less polite. On every wall, after all, there are books. Not only books, but mainly books. A brightly coloured patchwork of solid wallpaper made up of spines and covers. A few hundred feet of packed shelving. A great weight of printed paper.

I shrug an answer, normally. "No, but I've used them all, at one time or another." I could go on to explain, to sketch the different areas of interest, the old commitments and past intellectual passions or tasks. The Greek texts from the days I "did" A Level Classics. The two years' worth of philosophy. The novels and poems that survive from my undergraduate degree. The labour history from my research The theology volumes from a religious publisher I once did jobs for. The political books and pamphlets from past issues, crises and campaigns. The various clusters of volumes that recall once-active currents of fascination. It's a reasonable answer, as far as it goes.

Yes, I could say, each book is a trace of an episode, each one summons a small history. Sometimes the fly-leaf pins it down to an otherwise forgotten day: "Whitby, August '71" — a vivid find in the sole second-hand bookshop I came across during a dull holiday. Or "Warrington, July '67": a souvenir of a brief job in a town I haven't stopped in since, only seen again and again from the train. It was a habit, once, to buy a book in every new place that mattered, a kind of free association: Ernst Gombrich had no connection with Ambleside, except that I bought him there. Custom stales. For a few years now, I've not bothered to record the place, the date. Even the signature has gone. Each new book just finds its place on the appropriate crowded shelf. But still I buy them.

At one time, too, there were special days. The Penguin day of the month, when the new batch appeared in the bookshops down town. It meant a special bus-ride, a gamble that the new stock would actually be there on schedule, and a wasted bus-fare if it wasn't. Then I might squander a few shillings on a volume I'd dithered about the previous month, as consolation. In my mid-teens, Thursdays and Fridays also meant a special effort, to get the *Guardian* book-page and the *TLS*. It was pointless, though, trying to read the reviews on Sundays. Dad didn't go to work on Sundays (it was he who got the Thursday *Guardian* for me though he never read it) and no local newsagent would deliver the *Observer* or the *Sunday Times*, only the *People* or *Express*. I couldn't afford the Sundays anyway (or the books they reviewed), so I read them, if at all, on Mondays, in the local library.

Nostalgia tugs. The discovery and rediscovery of dusty secondhand bookshops. A whole Saturday examining an influx of old Everymans in a shop I thought I had exhausted, and a solemn sixpence or two finally exchanged for a bulging, tearing, brown paper bag. Towns took shape round certain streets, always a detour from the family outing, often a delay that could develop into impatience. Clutched treasures on the wet walk home.

It seemed incongruous at times. It seems exaggerated even now. I still register those eyebrows softly raised when the stranger walks in and the eyes begin their covert counting, soon abandoned. Looking round, alone, I sometimes start to share that surprise. It seems a ludicrous investment. The Inland Revenue think so too, year after year.

But a memory bites, behind it all, the nearest I can get to explanation. Aged eleven, sitting in the school library, a "free reading period". I forget what I was reading or what it led me to look for along the shelves. Something urgent enough to disturb my twelve-year-old neighbour at the table. His

145

irritation turned to smooth superiority as I explained, mentioning the title. "I have it," he said. I didn't quite understand: he certainly wasn't reading it. With precisely that arrogance that possession gives, he pushed back his chair and sauntered to a cupboard set below the shelves. "I keep my own books here," he said, unlocking double-doors. I stood behind him as he crouched and delved. I suppose my eyebrows softly lifted and my eyes began a mental count. I suppose his smile was smug, his gesture lordly, as he handed me the volume. What I registered, and remembered, was the insult latent in the favour, the condescension of superiority. The exact tone of the man of taste and wealth was already audible in that schoolboy's casual remark of privilege: "Do let me have it back in good condition." It soured the book. I returned it, only a few pages skimmed, when the bell rang.

He was middle-class, of course, according to my schoolboy definition. I was the son of a telephone engineer, grandson of a Liverpool docker. A scholarship boy (though we all were) in a grammar school that had seemed, till then, alien but unquestioned. It took some time for the experience to settle in, to cast slow light on other facets. That glimpse of private paperbacks bound in celluloid protection linked gradually with the strange futility of compulsory Saturday mornings spent fumbling with awkward fingers at a violin, and with the idiotic boredom of trying to catch an elongated ugly ball from an endless scrum called rugby, while a few miles away along the bus route the two best teams in the world played glorious, fast football. After two years of this, I switched schools.

But just before my thirteenth birthday, when Mum asked me what I wanted, I answered "Books," and produced a definite list. I even borrowed a typewriter and thudded out the letters, so she wouldn't get them wrong. They were copied from a Penguin catalogue, all the "Penguin Classics" I could recognise by title or by author: Virgil, *The Aeneid*, Homer, *The Iliad*, Herodotus, *The Histories*, Thucydides, *The Peloponnesian War*, Ovid, *Metamorphoses*, Xenophon, *The Persian Expedition*; the list extended. I knew what they looked like (warm brown borders for the Greeks, imperial purple for the Romans) and how much they cost: I included *Two Satyr Plays*

146

and Lucretius because they were only half-a-crown apiece, while Livy cost as much as those two put together. When I added up all the awkward 3/6d and 4/6d entries it came to an appalling £8-13s-6d. But there was also Christmas, and next year's birthday as well, so I let it stand. It would take a good few celebrations to work through that expensive list. In fact, it took only one year, and those volumes still resonate with hard-earned gratitude on my shelves.

Years later my mother told me how she had gone shopping, with the list in her hand, hesitantly trying out tentative pronunciations on equally puzzled shop-assistants. It was partly my typing, of course, but those names were from a different world, for her as for me. Only one bookshop in Liverpool, it seemed, in those days, actually offered immediate access to that world (there were others, as it happened, but it took a longish time to discover them.) Her shopping spree took courage and initiative as well as love.

It's the choice of books that now intrigues me. Those outlandish names I too could not pronounce (I still mistype Euripedes and Thucidydes). What had been latent in that moment in the schoolroom library was an anger of exclusion. A recognition that what was known as culture could be turned upon me as a weapon. A secret weapon kept locked in a private cupboard, access to which was only on sufferance. A temporary favour. Culture was then defined, in a deliberate gesture, as a matter of possession, physical, material possession. The first step in fighting back was, necessarily, defined in those same terms. The books had to be visibly there, under my own control, permanently. Once bought and inscribed they could not be locked away from me by anyone, did not have to be returned. But to maintain their rationale, as alien weapons appropriated, they had also to retain their strangeness, their unfamiliarity, their echo of a different world. Those remote and classical titles seemed to be the very inner fortress, the central redoubt I had to assault and expropriate. Once that was taken, I could work outwards, from behind the walls that seemed to be arranged as so many defences of a privileged and arrogant existence. But I didn't want to live in that redoubt. In any case, my fingers resisted the forcible stretching onto violin

147

strings, my body baulked at this slow, stubborn ridiculous game of territorial control and absurd gentlemanly regulations. So at first it seemed almost enough to thumb through the pages, arrange the volumes in a kind of order in the bedroom (Plutarch was then a problem: he had a brown-edged cover but wrote about the Romans). For a while, I only read them when there was nothing better to do. It took about two years before I had finally worked through the whole of that very first batch of Penguins.

About ten years later, I was reading Trotsky's *Literature and Revolution* when the following passage made me laugh out loud, a joke shared, a recognition acknowledged:

Though the proletariat is spiritually, and therefore, artistically, very sensitive, it is uneducated aesthetically. It is hardly reasonable to think that it can simply begin at the point where the bourgeois intelligentsia left off on the eve of the catastrophe. Just as an individual passes biologically and psychologically through the history of the race and, to some extent, of the entire animal world in his development from the embryo, so, to a certain extent, must the overwhelming majority of a new class which has only recently come out of pre-historic life, pass through the entire history of artistic culture. This class cannot begin the construction of a new culture without absorbing and assimilating the elements of the old cultures. This does not mean in the least that it is necessary to go through step by step, slowly and systematically, the entire past history of art. In so far as it concerns a social class and not a biologic individual, the process of absorption and transformation has a freer and more conscious character. But a new class cannot move forward without regard to the most important landmarks of the past.

Nowadays, when friends ask me if they can borrow a book, I'm sometimes tempted to say, with secret delight: "Keep it, it's yours." And then go out and buy another copy.'

*

The relation between class and culture, brought home to Armstrong for the first time in that passage, is later explored more closely in a piece entitled 'In a Glass Darkly'. This begins from a beer tankard given to Armstrong by a relative; he remembers what prompted the present — an incident in a pub where, as a teenager, he scandalised his non-drinking mother by being only too clearly well known to the barman — and then goes on to remember various 'locals' he has frequented over the years. That leads him, through a commentary on various changes in remembered 'working-class communities', back to the origins of the present licensing laws (imposed first on Glasgow munitions workers during World War One). He then turns unexpectedly to consider a set of wine glasses in his cupboard: this takes him back to the 'very strange experience' of being offered sherry at his first tutorial at university (at 9.30 in the morning!) but also to a more recent experience, bringing bottles of French wine through the customs after a holiday near Avignon. This abrupt juxtaposition neatly encompasses the two themes which are intertwined throughout this passage: class-solidarity (effected in different ways by different classes, on local, national and international levels) and 'class de-composition' (both in personal identity and in collective self-definition). But the whole passage ends with an anecdote of celebration: a shop-stewards' committee in the convenor's office in a Ford factory, drinking the health of their Belgian counterparts after coordinating by phone international 'black-ing' action during a dispute with Ford management over car exports. Among the mugs of tea on the desk lies a telephone receiver from which can be heard (at Company expense) the crackling noise of a parallel celebration in the Belgian factory. But the Belgians are drinking coffee and cognac.

Coffee turns up again in 'Filters', in which he remembers going round a coffee plantation in Brazil and where the overtly rapist attitudes of the landowner's teenage sons towards the adolescent Indian girls forced to work on the plantation leads him to explore his own sexism and the racism of a home city built upon the proceeds of the slave-trade. Sexism is again analysed in a piece prompted by some unused aftershave ('It smells'). Another factory appears in 'Rip Off', where he describes an idiosyncratic piece of metal 'sculpture' welded together from scrap ends during a tea-break in a South London steelworks; during that job a new million-pound pressing-machine went wildly wrong on a testing-run and shot out broken lengths of white-hot metal which gouged deep into the chest and forehead of a black worker, killing him immediately. From this conjunction of memories Armstrong probes the relations between 'useful' and 'useless' labour, between 'efficiency' and 'costs', between 'work' and 'art' — to end with a detailed description of a mammoth demonstration of workers for 'The Right to Work', which turns out to be a description of a print done by a South London worker, Dan Jones' 'March Against Unemployment', that now hangs on Armstrong's wall and which also appears in a new children's story-book he has just bought.

Some entangled relations between work and time are rather elliptically explored in a short piece entitled 'Clock on' which is worth quoting in full:

Clock On

'I awake each morning to find beside my bed a wristwatch, its tiny buzzing alarm long since quiet. Above my head, a loud alarm-clock, its ringing tone stifled long ago. Across the room, a radio is plugged into an automatic timer. But the radio is silent. I have probably turned it off an hour or so before. The timing mechanism is efficient. Both the alarm-clock and the wristwatch "work". All three will have delivered their noisy mechanical warnings: buzz, jangle, music. But it takes the telephone to penetrate my sleep sufficiently. The others I can evade. I flick them off and slide back into sleep. I can even talk for ten minutes on the phone and still awake an hour later, in mid-morning. The telephone conversation will have been only an oasis of coherence. I will still be late, almost, for my first appointment.

An anxious knocking on the door. My mother's voice: "You'll be late." My bed was just below the window. My shirt would be as stiff and chill as the white frost on the pane. The air in the room seemed fragile and icy-clear, so brittle that it might crack as I walked through it to the landing. The cold water from the tap seemed merely to slide across my skin like a glacier slipping across a marble landscape. My face was already frozen beneath it, the cheeks rigid in permafrost.

A normal winter morning, no particular hardship, just an ordinary, unheated council-house bedroom, the damp deep and permanent, the bomb-damage still visible in the cracks that trembled open when the front door slammed.

The walk to school crossed a double-carriageway. We timed our dash across the road so that the hot exhaust fumes from some great lorry would blast us as it passed, an inch or so away. A risky substitute for overcoats.

Later, I sat every morning on the upper deck of a stationary bus, waiting for its engine to vibrate and take me off to grammar school. Our side-road was a temporary terminus. I never discovered why. But it saved me from stamping thin soles onto hard paving stones outside the windy shelter round the corner. I sat hunched in gratefulness.

It wasn't always winter.

Years later, a crush of men waiting in the draught from a partly open sliding door, forty feet in height, the bleak end of the factory shed, a grey light falling on machines. They had stopped working but work wasn't over yet, until the minute-hand slowly clicked exactly to the hour. Then the clock-out cards plunged, punched, rang, and the gates opened wide to the street.

Later still, in the power station, machines hummed quietly. It was dark night outside. Bare bulbs lit the gangways, the iron catwalks. The generators whirred out electricity that travelled round the grid to light those very bulbs, and a large part of London with them. The deep late-running tube-trains rumbled far below us, driven by the power we registered on humming dials around us. An engineer lay dozing on a bench, waiting for the alarm-bells to ring. They rarely did. Waiting. Working. The night shift.

I write, much of the night. Nothing disturbs me till the dawn, a quiet, gradual event outside my windows. It is my own time, not even called to order by the more harmless routines of the day. Around dawn I switch the desklight off, set my various alarms, and plug in the timer on the radio, always optimistically. But the day — *their* day, it still seems to me — will begin without me. I work in my own time. A peculiar privilege. Or so it seems.

151

But I do not go south in the winter, even now. The watch, the clock, the radio, the light, the plug, remind me not to. Yet.'

*

Armstrong's radio appears in another context ('rowdiose wodhalooing' — a phrase from *Finnegans Wake*) which considers the role of records and the mass media generally, from memories of the Cavern Club in Beatles' days to analysis of a campaign for 'access' television in the late sixties. One well-played disc that allows a direct link to politics is the *Concert for Bangladesh* LP of 1971. The cheque for $243,418.50, raised by the concert and made out to 'United Nations Children's Fund for Relief to Refugee Children of Bangla Desh', reproduced in the sleeve notes to that LP, is later alluded to again, when Armstrong considers the associations of his own chequebook ('It does you, credit'). Money figures centrally in 'Roofing it' where he describes how he finally didn't buy a house, after taking us through the 'collusive network' of local capitalism in the form of estate agent, surveyor, solicitor, building society, bank, structural engineer, architect, builder, local council. That particular story is probably too familiar in everyone's autobiography to need telling — though, no, not, after all, everyone's. Sorry. One neatly informative piece, which brings together global capitalism (via Rank Xerox) and local police surveillance, begins from his filing-cabinet ('A light on the files') and spirals through memories of being interrogated in connection with the Angry Brigade to being taught a loathed italic handwriting in primary school (now he writes illegibly but takes a typewriter on holiday). I'm tempted to quote the whole of 'Being fashioned', about clothes, if only to adequately contextualise the mournful comment he remembers from a friend: 'I can't buy a new suit. I don't know who I am.' But the object which perhaps best sums up his preoccupations and brings out both the strengths and weaknesses of his procedure is his chess set. The piece is called

A check in the post

'Presents were always difficult. Particularly for me. Giving and receiving. The right combination of utility, appropriateness, price, pleasure. My parents solved it brilliantly once (though more than once). For my graduation they gave me a chess set. Not hand-made, but well-made. Not ivory, but wood. In an oblong wooden case that opened as a chess-board. 'Made in Poland', said the paper slip inside. I should have been able to tell, but couldn't, then: the inlaid design, the warm wood, the continental numbering of the squares. I have often used it, enjoyed it.

Chess had been an early adventure, the one skill my two years at grammar school had really taught me. I remember team matches, simultaneous games, even blindfold play. A boy in my class was expert, a Northern Junior Champion, as four brothers had been before him. His victories instructed my defeats. Years after, I met him again, mathematician, physicist, "defence" researcher.

Made of wood. For some reason, wood has always appealed. An Indian friend once surprised me by presenting me with a small, decorated box, as a leave-taking. An empty box, not even a cigarette box. She explained that my room was littered with small wooden boxes. I hadn't noticed. This box was from her home district, made and painted within a local craft tradition.

And Polish. Poland was a special myth in early childhood. I knew my American uncle was Polish. That was exotic. Something to do, for the child, with the possible puns: he was a polished pole. Perhaps.

My first published piece was about Poland. An editor gave me Kolakowski's *Marxism and Beyond* to review. I spent a month reading people called Zbigniew and Tadeusz, seeing films by Polanski and Munk, learning about the Lublin school of logic, the poor theatre of Grotowski, the political careerings of Gomulka. And Poland became slightly less exotic, no longer such a myth.

And I remembered. When I was twelve I had conflated Poland with Hungary, and this composite land had been confused, for a time, with all of "Eastern Europe". I was only just turned twelve. The day after my birthday British and French planes bombed Cairo. "Our" troops landed in Suez.

The news was full of it. Then the radio began mentioning another place: Budapest. And the 'Warsaw Pact'. And Poland. And "Soviet military units". It seemed that a new world war was to be my belated birthday present.

On the morning of November 4 1956 I sat curled in a cozy armchair in the front room, listening to the crackling of the radio, tuned to the small green lettering that read "Budapest". I have tried to check the text since and what the voice apparently said was:

(7.56 a.m.) "Attention, attention. You will now hear the manifesto of the Union of Hungarian Writers:

This is the Union of Hungarian Writers! To every writer in the world, to all scientists, to all writers' federations, to all science academies and associations, to the intelligentsia of the world! We ask all of you for help and support; there is but little time! You know the facts, there is no need to give you a special report! Help Hungary! Help the Hungarian writers, scientists, workers, peasants, and our intelligentsia! Help! Help! Help!"
(8.24 a.m.) "SOS! SOS! SOS! ..."

What I remember and have always remembered is a voice saying, again and again:

Do not forget us. Do not forget us. Do not forget us.

Then the silence.

The world seemed both smaller and larger. My school atlas began to make some sense. I was beginning to play chess and it seemed apposite. Two mirror-armies, two opposing powers, with bishops poised for long diagonal strikes, with brooding rooks grimly guarding respective territories, and prancing knights ready to engage in complicated diplomatic antics. Strategy. Tactics. Tension. But it was the pawns that most attracted me: pushed out into the empty chequered spaces, an expendable front-line but also, often, the key to the whole game, the surviving endgame players. I began to find out about Hungary, Czechoslovakia, Poland, but also, and more quickly, about Egypt, Kenya, Ghana, the Congo, Algeria, Indo-China.

Years later, looking for a play to produce, I read a work by

Conor Cruise O' Brien, called *Murderous Angels*, about Lumumba, Tshombe, Hammarskjold, and Belgian business interests. The sparse clarity of the plotting, the minimal set, the cold logic of the action, made me want to design and direct it as a game of chess. But by then I knew the analogue wasn't wholly adequate: I had met some of the "pawns" and my memory was full of them.

A clandestine New Year's Eve meeting of the guerrillas in Guatemala City. Caribbean radicals outside barbed-wire gates at an American military base. A Turkish poet pointing to a patch of ground where an anti-fascist had been gunned down the day before. That short burst of machine-gun fire one quiet evening in "Red" Bologna. The tight grip of an old woman in a Moscow subway as she insisted, in tearful, difficult English, "*Please* do not let your government start the war." A Catholic pub blasted into smouldering bricks in Belfast. The suddenly rigid shock of a South African activist as the door crashed open behind her. An iron bar from a blackleg's lorry swathing through a miners' picket at Dover docks. The silent concentration of a tired Sandinista in the strafed *barrios* of Managua. And yes, the wary determination and defiant singing of Solidarnosc steel-workers, at Nova Huta, outside Krakow, Poland.

Sitting here now, in the night, I can write about them. They seem connected, and remote. A few photographs, some letters, an address book. But now the conflict is more complicated, my maps are on a larger scale. And beside my chess set are two circulars from the morning mail. One is headed "Campaign for the Abolition of Torture: URGENT ACTION". Another "disappearance", this one in Argentina. I will send the requested, normal, telegram. The second is from Oxfam. A famine in Kampuchea, refugees in Somalia. I will send the inadequate, normal cheque. Tiny moves in a continuing deadly game played out by Superpowers.

But now at least I know that Budapest is not the capital of Poland.'

*

It is the unexpectedness of Armstrong's connections between objects and politics that makes us think, forces us, often, to

155

reflect further upon connections he doesn't make himself (his *American* uncle was Polish . . .). His own life, memories of which act as the formal link between the immediate object and the wider politics, is often left tantalisingly opaque, despite the details (*why* the attraction of wood and boxes?), yet it is, after all, the thread that binds these objects together. And that is where the basic presupposition of this book seems questionable — though admittedly it is I who have attributed that presupposition to it. If the basic strategy of the book is to make us consider the political as well as autobiographical significance of our own possessions, we have to find equivalents not just for Armstrong's objects but also for his experience. Here the 'looping' effect of his objects may well not find a parallel: each object seems to operate both as a culmination of an *already* political process and as a stimulus to a retrospective understanding of that process — so that his reaction to the schoolboy with the private library is *already* a 'class' reaction, just as the way he connects his coffee-filters to the conditions of plantation-workers in Latin America is possible because his visit to the plantation was already, it would seem, politically motivated: most of us, I'm sure, would have stayed on a Caribbean beach, not accompanied a demonstration. It's noticeable how many of his objects are in fact mementos of foreign places but they aren't holiday souvenirs. Reading the book, I began to take it, therefore, that he is most probably a roving political journalist, though he doesn't explicitly say so. What is certainly clear is that the places he visits were already saturated in politics for him, whereas, for example, my plastic leaning tower of Pisa conjures up no personal connections with, say, the Red Brigades. Many of the objects he probes are also presents from friends or relatives, but I doubt if those who gave him the objects could have anticipated his political response to them (the Indian friend's perception of his taste for boxes is surely a case in point). Were he to have focused upon much more ordinary, domestic, objects — such as a knife and fork — I doubt if he could have squeezed much more political significance out of them than Eliot did ('I have measured out my life in coffee spoons') — unless, as I suggested at the beginning of this review, he had adopted a much more direct mode of analysis, concerned with the actual conditions of production, distribution, etc., of those objects. He might thereby have written a more materialist book, but it wouldn't have been 'a materialist autobiography'.

In a curious way, therefore, I think the real persuasive force of the book comes not from Armstrong's chosen procedure, still less from his actual selection of objects, but rather from his accidental solution to that other problem I discussed earlier: the contemporary novelist's problem. By putting himself, as a de-classed international journalist, at the partly hidden centre of his book he has perhaps found a central character in whose life and work some of the major problems and most pressing contradictions of our own period can convincingly be seen to converge. This book doesn't actually follow that through, but, having discovered the possibility, he might now perhaps consider giving us a 'proper' autobiography.

Anne Arthur

Letters

Anon: *Dear Child*
reviewed by Nicola O'Connor

My first reaction to this unusual book was mildly cynical. It suffers from a considerable dose of whimsicality, gaucheness and sentimentality; I felt uncomfortable, even squeamish, reading it, in a way difficult to explain. My ambivalence may perhaps be shared if I simply quote the opening paragraphs. There's no contents page, preface, or other clues as to the kind of book it is, and no author's name is given, so these are literally the opening words:

Dear child,
 I'm afraid you don't know me, yet — but I'm your daddy! And if *you're* surprised, think how *I* felt when your mummy told me about you the day before yesterday! It was a pretty big shock, I can tell you. Well, I can't really tell you, yet. Which is one reason why I'm writing to you.
 You see, your mummy and you are going to be together from now on — but I can't be with you in quite the same way. But I do want to say hello from time to time. And this is my way of saying hello!
 Of course, you won't be able to read these letters for a little while yet, but your mummy will keep them for you and maybe you'll read them when you're older.

Et cetera. The style grates on me. It took me a page or so to be fully sure of the situation, but it's a simple and perhaps even attractive idea, in a cloying kind of way. The child is in the womb and the father is writing to it. The rest of the book is taken up with this one-sided correspondence, as the 'child' approaches birth. I'm still not wholly confident how I feel about the publishing of this — one hesitates for the appropriate word — 'collection'. Partly because I suspect a questionable commercial motivation: the book is very pleasantly produced, large print, generous margins, the kind of book certain people might well give as a present to 'expectant' fathers, and maybe the thought of such a market was foremost. Perhaps however my adverse response is mainly to the style, since I can imagine a quite appealing version of this idea. Certainly the lack of appropriate books for fathers-to-be is mentioned in that first letter as one reason for writing it:

Your mummy bought lots of books today, all about you! How you're gradually growing, and how big you'll soon be. What she should eat and how she should look after herself, so as to look after you.

   I was a little sad that I couldn't find anything especially for your daddy, except one small pamphlet. I know I'm not *very* important to you just now, but I did feel a bit left out of it all.

   When we got back from shopping, though, your mummy gave me a book she'd got from the library for me, which was very kind of her (you've got a good mummy, you know). It was the letters of a Frenchman, Jean de Lannoy, to his son — in 1465! Think of that! In it he says:

I realise that my son and I can never be of the same time, for he comes and I go ... Therefore I decided to write this letter to my son so that if I do not live to the day when he can understand me, at least he will know by letter what my lips could not say to him, as often it is with lovers, who when they are together for love they cannot speak.

I liked that — though it does seem funny that I don't even know whether you're my son or my daughter! That'll be your first surprise for us.

Given that sharp contrast between Jean de Lannoy's measured, adult style and the father's gooey prose, it's a relief that he regularly bases his letters upon some quotation or passage that has struck him. To be fair, the style does become more sure of itself — and perhaps the finding of an appropriate tone of voice and mode of address is genuinely a difficult part of assimilating the role of parent.

We gradually find out more about the family. It's the first child. Father is away from home a lot, working as a consultant engineer. The letters are therefore, in part, an indirect correspondence with the mother, though we learn relatively little about her, beyond the fact that she too works, in an architect's office. They live in a new town near London, seem fairly well-off, but have little active social life and not much local involvement or interests outside a familiar domestic horizon: a typical middle-class young couple, building their first home together. A privileged child?

There seems to be no particular pattern to the sequence of letters, though some register and respond to stages in the child's progress. There's an attractively silly letter congratulating the child on its first bout of kicking and fantasising about its future prospects as a World Cup goal-scorer. Another solemnly commiserates with the child when it suffers from hiccups during the fifth month. A certain amazement is recorded as the father finds out more about how the child is slowly assuming shape, as in the seventh week:

Dear child,
  Can I begin with a question? I'm told that you've been working very hard recently and that you've managed somehow to put together not only your arms and legs and your head, but also your eyes and your ears, your nose and lips and tongue, and even your fingers and thumbs! That's a lot of effort for a little child. But: how do you fit it all in??? I mean, you're only an inch long!

There's one letter where he includes an elaborate computer analysis of the 'odds' against the child being 'who you think you are': a quarter of a million egg-cells multiplied by 500 million sperm cells divided by a dozen or so, multiplied by the number of nights the parents made love, multiplied by the number of times they didn't, multiplied by the odds on the phone ringing. It's a wholly spurious calculation but a nicely teasing letter, which ends:

I don't want to worry you at this stage, but have you considered that you may not be you after all. That *would* be a pity!

161

The problem of finding appropriate reading material for fathers links a number of letters: one rather feels for him as he samples in turn Strindberg's *The Father*, Kafka's *Letter to his Father* and Freud on the Oedipus complex! A passage from Joyce's *Ulysses* particularly depresses him:

A father, said Stephen, battling against hopelessness, is a necessary evil ... Fatherhood, in the sense of conscious begetting, is unknown to man. It is a mystical estate, an apostolic sucession, from only begetter to only begotten. On that mystery and not on the madonna which the cunning Italian intellect flung to the mob of Europe the church is founded and founded irremovably because founded, like the world, macro- and microcosm, upon the void. Upon incertitude, upon unlikelihood. *Amor matris*, subjective and objective genitive, may be the only true thing in life. Paternity may be a legal fiction. Who is the father of any son that any son should love him or he any son?

This passage doubly worries him, because it also raises the issue of what kind of beliefs he has to offer to the child, what certainties or principles to live by, what moral code. He sidesteps this in the letter by trying to imagine the child successively muttering to itself in the sequence of languages and styles Joyce associates with the growth of the embryo in 'Oxen of the Sun'. Luckily, he doesn't try himself to emulate Joyce.

But he returns to the problem of fatherly example and parental advice in later letters, finding little to salvage from Halifax's *Advice to a Daughter* or Chesterfield's *Letters to his Son*. Yeats' poem 'A Prayer for my Daughter', perhaps surprisingly, wholly repulses and angers him, since he has begun to think seriously what differences the child's gender will make, for the child and for himself. This letter I found even moving, as it developed into a curiously passionate yet desperate expression of hope that by the time the child is an adult some of the age-old gender disparities will have dwindled away:

You will be labelled, dear child, labelled from birth. Your aunts and your uncles, your grandmas and grandads, will send you presents and cards — but blue for a boy and pink for a girl. And mummy and

162

daddy will label you too: a nice little girl, a good little boy. We will try, try hard, not to impose, not to define your roles in advance, not to limit you to what we expect. If you're a boy, I hope you enjoy cooking. If you're a girl, I'll buy you a carpentry set. But we won't succeed, not by ourselves. You will have to fight too — and fight us as well. And it will be hard to be you. But perhaps, just perhaps, not as hard as we think. You *are* a new time, entering the old time, you will *be* your own time just as you are your own eyes and ears. In that time you can perhaps mould a new world, in that time you can perhaps make your own expectations and live them.

This sense of eventual replacement by the coming child is very strong, particularly in the early letters. A passage from Gregory Bateson seems in an odd way positively to comfort the father as, in a rueful mood, he warns the tiny child about the massive amount it will one day have to learn, the sheer weight of cultural inheritance it will be expected to wear. The Bateson passage cuts right across this line of thought:

It is out of the random that organisms collect new mutations, and it is there that the stochastic learning gathers its solutions. Evolution leads to climax: ecological saturation of all the possibilities of differentiation. Learning leads to the overpacked mind. By return to the unlearned and mass-produced egg, the ongoing species again and again clears its memory banks to be ready for the new.

Yet the next letter begins, with a glance back at this passage:

Dear egg-head,
Do you feel like a holiday yet? Your daddy and mummy need a break, so we're going to one of our favourite places. We'll take you again when you're older — to Pisa. Not to see the tower: that may well have fallen over by the time you're big enough to know about it! But to see a tree. It's in the botanical gardens there, and it was planted in 1550. More than four hundred years ago. Lots of people have been to see it, Montaigne, Goethe, Liszt. It's perhaps the oldest living thing in Europe, and one day I would like you to see it, to touch it, to feel how old and how recent it is. The Renaissance is only as long ago as the lifetime of that tree. We can do a lot in a lifetime.

In a number of letters the closeness of the past becomes a theme, the sheer richness of the world the child will come into, but also the openness of the future, a sense of the incredible capacity of the future to be different while building upon that past. There's a delight in discovering a passage in Mme de Sévigne which might have been written yesterday, such is our deep continuity with the past:

Our daughter is a dark-haired little beauty. She is very pretty indeed. Here she comes. She give me sticky kisses, but she never screams. She kisses me, she recognises me, she laughs at me, she calls me just plain *Maman*. I simply adore her. I have had her hair cut: it is a happy-go-lucky style now which is just made for her. Her complexion, her chest and her little body are admirable. She does a hundred and one different things: she caresses, she slaps, she makes the sign of the cross, she begs pardon, she drops a curtsy, she blows a kiss, she shrugs her shoulders, she dances, she strokes, she holds her chin: in a word she is pretty in every particular. I watch her for hours on end.

Yet there is also a kind of anger about the past, which surfaces more and more as the nine months draws towards its end. One letter cites the infant mortality figures from different periods, including the horrifying fact of the Dublin Foundling Hospital admitting 10,272 infants in 1775-6, of whom only 45 survived. Clearly, such figures mainly stand in for an anxiety about the child and the mother, which begins to become more explicit as the letters increasingly disclose that 'complications' are developing in the pregnancy. Though the child, and through it the mother, is gently teased about a series of checks and tests, a genuine fear begins to tremble through the letters, and even at times a certain exasperation at the child for 'persisting in this peculiar position you have chosen to adopt':

I hope *you're* comfortable at least. Your mother certainly isn't! Now, tomorrow, could you please oblige us all by a considerate somersault. You won't get *out* that way!

But the child remains adamantly the wrong way.

If my review has so far made the book seem too much like a mere anthology, this is rather unfair to it — though it was the element that consciously interested me most. Yet by this stage I realised that I had become genuinely involved with the fate of this child: through the letters this unnamed 'you' had become a real recipient, a child one could address without expecting a reply, a real infant other. The increasingly sombre tone of the final weeks made me anxious and concerned for the outcome. More tests and efforts to right the child punctuate the gathering preparations for the birth: the father decorating and equipping a small spare room as a nursery, accompanying the mother on shopping raids, attending together the pre-natal clinic. But the letters become filled with a new seriousness as it becomes clear that the birth will have to take place in a special maternity unit in a large London hospital. One of the few glimpses of the wider world appears at this point: the father, reading his paper, sees for the first time the significance of two news items he would normally not notice, or connect:

A luxury private children's and women's hospital — intended to become the Great Ormond Street of the private sector — is to be opened near Harley Street next June. Every patient's room will have a private bathroom, telephone, television and piped oxygen. A special feature will be twin-bedded rooms, where parents, for an extra charge, can stay overnight with their sick child. Medical facilities will include a special baby care unit, two delivery suites, twin operating suites, radiology, ultra sound and an intensive care unit.

and:

Up to 6000 premature babies are likely to be deprived of the intensive care they need next year because of the shortage of hospital facilities, it was estimated yesterday. A senior paediatrician, who asked not to be named, described the situation as a 'disgrace'. Figures from the Neo-natal Medical Unit at St Mary's Hospital, Manchester, show that among the babies turned away because of lack of NHS care some 66 per cent died later, compared with only a 30 per cent death rate among those who were admitted.

He also notes a trade union advert stating that the cost of a single guided missile on a fighter aircraft would equip an intensive care unit. But the only other glimpse of that wider context is indirect. The father promises the child that he will buy a copy of every newspaper published on the day of birth, to keep for the child, but then scans that morning's diet of wars, rumours of wars, gathering tension, economic crisis, international hate and personal tragedy — and almost decides not to.

165

The caesarian operation is scheduled for three days after Christmas. The letter for Christmas Day is movingly simple:

Dear child,
A very happy Christmas. Looking forward to seeing you in your first new year.

Followed by a quotation from the apocryphal Gospel of James:

And he saddled the she-ass, and set her upon it, and his son led it, and Joseph followed after. And they drew near unto Bethlehem, within three miles. And Joseph turned himself about and saw her of a sad countenance and said within himself: Peradventure that which is within her paineth her. And again Joseph turned himself about and saw her laughing, and said unto her: Mary, what aileth thee that I see thy face at one time laughing and at another time sad? And Mary said unto Joseph: It is because I behold two peoples with mine eyes, the one weeping and lamenting and the other rejoicing and exulting.

And they came to the midst of the way, and Mary said unto him: Take me down from the ass, for that which is within me presseth me, to come forth. And he took her down from the ass and said unto her: Whither shall I take thee to hide thy shame? for the place is desert.

And he found a cave there and brought her into it, and set his sons by her: and he went forth and sought for a midwife of the Hebrews in the country of Bethlehem.

Now I Joseph was walking, and I walked not. And I looked up to the air and saw the air in amazement. And I looked up to the pole of the heaven and saw it standing still, and the birds of the air without motion. And I looked upon the earth and saw a dish set and workmen lying by it, and their hands were in the dish: and they that were chewing chewed not, and they that were lifting the food lifted it not, and they that put it to their mouths put it not thereto, but the faces of all of them were looking upward. And behold there were sheep being driven, and they went not forward but stood still; and the shepherd lifted his hand to smite them with his staff, and his hand remained up. And I looked upon the stream of the river and saw the mouths of the kids upon the water and they drank not.

And of a sudden all things moved onward in their course.

The Boxing Day letter opens:

Dear child,
Your daddy's done something very silly. He's in bed with

hepatitis, and he's going to be there for a week. And that means that you and your mummy have had to go into the hospital a bit sooner than we thought. I *hope* you'll both be alright, and I'm sure you will. But I won't be able to be there, after all. Please forgive me. After all this waiting, I will have to wait just a little longer to see you.

Will you do me a favour? Don't just cry when you take in your very first breath. Yell: PHONE DADDY!

They do phone. The last letter begins:

Dear, dear child!

Hello! You made it! You've arrived. They phoned five minutes ago (thanks!) and you're both fine.

Daddy is now going to cry.

The letter breaks off.

Below it is printed an unattributed paragraph:

This is an emergency announcement. At 10.47 a nuclear device was exploded over London. A Prime Ministerial message follows immediately. Please stay tuned to this wavelength.

I suppose it might happen that way, for somebody. December the 28th used to be the Feast of the Holy Innocents.

Nicola O'Connor

Poetry

Competition Result: *Four Quartets*

Since its first issue, *NCQ* has run a regular poetry competition, with simple rules. Contributors have been asked to take a well-known English poem and re-write it as an explicitly political poem.

Over the years, most entries have tended towards mere parody rather than displacement, but we have printed some memorably tongue-in-cheek pieces with the effect we had hoped for: that in any re-reading of the originals, they would be 'shadowed' by a memory of their political counterparts.

For this anniversary issue we set the rather difficult task of a line-by-line re-writing of *Four Quartets*, and we are pleased to print below the valiant winning versions of 'Burnt Norton' and 'East Coker', both by Jane Horner of Reading.

Her entry, though not wholly successful, did manage, in the judges' opinion, both to respect and to contest the original, falling into parody mainly at the points where *Four Quartets* itself deploys that tactic. We have no space to include her versions of 'Dry Salvages' and 'Little Gidding' but — in lieu of further *NCQ* competitions — readers may be tempted to complete the re-written version for themselves.

Though the usual prize of a free subscription to *NCQ* cannot, unfortunately, be awarded, as this is the last *NCQ*, we extend our thanks and congratulations to Ms Horner.

Editor

LEARNT TORSIONS

— but there is no competition —
There is only the fight
(T. S. Eliot)

par-odos: the way forward and the way back are never the same twice
(Caliban, *Dictionnaire*)

I

The history that is past and the history that is present
Will together, we presume, determine the history to come
And those histories are always before us.
For to be fixed in a permanent present
Is only a dead repetition, a fatal denial.
What might be and what can be
Are not merely some slight thought in advance
But practical, difficult, delicate paces before us.
What might be and what could be
Stem from determined decisions, from more than decision.
The calls of the dying stretch out at us
From brick walls trickling with blood,
Moments of misery, outrage and upsurge, courage defeated,
Efforts that failed. Such calls
Break on us still.
               Though to what effect
Stirring the pages in the autumn study —
A slight breeze on the brow?
                    Other places
Are vivid now, in deep lines of the mind,
Bitter times, but perhaps less blind and bitter
Than now: flags flying red
With the colour of blood, hoisted on walls
And high places, in cities beleaguered and dying,
Paris and Munich, Madrid, Prague and Turin,
The last achings of hope, and the first
Breeze of the future, light in cracked panes
And flames reaching higher, desires demanding to win.

We hear their defiance, muffled in cross-fire,
And the dead look like debts, awaiting redemption,
Promises drawn on ourselves:
A cart upended on cobbles, a rifle
Wrapped round with a rag, an arm clutching at air,
Stiff and drained white in the gutter,
A street silent and heavy with thunder.
These images amaze
Yet the pictures move in familiar ways
And the fingers clench, slowly, in pain
As the gaze moves on to the next:
A photo from Belsen, maybe a painting by Goya,
A map of some ruins, with radii dotted in ink.
Then the book is closed, and the heart is hopelessly empty.
No, says the mind, for the garden is lovely,
Peaceful and calm in the sun.
No! says the mind, for we cannot assign
The future, our future, to this.
What has been and what might be,
What others have done and might well do again
Impose one demand which is always insistent.

II

Guards and sappers in the mud
Dot the fields of Flanders;
The chilling in the blood
Freezes corpses in the trenches
Anticipating snipers' targets;
Fumbling fingers dropping rifles
As the bugle blows the dawn;
Barbed wire fences and the bullets
Tear the flesh of stumbling figures
In the gas-dark maze of morning;
And the shrieking and the dying
Drowned in whining of the shells
Bursting in the glare of rockets
And the choking at the throats —
As the generals peruse their menus.

171

At that peculiar moment, in those burning years, neither
   victory nor defeat
Neither for nor against; at that particular time, when the
   chance came,
But neither opportunism nor plot, and not at all a
   compromise,
When sudden decisions were taken. Neither forseen nor
   unexpected,
Neither gamble nor design. Except for that one chance, a
   strange and single instant,
There would be no change, and there has always been
   change.
We can only be ready, but we cannot say *when*,
And we cannot predict, nor determine, for that is dictation
Across unwritten pages of a history not yet fully
   deciphered:
The curious conjuncture of pressures and passion, the
   implosion of feeling
And the limits of patience, yet shaped every time
By the force of events, a pattern beyond us,
An instance beneath our control —
Yet not wholly anarchic; both a history made
And a history given, grasped
In the effort of partial intelligence,
Random in the impact of deep-buried tension.
So the chaining of the future to a hopeless past,
Implied in the weary reformist gesture,
Maintains a desperate, fragile, distortion
Which only endures for so long.
   Present demands and future perspectives
Leave but a tiny, diminishing space
For crucial decisions made under pressure;
But only after such risky adventure
Can the marvellous heave of the future be felt,
A gap opening up in the world,
A moment of promise, a promise of moments to follow.
An exhileration of time in the end.

III

These are only disaffected elements, we are told,
Time and again,
With a sneer: neither significant contributors
To the noble art of the feasible,
Labouring at margins of change,
Accretions of slow and patient amends,
Nor total rejection, disdain
Of all consequence, commitment beyond
Personal rapture or gain.
Neither reform nor revolt. Only a hardened
Tenacious grasp on the throat
Of structures, committees, campaigns and petitions,
Working like others, but concealing their aims,
Rabid fanatics with no comprehension
Of forms and conventions, of channels of protest,
Of ways of getting things done.
A slime on the face of compassion,
Again and again, we are told.
Selective protesters,
Picking our targets with care,
Ignoring the benefits, anxious to slur:
Cyprus and Aden, Oman and Belfast,
Racism, sexism, profit, corruption —
Why don't we go, and live over there?

Examine it slowly,
Look closely, with care: anger is there
But held in a grip like despair;
Desperate sorrow, torture and fear,
Repression, betrayal, oppression are near.
Who partakes of the profit,
Who lives in the clear, who gains from the pain?
Those who impose and those who oppose
Are both caught in the coils
And twist in the net,
Two sides of the knife. As knots tighten
And lungs constrict, the need erupts in us all:
To grasp hold of the knife, and cut our way clear.

The Thirties and Forties have deadened desires,
The Trials and the Camps have denuded our hopes;
The Long March awaits its new recruits
And the ships set forth for a silent coast,
Returning alone.

Will ever
The Sierra act again as our host, with banners unfurling
As middle-aged men in easy suits recall the bright days of
    their youth
And a thousand flourishing rifles are raised high in salute,
No longer in anger and pain?

V

Rhetoric moves, compassion moves,
Only for a time; what revives as emotion
Dies as refrain; of the momentary horror
Very little remains. Only by action, organised action,
Can changes be made and rendered secure.
This we all know
From the structures we live in.
Not only the buildings, designed and constructed,
But also the settled companies that built them,
Whether guilds or trades unions, banks or community
    trusts,
The hundreds of bricks or the mechanised belt,
The Cotswold village or the urban freeway — all are built,
As revolutions are built, from the ground. People are
    strained,
Crack, and sometimes break, under the burden,
Under the tension, slip, slide, resign,
Retire with uncertainties, cannot sustain the pace.
But some will not give in. Mocking voices,
Complacent and satisfied, or merely in genuine ignorance,
Constantly yap at them. The builder in a waste land
Is most despised by those who believe in a mirage,
The whining complaint of the nearly privileged,
The loud disclaimer of the already secure.

The details are obviously and always difficult,
As in the endless debates of the Central Committee.
Strategic choices are, of course, indispensable,
But not in themselves any guarantee of success;
The party, the leadership, are only a focus
For massive demands, for deeply embedded desires;
Tireless and disinterested, maybe,
But always replaceable
When caught in the cages of power,
Of personal kudos or dithering timidity.
Sudden, in a moment like madness,
While papers are still being shuffled,
Arises that incredible confident power
Of people demanding control —
And changing the forms of control for ever.
Marvellous the moments that matter
In a history yet to be made.

LEAST WORKER

I

Our births decide, to a large extent, our lives. In this society,
People live, and die, under exploitation, under employment,
Are bought and sold, retired, made 'redundant'; in their
    place
Is a new machine, or a cheaper worker, or an immigrant.
Old skills to new technologies, old products to new
    commodities,
Old needs to fresh investments, and every demand is
    turned into profit
Which is always means, aim and end,
Control over man and woman, necessities and pleasure.
People live and die, with a time fixed for working
And fixed times for leisure, time allocated
By the slow clicking of the factory clock,
By the endless murmuring of the TV programme,
A time bought and shaped by precarious weekly wage-slips.

Others' births dictate, to a large extent, our lives. How
    the few live
Affects us all, leaving still that deep inheritance
Of guarded, privileged, power, hidden from sight
Behind high walls round pleasant estates in the country
Or cased in deep vaults under imposing banks in the City,
Effective in quiet conversational boardrooms or in deep-
    carpeted offices
Smelling of wealth. At the subdued afternoon meeting
Calmly decisions are taken, by well-fed, satisfied minds,
And millions are shunted like empty trains
To wait for the next rich investor.

                                    In that ageing factory
If one does not go too close, if one need not get too close,
On the late afternoon shift, one can almost bear the
    broiling heat
Of the vivid furnace and the roaring rollers

To watch molten metal sliding into moulds
And workers stripped, swearing and sweating,
Struggling in the lurid light and aching fumes,
A dangerous, back-tearing job;
Two by two, in joint operations,
Grappling long soft lines of smelted steel
To be twisted and turned into tubes. Again and again to
    the furnace,
Arms raised against the flames and eyes searing in glare,
Viciously tired but with weary precision,
Curling white-hot snakes with clumsy asbestos paws,
Burnt palms and hardened fingers moving with practised
    skill
In guarded gestures long since learnt in a daily dance
With savage scorching injury. Keeping a rhythm,
The rhythm of the presses, the rhythm of the pressures,
The enormous pounding pressures of monstrous moving
    machinery,
The constant production and the continuous shifts,
The constant danger and the continuous exhaustion,
The repeated rhythm of afternoons, mornings and nights,
The endless alternation of shifts. Bodies ageing and aching.
Working and working. Injuries and death.

    Night ends, and another day
Prepares for heat or quietness. In a silent boardroom the
    night-cleaner
Empties the ashtrays and flowers. I am here,
Or there. Or elsewhere. Thanks to my birth.

II

'I wonder what the late shift is doing
With this sudden disturbance at the gates,
This loud rejection of the rates —
This rude insubordination on the floor —
This unprecedented hammering at my door!
Such total and determined solidarity
We've never had to face before!
Now thunderous acclamation, thunderous applause,

Greets every new outrageous clause
Proclaimed by rabid union negotiators
Outlining quite utopian realignments
Of the firm's basic governing agreements
Covering every aspect of employment —
They really want control and seem prepared to take it!!
Intend to run my factory for themselves, their friends and
    neighbours,
Producing things for use and not for profit!!!
Good God! Now they're breaking down my office!'

That was always a way of putting it — not very convincing,
A rhetorical flourish from a worn-out historical mould,
Leaving one still with the intractable problem
Of tactics and strategy. The pageantry does not matter.
It certainly won't be (I'll say it again) quite what one
    expected.
What then is the value of the long-pored over,
Long-argued about, finely-footnoted research into
Those previous revolutionary models? Have they misled
    us,
Or even misled themselves, those endlessly-detailed
    movements,
Leaving us only some paradigms of partial disaster?
Was their confidence only a misplaced commitment,
Their rational optimism only a product of bankrupt
    analysis,
Useless in these very different conditions we find ourselves
    facing
Or perhaps even try to ignore? There is, it must seem to
    us now,
At best only some limited lessons
To be drawn from any such previous experiment.
The theory imposes a practice, and is modified,
For the practice has to be changed every time,
And every historical breakthrough is a new and unforsee-
    able conjuncture
Of uneven developments. We can only fully predict

What has, as a matter of research, already happened.
At every conjecture, not only that crucial conjuncture,
But in all its developments, in every contradictory
  occasion,
On the edge of all possibilities, there can be no definitive
  future,
Though always the menace of memories, the threat of
  some terrible precedent,
Risking our own generation. We cannot rely on
The pattern of past events only, but rather their precise
  specificity,
Their very uniqueness, that peculiar unrepeatability
Of what we call history, or revolution, or tragedy.
The only confidence we can hope to acquire
Is the confidence of actual practice: and practice makes
  possible.

The ageing fingers firmly bend around the steel.

The chapped hands move calmly through the flame.

III

O hard, hard, hard. We all find it hard, of course,
The grinding daily routine, weary day after weary day,
The captains of industry, merchant bankers, newspaper
  editors,
The gentlemanly rulers, statesmen and speculators,
Distinguished civil servants, holders of many directorships,
Military controllers and TV pundits, all find it hard
To Make Ends Meet, even to Turn an Honest Penny,
After Tax, in the Office, down in the City, on the
  Exchange,
And slender the returns and gone the incentive.
And we all moan with them, after the terrible Budget,
Or the IMF conditions — though there is always someone
  to blame.
They say, in the press, be moderate, and work very much
  harder

For that will be in the National Interest. And when, on the
   telly,
The interviewers await, for the Prime Minister to appear,
With a grim frown in the eyes and barely restrained anger
   under the voice,
Then we know that the union militants, that same
   ubiquitous band,
(And with them the interests of millions) are about to be
   blamed once again —
Or when, on the front page, the headlines loom larger in
   red
And the daily ignorance is fed once again with lies and with
   silence,
And the facile analysis deepens into frothing hysteria,
Leaving only an empty wail of reaction;
Or when, on the radio, the News offers again the same
   stale old distortions —
Then we are told, be patient, and work without strikes
For strikes are always the wrong way to proceed; work
   without pay-rises
For pay-rises will just bring inflation; there are still
   productivity-bonuses
But the pay and the products and even the work may well
   go to others.
So work without power, for you are not ready for power.
Being moderate will bring us prosperity, though prosperity
   will somehow bring unemployment as well.
Long queues at the Labour Exchange, but excitement on
   the Stock Exchange.
A means test for school milk, but an increase in dividends.
A rise in prescription charges, but a pay-rise for the
   police —
All perfectly obvious, and no longer requiring analysis; it's
   the usual
Crisis continuing.

   You will say I am mouthing
Familiar *marxisant* platitudes. Do I need to say them
   again?

180

Do you need to hear them again? In order to defend what
   we've got,
To keep what we've fought for, to have what we made in
   the first place,
   We must take what was ours at the start.
In order to make what we need,
   We now need to make what nobody needs.
In order to dispossess those who never produce
   We must produce for those who never possess.
In order to wholly become what we all can become
   We must endure what no-one can wholly become
For what you are constantly told is the most basic of lies,
And what you can easily make is what you do not yet have,
And what you can become is only what you are prevented
   from being.

IV

'The militant striker tests the deal
That keeps him working overtime;
Behind the laundered balance-sheet the real
Division of social labour-time
Perpetuates the capitalist pantomime

In which the only profits are our losses
If we obey this system's rules
Whose constant care is for the bosses
Not for those who wield the tools;
Such tame obedience leaves us fools.

The whole industrial product should, by right,
Go to those who give it use;
But for that we'll have to fight
Since to save his private golden goose
Any boss will gladly draw the noose!

Slaughtering the guy who makes the goods
Seems a futile, stupid action.
But the deadly lesson that these hoods

181

Have learnt with dirty satisfaction
Is how to smash a militant fraction —

So the whole work-force must make it plain,
Each of us must have the resolution,
Not to live and work for private gain;
We know the ultimate solution
Is either death — or what we call a Revolution!'

V

So here we are, perhaps half-way there, having tried twenty
    times already,
Twenty attempts partly successful, the efforts of previous
    workers,
From Diggers to Sans-culottes and Chartists, and every
    revolt
Builds on the others but is a different kind of advance,
Since we can only consolidate facets of freedom
While a system remains that denies us the whole
And those facets can soon be absorbed. So each further
    effort
Demands its peculiar tactic, its shift in perspective,
Though the ultimate aim remains stubbornly the same
In the elusive continuity of struggle, the repeated
    trajectory
Of classes in conflict. And what we manage to gain
Through solidarity and strength, has often been hoped for
By others, who died long before, by men and by women whom
    we cannot
Redeem — for their suffering is over —
Though their aims and their words we can echo
In slogans their ghosts might applaud, though spoken
Under conditions they could not foresee. And perhaps
    neither our phrases nor actions
Will really outlast us, like theirs. For us, as for them,
    perhaps it's the trying that matters.

A hope is what one builds from. As history lengthens

The problems seem more intractable, the prospect more
   clouded
Of possible, actual. Not the local insurrection
Surrounded, with a long pause for development,
But a global reaction to every conjuncture
And not one reaction only but an endless variety
Re-shaping all other conjunctures, re-making the global
   occasion.
Here then is a time for hesitation, as the rifles are cocked,
But also a time for instant decision, as bombers take off
(A time to end all time, this time).
Sudden revolts can strangle themselves
When only the here and the now matter.
But revolutions are strangled at birth
When the here and the now matter no longer.
We must acknowledge that now and yet we are here
In a deeper perplexity,
More desperate entanglements, as a whole globe turns in
   our view
While the endless cries fill the air-waves in millions,
A world's hunger lapping loud in the silence of space,
A flicker of pain in the dark. Our lives have already, in part,
   decided our ends.

Essays

J. D. Hutton: *A Matter of Time*
reviewed by Antonio Ford

'Economy of time, this is wherein ultimately all economy resolves itself.' This laconic claim by Marx, in the *Grundrisse*, forms the epigraph to Jenny Hutton's new work. I rather wish that she had attended to its implications in her own writing: ironically, her book is approximately two-thirds longer than it need have been — a fact, however, which she has the grace at one point to acknowledge, even to exploit.

The first part is the main culprit. In three main sections she surveys an immense field, much of which this reviewer found yawningly familiar: the development of coinage, measurement and abstract philosophical thought in early Greek civilisation; the gradual mechanisation of the world-picture from late antiquity to the seventeenth century and the (linked) re-definition of the virtue of 'temperance'; the slow construction of a time-discipline appropriate to industrial capitalism from the late middle ages to the early twentieth century, from the invention of mechanical clocks to the imposition of the production conveyor-belt. It is this last development which seems most germane to her theme, and her excursions into the various preconditions for our present dominant sense of time were surely unnecessary and a little self-indulgent. One can presumably recognise what is at stake in Franklin's advice to young tradesmen, that 'time is money', without relating it to Newton's cosmology or his time at the Royal Mint, still less to any putative links between Lydian merchants, pre-Socratic philosophers and Aristotle's *Physics*. Nor do we need to know, for example, that the expansion of railways in mid-nineteenth-century Britain involved the extension of 'London time' to the whole country, in order to appreciate the fact that a complex industrial and commercial economy ideally requires a uniform time-base from which to coordinate its interconnections. Far from historically illuminating for me the 'social homogenisation and thrifty intensification of time-awareness' (a characteristically jumbled phrase from p.384), Ms Hutton's initial 400 pages merely reinforced my phenomenological endorsement of 'capitalist time' in the form of a deeply felt and growing impatience. Any reader already familiar with the work of, say, George Thomson, Alfred Sohn-Rethel, E. J. Dijksterhuis, E. P. Thompson, David Landes and Nigel Thrift, is strongly advised to begin Ms Hutton's volume at p. 405.

Here the argument begins to bite, mildly. Her basic point is that at the core of Marx's economic analysis of capitalism is a concept, that of 'socially necessary labour-time', which is deeply 'impregnated' (her curious word) with a 'capitalist conceptualisation of time'. One might murmur that this seems precisely apposite to any accurate analysis of capitalism, but Ms Hutton prefers to regard this particular notion as having 'latently deflected' (*sic*!) most nineteenth-and twentieth-century European attempts to 'conceptualise socialism'. I would myself have thought that the emphasis of marxism was not to 'conceptualise' the world but actually to change it, but her formulation has some irritant value. Fortunately, she is only indirectly concerned with the entangled debate on the intellectual credibility of Marx's so-called 'labour theory of value'; her concern is rather that attempts to derive some relatively concrete model of a post-capitalist economy, including those derived from Marx's analysis of capitalism, have retained a reliance upon 'socially necessary labour-time', in some form or another, as a crucial conceptual prop.

She first of all locates this covert appeal behind not only some rightly-forgotten nineteenth-century 'utopian' programmes for the replacement of money by 'labourtokens' but also such familiar 'Labourist rhetorical priorities' as the 'equalisation' of wealth and income. Both of these she sees as mere variations upon an underlying triple equation of money,

labour and time, all three conceived along an axis of homogeneous measurement units. She next analyses the emergence
of Soviet economic planning in the 1920s, linking it both to the
Taylorisation of factory work-processes and to the extraordinary proliferation of officially encouraged 'time-budget'
sociological studies in the early Soviet Union. Here again she
claims that the 'key operative concept' was the 'abstractly
homogeneous character of time', with time as both the
immediate measure of labour-efficiency and the ultimate
measure of money, itself the primary 'organisational means' of
State allocation of productive resources to 'socially necessary
labour'. In this analysis, however, a certain fissure appears
between 'socially necessary labour' and 'labour-time', with
'homogeneous time' as the core concept of State planning
operating as an 'organisational mediation', whether directly in
the form of Five-Year Plans or indirectly in the exaltation of
Stakhanovite work-norms: the 'primary drive of the entire
Soviet economic motor' was, she claims, 'a race against
abstract time'. (I would myself have thought it mainly a race
for security against far from abstract Western hostility.) In a
brief aside she indicates that this alleged fissure between
socially necessary labour and labour-time took a radically
different form in the Chinese Cultural Revolution, but she
postpones discussion of this and returns instead to Western
Europe and the present, suggesting a 'reverse parallel' (whatever contorted geometry that term might derive from) with
the Soviet experience. In the wake of massive and long-term
structural unemployment (those easy phrases ...) she maintains that most 'socialists' (*her* scare quotes) have proposed
merely short-term demands focused upon a reduction in
'average labour-time' as a means to a 'redistribution of
socially-available necessary labour' (i.e. crudely but less con-
ceptually put: job-sharing) while retaining an equation between labour-time and money (i.e. minimal loss of average pay)
as an organisational means of somewhat covertly redistributing income. But this she sees as merely 'capitalist labour-
time allocation stood on its head' (another appealingly clumsy
phrasing!) and in any case as in itself both politically unlikely
and economically unviable, since such a demand implies both

the *pre*-condition of adequate coercive power over international capitalist enterprises and a continued endemic misfit between total purchasing power and total earned income (i.e., in her view, an inflation – deflation cycle). The logical resolution of this 'incoherence', according to Ms Hutton, would be State control of capitalist enterprise and a fully 'planned' economy — but that is precisely the recipe which informed both early Soviet and traditional Labour-socialist thinking, i.e. for Ms Hutton most left responses to the current crisis of employment embed yet more permutations upon an underlying economic model fundamentally shaped by the insidious notion of 'socially necessary labour-time'.

By this point in her lengthy but not very lucid discussion I was both irritated and intrigued. Ms Hutton seemed to have argued herself into an impossible corner. If her overall argument was correct then only an abandonment of the very notion of 'socially necessary labour-time' in any form whatsoever could satisfy her idea of socialism, yet *any* 'conceptualisation' of an economic *system* would seem to require *some* notion of overall social allocation of jobs and with it, therefore, of 'labour-time'. This is what intrigued me. What irritated me was the slipperiness (to be kind) of her actual arguments. For example, I am simply not convinced that a sensible redeployment of labour, eradicating 'overtime', reducing average weekly hours, extending job-sharing schemes and the like, while maintaining a firm incomes policy and (perhaps) a national minimum wage, would necessarily involve either coercive direction of industry or an unstable national currency; such a programme seems to me eminently rational and pragmatic. I can see that it would qualify neither as Ms Hutton's 'socialism' nor as a long-term solution to structural unemployment, but that is no justification for cavalier dismissal. Nor do I admit the 'parallel' she draws between the alleged 'logic' of Labour Party socialism and the basic model of Soviet planning; the latter has more in common with the early, forced phases of capitalist industrialisation (as her own Part I, section (iii) should have reminded her), while the former is characterised by a humane flexibility rather than by any rigid 'logic'. However, the details of her 'arguments' are perhaps less important than the peculiarity of her own 'logic'. It would seem that any implicit reliance upon a conception of time as homogeneous, as composed of abstractly equatable units, is enough to characterise an economic system for Ms Hutton as 'impregnated' with capitalism — presumably implying that capitalism would re-emerge from the womb of any such system. Yet on her own evidence — a full 400 pages of it — that very notion of time not only pre-dates capitalism but also deeply permeates the whole fabric of Western thought. Which is why, despite my impatience and irritation, I remained intrigued enough to persevere with the next section of this sprawling volume.

It begins abruptly, even impolitely, with a peculiarly silly question: 'How long has it taken you to read this far?' It proceeds to even sillier questions, such as 'How long did it take you to understand the argument on page 174?' I confess that I found it difficult even to locate an argument on page 174 — to which, no doubt, Ms Hutton would respond by asking me how long I looked for one or how long it took me not to find one! The point of these questions is presumably the simple-minded one that each reader will have a different answer, or even that an 'answer' is impossible to give (does one include coffee-breaks, answering the phone, checking a reference, going off to read a cited article previously unknown to one — or just calculate the physical turning of the pages?), yet I reject the further implication that the obvious incommensurability of different readers' rates of reading and comprehension somehow undermines the notion that time is homogeneous, since whatever answer one gave would still have to be couched in terms of some public unit of measurement. I admit, warily, that an appropriate (if, in this case, horrifying) answer might be 'a lifetime', but even a lifetime is measurable in years — insurance companies do it all the time. But if Ms Hutton thinks these peculiar questions are relevant to the problem of organising an economic system I remain wholly sceptical.

Nor does her next series of questions at all persuade me. She asks, for example, 'How long did it take you to mend the fence/clear out the attic/wallpaper the bedroom?' Again, these seem to me stupendously inept questions in this context, not only because in my own case such factors as personal skill, degrees of motivation and temperamental procrastination are involved, but because one *could* reasonably assimilate such tasks to a wage-rate based upon how long the job *ought* to take a competent professional. If Ms Hutton intends to suggest some qualitative difference (apart from sheer frustration) between my use of my 'own' time on such chores and the time taken by an employed gardener or decorator, then she is merely reminding us that in some cultures 'time' is indeed conceived of as task-time rather than wage-time.

I admit some puzzlement or doubt as to the very validity of her next series of questions, which are variations upon: 'How long did it take for you to have your last idea?' The precise formulation is odd here: not 'how long did it take you' but '*for* you' — implying perhaps that some at least of that immeasurable time (a point I partly concede) was not only 'my' time, since arguably some ideas are historically unthinkable before the development of other ideas: one couldn't have an 'idea' in nuclear physics before the discovery of the atom. But again the wider claim Ms Hutton seems to be suggesting is surely misguided: we can and do assign a certain measurable temporality even to the process of thinking, by, for example, commissioning research within a firm deadline and expecting it to be met (Kennedy's promise to land a man on the moon in ten years), and we can often, in our own case at least, estimate fairly precisely how long a certain intellectual task will take (writing this review for instance). Moreover, we have conventional ways of paying for intellectual work, even — or particularly — when it has involved a long period of gestation or prior dedication, training and practice, as in the case of painters, lawyers, professors, or even reviewers. Admittedly, our sense of the exact 'value' of such work is dictated not by 'how long' it took but by its artistic quality, its competence, its intellectual worth, etc.

Ms Hutton would probably assimilate all of these distinct criteria of quality to the marxist notion of 'use-value', since her next step is to return to Marx. Much of this is familiar enough. She makes the usual points, that for Marx capitalism is geared to the production of exchange-values rather than use-values, that labour-power is a commodity, and that the main 'contradiction' developing within capitalism is that between the material forces of production and the social relations of production. She does a rather tedious job of explaining her own understanding of these notoriously opaque terms, devoting a surprising number of pages to elucidation of a theory which she seemed earlier to regard as crucially flawed for her main purpose. Some aspects of her account were, however, unfamiliar and one or two controversial. I was, for example, struck by her use of a passage from *The German Ideology*:

with a communist organisation of society, there disappears the subordination of the artist to local and national narrowness, which arises entirely from division of labour, and also the subordination of the artist to some definite art, thanks to which he is exclusively a painter, sculptor, etc., the very name of his activity adequately expressing the narrowness of his professional development and his dependence on division of labour. In a communist society there are no painters but at most people who engage in painting among other activities.

Rather amusingly, she amends this passage to apply variously to plumbers, physicists and pole-vaulters, her case being that for Marx a communist society is not organised on the basis of job-allocation or even diverse 'part-time' activities, but that the very concept of 'a definitely-named job-definition' (her usual verbal goulash) has been 'surpassed'. (Quite what this would mean for those of us who prefer the intense Englishness of a Constable to the rootless talent of a Picasso she doesn't say. Nor could she find a place for my local plumber who alone understands the intricacies of my Edwardian hot-water system, but let that pass.)

More surprising than this predictable utopian woolliness is an unusually sustained argument in which she seeks to show that in Marx's theory the real motor of history is — of all things — 'ideas'. Her reading of Marx puts a quite rigorous emphasis upon the 'primacy of the material forces of production' in any development of the 'preconditions of social change' but, as she puts it with rare colloquial vigour, 'material

191

forces of production are of no earthly use if no-one has any idea what to do with them.' This logically leads her to the claim that it is 'new ideas' about what to use in production and how to use it that underpin any major development of production, though she also recognises that the emergence of such 'new ideas' is often closely connected with actual production and is inevitably shaped by human desires, needs and curiosity, all 'profoundly produced from within an existing social matrix yet also premissed upon a proleptic idea of possibilities not currently contained within that matrix' (I much prefer her colloquial prose). What more orthodox marxist materialists or determinists will make of this argument I don't know — but she makes effective use of Marx's own writings as an example of a 'new idea crystallised within yet pointing beyond the parameters of a particular socio-intellectual paradigm' (ugh). Presumably for her the notion of 'socially necessary labour-time' is precisely an index to Marx's own 'intrication' (!) within the 'matrix' he 'proleptically surpassed'.

After 550 pages of this coagulated prose, it was at least a relief to reach the final section of the book.

It opens promisingly, with a joke: that magnificent exchange between Eccles and Bluebottle in *A Punch Up the Conker*, which begins:

Bluebottle:	What time is it, Eccles?
Eccles:	Just a minute. I've got it written down here on a piece of paper. A nice man wrote the time down for me this morning.
Bluebottle:	Oh. Then why do you carry it around with you, Eccles?
Eccles:	Well. If any body asks me the time I can show it to them.
Bluebottle:	Wait a minute, Eccles, my good man.
Eccles:	What is it, fellow?
Bluebottle:	It's writted on this bit of paper, what it is 8 o'clock, is writted.
Eccles:	I know that, my good fellow. That's right. When I asked the fellow to write it down it was 8 o'clock.
Bluebottle:	Well then, supposing when somebody asks you the time it isn't 8 o'clock?
Eccles:	Then I don't show it to them.

Essays

Bluebottle:	Oh. Well, how do you know when it's 8 o'clock?
Eccles:	I've got it written down on a piece of paper.
Bluebottle:	I wish I could afford a piece of paper with the time written on. Here, Eccles, let me hold that piece of paper to my ear would you ... Here, this piece of paper ain't going.
Eccles:	What! I've been sold a forgery!
Bluebottle:	No wonder it stopped at 8 o'clock.
Eccles:	Oh dear.
Bluebottle:	You should get one of them things my grandad's got. His firm gave it to him when he retired. It's one of them things what it is that wakes you up at 8 o'clock, boils the kettule and pours a cup of tea.
Eccles:	Oh yea — what's it called ... erm ...?
Bluebottle:	My grandma.
Eccles:	Wait a minute. How does she know when it's 8 o'clock?
Bluebottle:	She's got it written down on a piece of paper.

— and so on. (Sadly, BBC copyright fees deter me from quoting more.)

Ms Hutton poses two linked questions about this exchange: how are jokes produced and distributed? I confess, as indeed she does, to a certain bafflement as to how jokes are 'originally' produced (and perhaps neither Freud nor Spike Milligan could help us very much), but I accept her fairly harmless claim that the 'distribution' of jokes normally involves a kind of re-production rather than simple repetition and that this re-production usually employs only the resources of our own physical bodies. The implications of this banality fascinate Ms Hutton sufficiently for her to spend several pages elaborating it, but the point is reasonably obvious. She next extends the same basic analysis to songs, and again I have no major quarrel with her. But she then advances to the 're-production' of what she calls 'art-ideas'. I would be tempted to characterise this passage as an unabashed avowal of artistic plagiarism.

She recounts how, as a student, she used to prowl art galleries and exhibitions looking for aesthetically pleasing modern sculptures and paintings which she was able to 'make for herself' out of scrap materials at home! I doubt if her miniature Anthony Caros or recreated Mondriaans gave much aesthetic pleasure or edification to anyone else, but in principle her claim seems valid (it is one of my objections to much modern art): that the basic or even detailed 'idea', scheme or formal pattern of a particular work of art could be deliberately reconstructed from easily available materials, with relatively little practical 'skill' involved. That the plagiarist (or forger) could introduce individual variations seems to her simply on a par with a personal rendition of a folk-song or phrasing of a joke. Her next target (or victim) for appropriative imitation seems to have been modern furniture, and even interior design, in equipping her student bed-sit. No doubt such practices are more common than the proprietors of Habitat would care to think and are, I suppose, encouraged by an early addiction to knitting or dress-making from *Vogue* patterns. Ms Hutton traces her ethically dubious career along these lines to encompass a rather surprising, even impressive, range of other people's designs and commodities. Her serious intent, over and above mere autobiographical self-congratulation, begins to emerge as she successively lists, with each new 'acquisition', the tools she also purchased, borrowed or — it seems — made for herself (on the basis no doubt of thoughtful visits to her local tool-merchant or crafty scanning of manufacturers' catalogues!). From this point, however, it is difficult to tell how far she departs from veracious anecdote and ventures into fantasy. Faced with a tricky spot of welding, she perhaps did have recourse to the equipment in her local school's handi-crafts workshop (as it happens, domestic oxyacetylane welders can be hired anyway, at least in the States), but I am disinclined to believe that she could ever have 'borrowed' the facilities of an old Government Retraining Centre to make a new door for her car, or that she made herself a working telephone (outgoing calls only, but uncharged) 'with the help of a friend'. Certainly by this time she must have exhausted, even ex-ceeded, the range of do-it-yourself projects catalogued in the *Readers' Digest Home Maintenance Manual*, ambitiously com-prehensive as that is.

It should now be apparent what her basic point is: that in most of our purchases of durable commodities we certainly pay for materials and for someone else's labour-time but we also pay for the knowledge and skill (the 'idea' of the object, in her terms) and for the machines and tools used, yet we can relatively easily appropriate much of the design-knowledge and even skill and we can often gain access to the necessary tools and machines. Two proposals emerge here, which for Ms Hutton are apparently steps on the way to socialism: that there should be publicly owned 'workshops' equipped with a wide range of tools and machines, and secondly that the requisite 'production knowledge' should be widely and freely available. She concentrates first on the latter aspect. There are three main ways, she argues, in which this aim can be achieved. First, by an emphasis upon production knowledge in schools, aimed *not* at 'training for jobs' but, in the first instance, at domestic do-it-yourself competence, confidence and even self-sufficiency; this she envisages in a concrete form, of a school undertaking, for example, to build, equip and maintain actual houses for old age pensioners. Second, she wants a 'redesign programme' giving priority to the re-design of all common articles of use so that they can be not only maintained but actually made with relatively little technical expertise and with tools and machines that can be made easily available for public use. Again, the educational sector is to play a role, with redesign commissions along these lines to technical colleges, art schools and universities. Third, she proposes an 'access programme', in which all production knowledge is made publicly and freely available, both in the form of computer data-banks and through a register of available 'teaching' personnel, both of these coordinated through the network of public workshops. These latter she envisages, it seems, as a cross between a small-batch production factory and an adult education technical centre, but based on the principle that anyone can use their facilities to make rather than buy what they want. The problem of 'payment' for materials and facilities she postpones.

In themselves, these are not particularly 'utopian' proposals. They indeed extrapolate from some familar features or growing tendencies in our present 'socio-intellectual matrix'. Secondary education has long imposed a certain amount of 'workshop' knowledge, not to speak of traditional 'domestic science' upon reluctant pupils. The DIY 'industry' is already significant, involving a considerable degree of incipient 're-design' (quite startlingly in such areas as plumbing), while the general de-skilling of many production-line jobs in the wake of the microelectronics revolution does, I suppose, have the kind of reverse-side potential Ms Hutton clearly relies upon. The increasingly sophisticated development of multi-function robotics, numerically-controlled machine-tools, computer-aided design, modular instrumentation and terotechnology, leading to radically reduced maintenance requirements in factories, does perhaps make the provision of small-scale and very versatile 'workshops' feasible. The even more rapid advances in information technology certainly indicate the technical possibility of a vast extension of instantly-available production-patterns, instruction-sets, and even feedback-controlled computer-assisted production machines reprogrammable for a wide range of products, upon which any computer-literate person (or even, given effective graphics, VDU-reader) could successfully perform a reasonably complicated production-process.

Nevertheless, the convergent implications of Ms Hutton's proposals are, I think, very radical indeed. The very term she favours, 'work-shops', indicates a fusion of activities with rather drastic implications for the local High Street or shopping precinct, not only for proprietors but for distributors, packaging companies, accountants, advertisers and sales-assistants. By, in effect, cutting out all 'middle-men' between 'producer' and 'consumer' (so far, though, only in consumer durables?) a very extensive re-distribution of social labour is implied, and with it a far-reaching re-organisation of individual and social 'time'. For example, a great deal of time is currently absorbed in the transportation of finished products, in stock-taking, display, etc., and in 'shopping around' for the 'right' product. If one were able simply to enter a workshop and 'reproduce' what one wanted from an available pattern or electronic template (much as one can now mix one's own choice of decorating paints in some shops), the effect could be as devastating as the impact of cassette-recorders on the record industry or of videotapes on cinema attendance. Yet the total 'time' involved for the individual re-producer in, say, fully equipping a house might not be very great — and it would be time directly involved in production for use not for exchange. Presumably, too, it would be open to any individual to feed any bright new ideas for making products into the general data-bank.

Ms Hutton is clearly attracted by these last points, and they apparently override for her the loss (not least in social time) of economies of scale in such a dispersed organisation of production. A number of other obvious problems she does, however, consider. The first is the provision of such workshops and the control of them. Here it seems that her proposals are deliberately 'transitional', envisaged as able to be developed from the already-present possibilities towards an ultimately very different future. It is also clear that her 'present' is, quite decisively, the *most* advanced form of technological industrial capitalism: one could hardly implement her 'idea' in much of the Third World! Thus, she has no hesitation in seeing the building and equipping of such workshops as the initial responsibility of national and local government, arguing that the present level of government financing of industry, in grants, taxation provision and direct investment (amounting in the UK to over 50 per cent of industrial capital investment) makes a gradually extending programme of such workshops perfectly feasible. She applies the same argument to a redirection of present government-sponsored research and development towards commissioned redesign projects leading to government-held patents. But she also envisages the building and equipping of such centres as eventually shaped by the same production-for-use principle: that the resources of one centre would enable another to be built by those demanding one in their more immediate locality (presumably when the queues for use of the resources become as long as the present dole queues!).

Forms of 'payment' for use of workshop facilities cause her little hesitation. She is naively optimistic about the development of 'alternative' renewable energy sources for such workshops, listing a locally variable repertoire or 'cocktail' of solar, wind, wave, hot-rock and biomass forces as making possible a major reliance upon workshop-generated power and thus reducing energy 'costs' to a minimum. Second, she wants an extension of the 'grant support' principle to cover the remaining energy and maintenance costs of such centres on a par with hospitals, schools, municipal sports facilities, etc. For the 'cost' of materials (including the transportation costs of basic 'raw' materials for each centre) she finds herself reaching for what is surely her own variation upon a scheme based on 'socially necessary labour-time'. She proposes, in effect, a redirection of labour into the production of 'primary materials', with work in a 'primary industry' (the level at which the workshops themselves are 'supplied') as one component of a 'redivision of labour-lifetime' (a dishonestly fudging phrase). She apparently sees us all as 'qualifying' for use of workshop materials by virtue of some contribution to 'primary' production at some (limited) period of our lives, rather as one might now be 'entitled' to three years of higher education at some self-chosen moment in a life. The traditional, and bankrupt, character of *this* 'idea' is partly obfuscated by her elaboration of a number of allied notions.

The central claim here is that an economy reduced to *paid* labour *only* in 'primary' production, with a great many secondary and finished-product sectors effectively eradicated, would be amenable to 'price calculation' upon a Sraffian model, i.e. by a system of social accounting derived directly from the concrete physical data of production, as in Sraffa's *The Production of Commodities by Commodities*. In a sense, she argues that while Marx's correct analysis of capitalism has proved inappropriate for conceptualising socialism, Sraffa's inadequate model of capitalism can be developed to provide a basic model of a socialist economy. To achieve this bizarre reading of Sraffa's (deceptively simple) argument she particularly insists upon four aspects of his analysis. First, that the terms 'profit' and 'wages' in Sraffa's terminology can be systematically replaced by 'social appropriation' ('taxes'?) and 'personal income', without modifying the logic of his case. Second, that her notion of 'primary' production can be successfully approximated to Sraffa's term 'basic commodity'. Third, that Sraffa's theoretical proof that

198

in any actual economic system there is embedded a miniature
standard system which can be brought to light by chipping off the
unwanted parts (para. 26)

offers a real practical basis for price calculation within a
'reduced' economic system of the kind she sketches. Lastly,
that Sraffa's insistence that

the rate of profits, as a ratio, has a significance which is independent
of any prices, and can well be 'given' before the prices are fixed. It is
accordingly susceptible of being determined from outside the system
of production, in particular by the level of the money rates of interest
(para. 44)

suggests the feasibility, within her system, of determining the
overall proportion or ratio of 'social appropriation' to
'personal income', *and* the level of 'wages' and 'prices'
(exchange ratios), by deliberately political decisions, guided by
physical data calculations — i.e. the required capacity of the
'primary' production sectors.

As a non-economist, all I can do is relay Ms Hutton's basic
points, as I glimmeringly understand them, and humbly
recommend that you read Sraffa for yourself, bearing them
critically in mind. But I at least remain unconvinced, certainly
by her third and fourth points. I am also wholly sceptical
concerning her 'practical' application of this theoretical
position: she elaborates a notion of 'regional standard
systems' or sub-systems (the terms are derived from Sraffa),
based, it would seem, not upon geographical regions but upon
composite 'units' of democratic control defined according to
approximate self-sufficiency in primary production. This
seems to imply that one might live in Manchester but be a
'citizen' of the same political 'unit' or constituency as an area
of Wales (providing water reservoirs), a percentage of Sheffield
steel-mills and a number of East Anglian farms! Not even
Athenian democracy, in all its complexities of citizen
identification, ever tried to operate quite such an outrageously
unwieldly structure!

It should be clear that Ms Hutton's harmless *Goon Show*
joke has finally led her to the usual utopian absurdities, and it

seems pointless to pursue her wilder fancies into the realms of, for example, agriculture and international finance, or to recapitulate her familiar programmes for workers' control of primary production. To her credit she disarmingly remarks that

> detailed utopias only seem impossibly complex to those who have never seriously attempted a systematic description of how our present economic, political and social system manages to continue functioning even for a short period of time.

She also recognises that her own portrait of the future is partial, incomplete and provisional, neither a manifesto nor a programme but a 'perspective'. Some conclusions may however be drawn from this ambitious, if largely futile, book.

The first is that the demise of socialist 'utopian' thinking and imagination has perhaps been unfortunate, even for non-socialists, if only because any single attempt without a tradition to support it must seem mere wishful thinking. Perhaps a deluge of personal and idiosyncratic utopias is a prerequisite for any coherent sense of a feasible alternative future. (There were some 200 'utopias' published in the last decades of the nineteenth century, providing a context for such brave attempts as William Morris's). The elaboration of multiple contending utopias, extrapolating from different major emphases within the socialist tradition (as many SF dystopias have extrapolated facets of capitalism), may be necessary before a sensible sifting of the feasible and attractive from the idiotic and repugnant can occur. Ms Hutton's emphases seem to me interesting as starting-points: a serious consideration of 'production for use', an underlining of the need to socialise 'production knowledge', a deliberate programme of technical re-design rather than mere extrapolation from the existing horizon and priorities of technology, and perhaps her attempt at an appropriation of Sraffa. I am less persuaded by her theoretical starting-point. Her apparent repudiation of 'homogeneous time' seems to me (insofar as I find it intelligible at all) largely a disguised aversion to *any* economic thinking which deploys an abstraction from 'concrete' labour to yield a viable account of how ultimately

Essays

we measure 'exchange-values'. The logic of her position is indeed that she thinks primarily, and even parochially, in terms of individual or domestic 'use', whereas the traditional emphasis upon 'socially necessary labour-time' is also a way of confronting that level of social needs which are definable in practice only through the political processes which she largely displaces from the centre of her analysis. The articulation of or interaction between those perspectives is formidably difficult to formulate, but Ms Hutton seems only to have considered one, lop-sided, element within that complex dialectical process of transformation so ably summarised, for example, by Mr Peregrine Anderson:

Crises within modes of production are not identical with confrontations between classes. The two may or may not fuse, according to the historical situation. The *onset* of major economic crises, whether under feudalism or capitalism, has typically taken all social classes unawares, deriving from structural depths below those of direct conflict between them. The resolution of such crises, on the other hand, has no less typically been the outcome of prolonged war between classes.

Oddly enough, Ms Hutton somewhat redresses the balance in the body of her book by returning in an Epilogue to her postponed discussion of the Chinese Cultural Revolution, where she seeks to show that some of the basic principles she has advocated were actually implemented, however unevenly and briefly, in a society with a radically different level of technological development. In particular, she emphasises the role of 'do-it-yourself' technical innovation and the appropriation of production 'ideas'. Personally, I do not expect, or hope, to see the transplantation of such a cultural revolution into England. It is far more likely, in my view, that an enterprising capitalist will soon open a 'workshop' very much along Ms Hutton's lines — but on a commercially profitable basis and as an extension rather than subversion of existing capitalist priorities. And I suspect that any 'users' would be very heavily charged indeed for real access to any effective 'production knowledge'. Trade secrets are even more tightly protected than State secrets! If such a capitalist workshop

201

were to develop it's possible, I suppose, that the entrepreneur involved would actually be fostering socialism 'unawares'. But I rather doubt it.

Antonio Ford

Drama

Margaret Yates: *Strange Meetings*

Editorial note

Usually *NCQ* has only carried reviews of theatre performances (imagined, of course). For this last issue, however, Margaret Yates has given us a full-length script of one part of her trilogy, *Suggestions*. In a letter she writes:

In a sense, every drama script is simply an outline or sketch of an *imagined* work: the performance is the play, not the script, so in reading this script your readers will in any case have to imagine the play for themselves. But *Strange Meetings* is perhaps right for *NCQ* for other reasons as well. It's the final play of a trilogy that I doubt will ever be performed! The first part is a music drama based on the *Medea* and designed for operatic treatment on a large open stage. The resources needed just for Act I include a massed African choir and thirty black dancers, and for Act II a quartet with the musical virtuosity of Fires of London. The title role has to be played by a black actress – singer. The middle play is a political pantomime for kids and adults, designed for a proscenium arch stage, and tells the story of the development of feudalism and capitalism into communism through the antics of magic toys on Xmas Eve. The leading roles include a ballerina, a 30 foot golliwog and sixteen six-year-olds. The three plays were written to be seen together at the same venue — i.e. they would have to be done at the National all at the same time. *Black M'dea* in the Olivier, *'Twas Xmas, Eve* in the Lyttleton and *Strange Meetings* in the Cottesloe. Obviously this isn't going to happen! The scripts of the other two would be unimaginable without the music and the props, so all I can give you is *Strange Meetings* — and even in that you'll have to imagine the visuals. But you're welcome to it if you want to use it.

We asked Margaret to provide a note on the set she had in mind. We leave you to imagine the rest.

Strange Meetings

Note: Seating in the auditorium is arranged so that the audience is banked in two steeply-raked tiers facing each other across a fairly narrow, oblong playing area. The general arrangement and dimensions are those appropriate to, say, a table tennis tournament. At either end of the playing arena is a large screen, almost abutting onto the edges of the seating tiers, and thereby not quite enclosing the whole area. Rising from behind the back row of each tier is a narrow screen, running the length of the seating. When slides are back-projected onto these four screens they combine to create the impression of a scenery box which encloses both audience and actors. The screens are edged in black which acts as a picture-frame. Actors' entrances are from the spaces between the foot of an end-screen and the seating (1, 2, 3, 4). Acting spots are indicated by A, B, C in diagram: Waist-high panels in front of front audience rows. At C there is a table and chair. When chairs are brought to A and B they are wooden, with strutted backs, as is the chair at C. Lighting is by almost vertical over-head spots, supplemented by discreet highlighting for features.

Programme notes should not identify characters; simply list nine actors. The programme might include Wilfred Owen's poem, 'Strange Meeting'.

The audience arrive and take their places. Normal house-lighting. All screens are blank. No house music.

When audience is settled, OLD MAN *enters from 1; as he makes his way slowly to his seat at C, house-lights fade, until only C is lit by an overhead spot: fairly harsh and concentrated white light.*

OLD MAN *is dressed in heavy, long black overcoat which reaches to below his knees, black trousers and shoes, black trilby; he wears dark glasses and uses a heavy, rather dirty, white stick, with which he taps his way; he is nearly blind, old and feeble but*

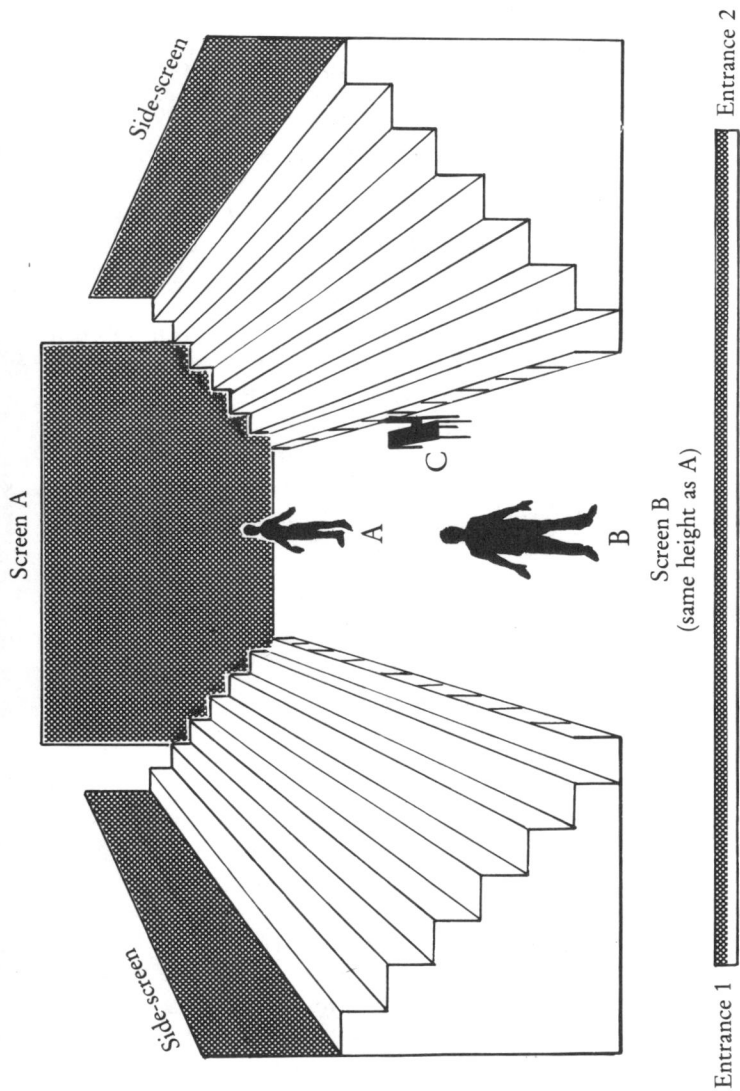

Seating arrangement and set for Strange Meetings

still erect; his appearance and entrance should be slightly chilling and sinister.

He sits behind table. Pause. Suddenly he taps loudly, twice, on floor with upright stick. Spots at A and B snap on; white harsh light.

In spot B is CARDINAL, *in resplendent red robes of a Prince of the Roman Curia. Tall, dignified, middle-aged, well-preserved; a Renaissance diplomat, with an easy but professional smile upon his lips.* CARDINAL (C) *looks across towards spot A.*

Almost immediately, PROTESTANT (P) *steps into spot A. P is dressed in the soft black garb and hat of portraits of Martin Luther. In his mid-thirties, a set, rather grim face, wary eyes, powerful but not elegant figure. He faces* CARDINAL *with a hostile but unawed expression.*

As the dialogue begins, OLD MAN *unobtrusively places stick across table in front of him, though still gripping the handle-end. His light dims considerably; the audience should amost become unaware of him as the scene proceeds.*

The exchange between C and P that follows could be described variously: as one game in a world championship series between two chess Grand Masters, in which P is the challenger with a difficult task; as a scholastic disputation on a quaestio, *between two personal rivals; as an exhibition darts match in which each is the true target of the other's darts. Every word uttered is deliberate and calculated. There is a pause between each response, though P pauses to consider his exact reply, while C, swifter at repartee, pauses to adjust his manner and expression to reinforce his verbal effects. C is almost* benign, *the silk glove extended over the claw. P is defensive and tense, but waiting for the opening, the weak spot to hit back at. C lobs the ball with pin-point precision to the bye-line corners, P serves hard fast aces if he can.*

There was a deadly game of reputation played between Renaissance diplomats and scholars: capping each other's Latin quotations. Both C and P have played this game many times. C's touch is much the lighter, ironic, mock-friendly.

C serves first. Each player waits for the ball to bounce. The audience follows the play; C may, slightly, acknowledge their responses; P ignores them.

C: You know the accusation?
P: I have heard the allegation.
C: You always twisted words.
P: It is better than twisting bodies.
C: Only to straighten minds.
P: Your mind leads straight to perdition.
C: You think you can decide these things?
P: I know they are decided.
C: For you — too.
P: I am sure of that.
C: Ah, *now* you are, perhaps.
P: Always, from before time.
C: Tut, tut. You forget your scholastic training. From
    before time, indeed. A logical slip?
P: A necessary metaphor.
C: Ah. Your usual excuse: necessity.
P: Necessity excuses no one.
C: Oh? But God does?
P: You claim to speak for God?
C: No. (*a drawled vowel*) I endeavour to speak to Him.
P: You have heard his reply.
C: From the mouths of babes. (*insult*) How *are* the children,
    brother Mar ... or should I say 'father?
P: Call no man father, (*slight pause*) Your Eminence.
C: You make it sound like a depression. Have you recovered
    from your ... illness, shall we say?
P: One does not recover. One is saved.
C: And many are damned?
P: Only the chosen ones.
C: Choice? What happened to necessity?
P: Free choice is the knowledge of necessity.
C: Surely a divine attribute — only.
P: We can be taught that knowledge.
C: Indeed. By one who has authority to teach.
P: The many can read for themselves, given the right
    Book.
C: Of course. And how are sales going?
P: Fruitfully.
C: What a delightfully laconic style you have. Your eyes

must ache with weariness — with all your writing and translating.

P: Not when God guides the pen: his yoke is easy, his burden light.

C: I see you take the role of prophet (*'profit'*) seriously.

P: I am merely a labourer in the vineyard.

C: Ah yes, I remember your liking for wine — it was wine, wasn't it? ... and singing too, of course.

P: In my own tongue, yes.

C: Ah, the tongue. What strange tastes you have.

P: I have tasted of the Lord and have been nourished by his Word.

C: You have tasted of the Lord ... isn't that heresy? For you, I mean.

P: 'Heresy' is always the accusation of the powerful.

C: And is God powerless — even on earth?

P: He came amongst us as a babe, not as a proud prince.

C: Always back to babies. You feel so strongly for them — even in Hell?

P: Water cannot cleanse even a baby's soul of sin.

C: Not even the great river of God's good grace? Directed through its chosen channels, of course.

P: Grace is a gift; we cannot plumb the depths of God's decisions nor control his wishes.

C: 'Plumb' the depths ... always the homely metaphor. I trust you find your fine new house sufficiently ... er ... well provided, after the hardships of the monastery, I mean.

P: God will provide. It is in his mansion that we dwell.

C: Such humble confidence in Providence. I do approve. There are many rooms in the House of God, but it *is* one House, is it not? A house divided against itself ... But you know the scriptures.

P: A house built on sand ... Do *you* know the words that follow?

C: The sands of time may prove a more reliable foundation than mere speculative enterprise. A long-established firm is surely more worthy, and deserving, of credit than the overnight business of a ... *nouveau riche*?

P: A bank may still be issuing worthless coinage long after its coffers are empty — though yours are, I hear, somewhat overflowing with the more material assets of your profession.

C: The poor we have always with us. It is as well to keep something back — in reserve. You must know yourself the difficulties of long-term planning — particularly on a meagre capital.

P: Is thirty years a long time in the sight of God? His mission was only made public after thirty years.

C: Yes — though first, if I recall, to some chosen apostles, who should continue that mission. Three years is not, indeed, a long time in the eyes of faith, but enough to ensure a permanent succession.

P: The eyes of faith see through the holes in history. They see an empty tomb which is always present.

C: There are other holes, which await the blind leading the blind. We can trust none of our five senses, not even over such simple matters as food and drink.

P: Agreed: the bread may become dry and stale, weighing like a brick upon the belly; the wine may be poisoned by being kept too long in old and cracked containers. Then one can only vomit up the old corruptions.

C.: Oh, these medical metaphors. Tut, tut. Are they really necessary? They turn my bowels ... Yours are functioning well, I hope. Oh — my apologies. I shall keep to fundamentals. You do remember your Fundamental Theology? It comes just before Moral Theology in those textbooks I once taught you how to read.

P: I am eternally grateful for the clear way in which you showed me the nature of my own ignorance. Enlightenment came soon after.

C: In a sudden flush, bringing rain. You recall the old questions, the old answers? 'Who made you? 'God made me.' 'Why did God make you?' God made me to know Him, to love Him, and to serve Him in this world, and to be happy with Him for ever in the next'. Your new catechism begins on a more tentative note, I take it: perhaps (*pause*) 'Why did God make you?' Answer: 'Well,

it depends. Either to know him, love him and serve him, or
— quite possibly — in order that I should remain in
darkest ignorance, never know his love, and fail miserably
to do him anything other than a disservice, however hard
I might try; and as for the next world —.' Well, I can
hardly go on. It *does* seem a peculiar 'Either/Or' for a
father to offer his children: an amazingly *easy* choice to
make, one would think, even on one's own account —
but a deeply dark dilemma, or not even that, if one is
already impaled on the wrong end of the Or. I fumble my
metaphors. Forgive me. They are your *forte*, not mine. *I
am a theologian.*

P: It is not always the worst fathers who make decisions for
their children; we condemn them to life itself, in this vale
of sorrows and tears, even by begetting them.

C: Is *that* a matter of *choice*? I am purely ignorant in these
private matters. What does one do? Withhold assent?
The wish being father to the child? Or are you — surely
not? — condoning contraceptive practices and pre-
cautions? Where would such a position end, I ask myself?

P: The old masturbatory circle of the self-questioner. Your
theological certainties will end in rational doubt. Your
lucidity lights a flame in a furnace that will temper
scepticism to a hard unbending steel. Only the sword of
infinite faith can cut the intricate tangle of your casuis-
tries. Only a leap into the black night of deadening
despair can bring the trusting soul to the revelation of
morning light — and in that depth of darkness the *only*
weapons are the sword of faith and the buckler of hope,
and those weapons are God-forged and God-alone-given.

C: The rhythm of your military metaphors really does suggest a new art form. Perhaps you should take up music —
oh, of course, you have, once, already. Or perhaps the
stage — an arena of dim spots where ignorant armies clash
by night. Or perhaps combine the two? Now that does
have indistinct possibilities ... I must mention it to the
Liturgical Commission next time I tread the pilgrims'
road to the Eternal City. It would make a change from
the baroque amusements of Benediction — of which I

believe you extremely disapprove; true, such remon-
strances of affection should really be kept where they
belong: among domestics.

P: You cannot shrug off the fear and trembling of the soul
by the ironies of the wordly-wise; your complacency is
curling at the edges; your disdain deadens you and all you
touch; your great resounding edifice is a hollow dome
that will crumble silently into dust; you are old, Father
Cardinal, and your hinges rusty, they creak with the
ravages of time, and you too will face the final dis-
solution. Consider death, and leave your dying citadel:
only the individual can be saved, by that mighty calling
which has preceded us from all eternity and reaches our
ears only in that last extremity. The cold is already upon
you: the ice of hell awaits you and there you shall *know*
that your kind were always damned; you are determined
unto everlasting death.

C: Oh dear. The spirit shudders even as you speak. 'The ice
of hell' — a chilling phrase I have somewhere heard
before — though in your frothing mouth it fades to a
frosty dip in a frozen pond before breakfast every morning. Your rhetoric evokes a constant crisis. That is mere
inflation of the lungs and afflatus of the wind. There is
no coming crisis. The world continues on its well-heeled
paths, and your flaming chariot of new-found fervour will
crash, like all the others, into the grimy ditch that
beckons all travellers who take time by the ears and force
its pace beyond the steady rhythm of the turning days.
You cannot match the majestic march of Rome; you may
whip the horses of your ambition, pride and envy, but
you will not tilt the earth you travel. Heaven's found-
ations are secure on earth; the centre of the world is
known, and the eternal avenue to the divine is direct, a
well-worn route that millions before you and after you
gladly recognise; all roads lead *there*, and you cannot
turn the globe around or upside down to mark a new spot
on the map of human history and divine discretion with
your puny appeal to cowardly conscience against age-old
authority. We are firm. We will *not* be moved. We remain

while you sputter out and vanish. We are permanent,
you a mere bagatelle among the winds that blow//

(*At or just before*// OLD MAN *lifts stick and crashes it onto
table: the loud report should make the audience jump. At the
crash* C's *light snaps out and he stops in mid-sentence.* P's *light
remains on.*)

P: (*his face softens for the first time*) Get you gone (*his own
light begins to fade*) — though perhaps with blessings on
your hoary head. (*There is sadness in his voice and expression as his light fades quickly to blackout. He remains
standing, looking at the darkness where* C *had been.*)

Now only the OLD MAN's *light is on, at* C. *The* OLD MAN *is
impassive, fist clenched on stick, staring with unseeing eyes
ahead. Brief pause.* C *and* P *both exit in the darkness.*
*Faintly, we hear monastic voices chanting Gregorian chant:
the Alleluia for Easter Sunday (Gregorian, Mode 7).* OLD
MAN *relaxes slightly; his stick returns to the vertical, at his side.*

Music	Screens
Alleluia increases in volume, though still heard as distant: 'Alleluia, Alleluia. Pascha nostrum immolatis est Christus.'	*A and B: Exterior shots of ruined Tintern Abbey amid green foliage.* *Sides: tops of trees against blue summer skies.*
Overlapped into: Sequence for Easter Sunday, Gregorian Chant (Mode 1): slightly louder and nearer; if not whole of sequence, include italicised phrases:	*Overlapped into: Interior shots of Gothic Cathedral:* *A and B: East and West shots of nave, emphasis on warm stone pillars and arches. Canterbury perhaps.*
'Victimae Paschali laudes immolent Christiani.	
Agnus redemit oves: Christus innocens Patri reconciliavit peccatores.	*Sides: Effect of stained glass. Audience are inside warmly-lit cathedral.*
Mors et vita duello conflixere mirando: dux vitae mortuus regnat vivus.	

212

Dic nobis Maria, quid vidisti
in via?
Sepulchrum Christi viventis
et gloriam vidi resurgentis.
Angelicos testes, sudarium et
vestes.
Surrexit Christus spes mea:
praecedet suos in
Galilaeam.
Scimus Christum surrexisse a
mortuis vere: tu nobis,
Victor Rex miserere.
Amen.
Alleluia.
*Modulates to louder volume
as, next:*
*Palestrina, Missa Papae
Marcelli, polyphonic* Agnus
Dei, *whole or in part:*
Agnus Dei, who tollis peccata
mundi,
miserere nobis. (*bis*)
Agnus Dei, qui tollis peccata
mundi,
dona nobis pacem.
*Modulates to louder volume
as, next: Eine Feste Burg (A
Mighty Fortress is our
God,) massed choir sung in
German; whole or part,
from the beginning.*

*Screens continue with
interior of cathedral
effect. Perhaps changing
shots, different
cathedrals: Chartre,
Notre Dame.
Peaceful effect.*

*Changes first to exterior
shots of St Peter's,
Rome; then interior
shots; light is mono-
chrome blue-white tint,
not bright.*

*Changes to interior
shots of, for example,
Chapel of Emmanuel
College, Cambridge,
rather dark brown
colours, slightly gloomy.*

*Fades and is overlapped
with exterior shots of
new Westminster Bank
Building, London, seen
first from East End,
then as towering over
City.*

213

Music and screens fade out. Only C lit. OLD MAN *getting impatient.*

OLD MAN *strikes stick sharply on floor, twice, impatiently. Spots at A and B fade up rapidly, revealing CAVALIER-KING (C) seated in B; A is empty, no chair. Pause.* PURITAN *steps into spot at A and stands, regarding* CAVALIER.
CAVALIER *is dressed as in portraits of Charles II.*
PURITAN *is dressed as in portraits of Cromwell.*
C is richly dressed, well-fed, a rather beaming countenance but also a somewhat distracted expression at times; socially graceful but a lot on his mind; if he wears a small crown, he might wear it slightly askew, and adjust it occasionally without much success. P is brooding, bitter, wary; his face shows years of worry and responsibility, but he is used to commanding and enjoys the masochism of power. He wears a hat, and keeps it on.

The exchange that follows might be likened to a 'carpeting' before a headmaster whose combination of a 'liberal' approach with incompetence evokes only veiled contempt from the intelligent sixth-former before him, caught breaking a major, but silly, rule; or a contest between a wily and deceptive spin bowler, a Tommy Cooper of cricket who distracts and disarms the batsman by apparent tomfoolery, and a straight-bat stone-waller very much on his guard – both know about googlies; it remains unclear, till the end, whether C is a childish nincompoop or is teasing P by treating him as a child. C may play to the gallery, return audience laughter with a graceful smile; P disdains such theatricals.

C opens the proceedings. As dialogue commences, OLD MAN's *light dims slightly; the spots at A and B are softer than before, but are still well defined.*

C: My *dear* Oliver. This *is* an unexpected pleasure.
P: Perhaps for you.
C: I see you still have your old world manners.
P: Of course.
C: Not even courtesy for a king?
P: You expect the defeated to be courteous?
C: It's the very least one might ask.
P: But I am not defeated.

C: Oh, come, come, Oliver. Has your memory so faded with the mere passing of time?

P: Have you forgotten the future?

C: Now, that somewhat tortuous question is a tiny bit too metaphysical for my poor head.

P: Be thankful that you still have one.

C: Ah, the unkindest cut of all! A wry stroke indeed. When *did* you last see my father?

P: I met him but seldom.

C: And I thought you knew him *so* well.

P: Only towards the end of his life.

C: To which *you* contributed *so* much.

P: Perhaps.

C: Come, you are too too modest (*French pronunciation*)

P: My enemies did not think so.

C: (*slight drawl*)Nor your friends either, I hear.

P: Some people will dig for dirt wherever they can find it. They stop when they strike hard, unyielding rock.

C: I hadn't thought such earthy talk was in your line at all. I had imagined you would rather burn with a hard pure gem of flashing light than be a solid rock of ages.

P: Fire tempers steel; but it is the rock that makes the bright sparks fly.

C: That's good, very good. You know, my dear chap, you really could have had quite a respectable career as a social epigrammatist, specialising in dark taciturnities. I would have welcomed you among my Court wits with open arms — provided you weren't wearing your sword at the time, of course. But I remember now, you employed a mere secretary for such lowly pursuits as turning phrases into more phrases, did you not?

P: Indeed. But writing is not a pursuit of the low; it seeks the higher.

C: And has its own justifications too, of course. And that secretary himself had a secretary, if I remember. A quite *marvellous* arrangement. I only wish *I* could afford such extravagances — or was it thrift in your case? I never can work out the complex ethics of bureaucratic expenditure. My poor father had a rather similar problem. Now I have Secretaries, but all *they* seem to do is scribble away for their *own* pleasures; I never seem to see anything they write.

P: Perhaps others do.

C: Do what? Oh, I see, see what they write. No, I can't think so. After all, I am the king. Things ought to come to me in the end; the fast buck stops in my pocket, as they say. No, I'm sure there's a much better explanation: they're all posthumists these days, that's what it is. It's a new craze: deliberately planning to become fashionable and popular when one is no longer there — a kind of planned obsolescence in reverse. How peculiar to be a posthumist.

(*That doesn't sound quite right to him: sotto voce, he practises the rhythm, trying to get it near: 'How peculiar to meet Mr Pepys, Mr Elyot, etc.*)

P: Aren't we all?

C: All what? Oh, posthumists. Are we? Were *you*? I thought *you* were a ranter, or a raver, or a rocker, — no, what *was* the word? Still, I'll forget it again even if I do remember it — so why waste the time before and time after trying to remember just for the sake of the time-in-between, that's what I say. *I* think you're just being gloomy, that's all, pondering on the mess your secretaries left your papers in, so that it'll be rocks of ages ... er ... lots of rages ... er ... oh, ages and ages, before anyone edits them, so you won't get a penny's worth of royalties after all. Oh, I'm sorry — was that a joke in aristocratically poor taste?

P: It was 'Puritan'.

C: '*Puerile*'? What was? The joke? Oh, no, of course. "*Puritan*'. *That* was the word I was looking for. Now, what does it mean? No, why was I looking for it? Can't remember. Never mind. Oh yes I do — You know, I really *do* need a secretary, to remind me of the things I forget just as I've remembered them — or the other way round. Any way — up or down — it's the same thing — I wanted to put a *label* on you, that was it, so I don't forget you. Nothing personal, of course. I do it to all my

friends ... well, to people I ... er ... want to remember.
That's why I give out so many titles. Don't *you* find it
easier to put a title to a face? I mean rather than remember whether some bloke is called Percy or Gordon or
George or Bysshe, it's much easier just to say 'My
Lord' — and then if they're not a Lord they don't mind
anyway: they think you're just dropping a sly hint that
you'd look favourably on a fast buck coming your way in
exchange for a real Lordship. Bishops tell me they find it
convenient the other way round too, as it were — not the
fast buck, the title. I mean, they don't have to remember
who they are, just where they come from — you know,
'Dear Sir ... signed: Portsmouth.' Bishops have such
short memories, it helps. And you don't even have to
know who you're writing to these days ... er ... to whom
you're writing ... just call them all 'Sir', even if he *is* a
Madam. Oh, I am sorry; I hope that didn't offend your
Puritan sensibilia. It *was* just a tiny bit risqué — I don't
know if you spotted that?

P: I am used to risks; the Fall itself was a risk.
C: Eh? whose fall? Have you had a bad fall? Oh, *our* Fall.
Glory be, yes. What a risk? — but think of the insurance
money. No, I'm sorry, I really am; I shouldn't joke about
serious things, I know. But you can't make jokes about
funny things, can you? I mean, if they're funny in the first
place, what's the point of making a joke about them. In
any case, the Fall wasn't entirely serious, was it? No, I
don't mean it was a joke — far from it — though I know
some people do have a peculiar sense of humour. No, I
mean it wasn't entirely *gloomy*, there was a bright cloud
in the hiding, as the Latin poet said ... er ... 'O Happy
Felix'.
P: O *felix culpa*.
C: Was *that* his name? Lord Culpa, was it? Yes, much better
than mere Fred Culpepper, or whatever. Yes, I remember:
'And ye shall become like Lords of the earth.' Yes, what a
elevation! 'The House of Lords of the Earth.' I must
change the name. Can you imagine having *that* address on
your headed notepaper? But of course you never dealt

217

with these things when you were alive and well and ... er ... you know, notepaper, newspaper, bogpaper: you left all that to your amanuenses. But think of it — where was I? Portsmouth? No, the House of Lords. Can you imagine the *ease* of one's daily correspondence — address: just 'House of Lords of the Earth' — just that, no difficult numbers or streets to remember, don't even have to put 'London' in; I mean, there isn't going to be a House of Lords of the Earth anywhere else, is there, particularly now that we've got the Navy off the rocks? That reminds me — what of? rocks ... secretary ... oh, yes, Posthumists. Yes, just begin: 'Dear Sir' and sign yourself: 'Portsmouth', brackets, 'Posthumous', close brackets. Makes 'Colonel (Retd)' look positively self-effacing — or is it the other way round? Er ... were *you* a colonel, er, Colonel? — or if you weren't, were you a colonel, Oliver? I mean, should I call you 'Oliver' or 'Colonel', or 'Ollie', or 'Crummie', or ... er ... what?

P: Lord Protector.

C: Protect *her*? Who?? You mean my dear Nell? No. Oh, you mean I should call *you* 'Lord Protector'? But I can't do that: it'd be treason, and you wouldn't want *two* kings tried for treason in succession, would you now? Oh well, perhaps you would. But it would be a difficult line to follow, I can tell you. Bad enough as it is, trying to produce royal babies of the right size, sex, shape and religion to order. Can't be done, I tell you. There's a limit to man's capacities. I speak generally, of course, scientifically — no offence to present persons excepted, ... (*shrugs it off; can't correct every mistake*) You have been introduced into the Royal Society, have you? Phenomena like fossils offer a fascinating field for one's retirement, I feel. (*He just carries this sentence off, with relief.*) I must write you a letter of introduction: 'Dear Sir, I hereby recommend an old friend, Oliver ...' — sorry, was it *Colonel* Oliver?

P: (*grim tone*) Lord Protector.

C: Oh, I *see*. You were a Lord Protector, not a Colonel. Is that above or below a General? I can never remember ranks, orders, hierarchies, all that nonsense. I mean, I know where *I* am, of course; I'm the King. Forget me own name before I'd forget that. (*Distracted by trying to remember his own name; apparently fails*)

P: (*angry*) Above.

C: (*looks up*) What? Where? Oh, sorry. Thought you meant there was something up there you were warning me about.

P: (*tight-lipped*) There *is*. The Almighty God.

C: (*faint* Oh? *as he cranes upwards. Pause. Looks down. Innocent:*) Is that all?

P: And His Vengeance coming like a thunderbolt upon the heavens to seek out the wicked and to punish their evil wrong-doings, to mortify their flesh and to chastise their spirit!

C: (*hurt, telling-off*) Now, that kind of language is a bit sharp for my taste, thank you very much. It's distinctly intolerant. And I am trying very hard to encourage religious toleration. You should discourage this tendency to intolerance in yourself. You won't *fit*, you know, if you go around talking like that all the time.

P: I do not wish to *fit* ...

C: (*interrupts*) Well, I know Lords are allowed to be *eccentric*, but that's a different matter from not *fitting*. I mean, if you want to be Lord Protector or Lord Putney or wherever it was, you'll *have* to fit, won't you; at least, you can't disturb the place you fit *into*; after all, you're only keeping it warm for somebody else to come after you. You may have children of your own one day — *and* of Lady Oliver's. Oh, I'm so *sorry*: that was in distinctly bad taste — and you a Lord. Fancy my making a joke like that to Lord Putney!

P: (*so angry he can hardly say it*) PROTECTOR, *not Putney!* The Lord Protector is not like the Lord Portsmouth. It's a political *concept*, not a public house coach-stop, *you idiot*!

C: (*hurt*) I am *not* an idiot. I'm a king. I know I can't vote, but that's not because I'm a king ... (*quick correction*) because I'm an idiot. (*that sounds wrong too; worried, gives up*) Anyway, I don't see why *you* should get so angry. Here I am, trying very hard to make polite, innocuous conversation, as one should in the presence of royalty, and you go losing your temper. Why? Don't you want to be Lord ... er ... Wherever-You-Like?

P: (*very slowly, grimly, quietly*) I am coming to the conclusion that it might greatly benefit mankind if there were no more Lords of the Earth at all, ever again.

C: Oh, you can't say that. What about that lovely address, for a start, with nobody to write letters to it from ... er ... from which ... Oh, never mind. And if you abolished all their Lordships, I'd have to remember all those names again. And I've got a memory like a ... er ... like a ... you know, the thing you put strains in. No, that's wrong. Anyway, I do *try* to remember names and things. Like *your* name, for example. I made a great effort when you came in just now, racked my brain and said: 'My dear Oliver,' I said, with my royal heart quivering right down inside my noble tootsies in case you weren't an Olive at all, but a Tommy or a Lorry or a Charlie or something. But it would be *so* much easier if I could just call you 'My Lord'. Would you mind terribly? I mean, it would be easier if I could just call *everybody* 'My Lord'. In fact, that's what we'll do! Let's not abolish the House of Lords; let's just circulate the peers, so that everybody can have an ego trip. Come to think of it, I'm already moving in that direction, you know — selling 'em off like hot sieves. I'll just speed it up, and charge even cheaper rates. Then even the very poorest people, chambermaids and bankers and ... er ... footmen and ... (*can't think of any other 'people'*) they could *all* afford to be Lords and Ladies, for, say, twenty minutes or so. Soon the whole country would be populated with Lords and ex-Lords and Lords-in-waiting. England would be known to the whole civilised world as Lords-ground. There, how would *that* suit you?

P: You twist my aspirations. You insult my ideals. I say that *no* man should be a Lord over others.

C: (*having considered the painful process of having one's*

aspirations twisted, is conciliatory and penitent) I've offended you, I can see. Look, I *am* sorry. I'll lend you Nellie for a night to make up for it — very cheap rate, and a real lady. Oh, sorry, there I go again: I forgot you were a Puritan. What *is* a Puritan, old Ollie? Sorry, no — don't answer that — it might take all night, and I've better things ... Sorry. But there was one thing you might explain for me. Something I wanted to ask you. Now what was it? I'll remember it soon. *(immense concentration)* It's coming, it's coming ... No joke, no joke! ... Ah yes! You said — and I quote — 'I am coming to the conclusion that it might greatly benefit mankind if there were no more Lords of the Earth at all, ever again.' Did I get that right? Now, answer me Ollie, answer me honestly and truly. *Why* did you say such a cruel and hurtful thing to me, your own poor little harmless king?

P: *(looks long and hard at C, who adopts encouraging listening attitude, respectfully expectant; finally, P decides it might just be worth trying to speak seriously to this misguided fool)*

I have pondered well these things in the privacy of my heart. If you are indeed a serious seeker after Truth, listen unto what I say and consider your conscience. For there is but one Lord of all the earth and of all that lives and crawls thereon. In his eyes we are but as the grass that groweth unless we acknowledge his ways and follow his paths. But in the beginning when God made the earth and made the heavens he placed man upon the land to till it and to make it fruitful, as a service to the Lord God Almighty. And in those days there was no division upon the face of the land. Adam was sole master under God, his sole helpmeet Eve, who was placed under his care and authority, But all authority cometh from God, though the *form* of that authority hath been made by man, by fallen man ejected from the Garden in sorrow and in misery. For we are but fallen and all the works of man are tainted with sin. Yet we have built upon the earth great towers of pride and it was in the fullness of our pride that we confirmed our Fall. For Pride is of the Devil not of

221

God. But what else is human lordship if not pride? For the King struts upon the earth in all his glory, though glory is of God alone. And the great princes of the earth parade their power, but God alone has power of himself. And the lords of the land proclaim their possession, though the land belongs to God alone. God may give as it pleaseth him, and as he gives so may he take away. For the land is given only to bear fruit and to flourish, and we hold it only to do him service. And those who waste the produce of the earth in wanton luxury and in evil-living do betray that gift of God; and those who seek not the golden yield of the soil but trample bare the forests and fields in pursuit of private pleasures are false to the Lord God who gave the meadow and the pasture for tilling and for feeding his flock; and those who leave the land fallow without good cause spurn the commandment of the Lord, that it should be fruitful from the sweat of our brow and from the labour of our hands. Yet who is it who labours and sweats in the vineyards of the Lord? It is not the king and his nobles, nor the fine ladies and foppish princes of your courts, but the gentlemen and commoners who toil and bend their backs, who nurse and nourish the soil and reap the ripe fruits of the glebe. It is they who keep covenant with the one Lord of the Earth, it is they who follow in his paths. Your pride is that of fallen men; your greatness on this earth proclaims your littleness in the sight of heaven. It is the poor and humble who are the true saints beneath the gaze of God, they upon whom his eye rests with the loving forgiveness of a Father for his children, for it is the children of God who are the new saints on earth and over such children no one but the Father hath authority. And we are made saints not by the hierarchies of men but by true faith, not by the baubles of rank and title but by righteousness and loving kindness. And in becoming saints we cast off sinful pride, we tumble down the tower of Babel and with it all the temples built by fallen men to their own pride and disobedience: we acknowledge no master but the Lord God alone and Him only do we serve. Let there be no

Lord but one Lord, the Father and Creator of all the little world of men. For we are but men, *not* lords.

C: (*pause*) Ollie, I am deeply and truly impressed. Spoken like a real rocker ... er ... ranter. You do surprise me. I thought you left such rhetoric to your speech writers. But have you not become a tiny bit carried away by your own phrasemongering? A pardonable offence, of course. The tongue too has its pride and its pleasures. Let me bring you gently back to earth — if I may put it that way. (*slight pause*) Now, I do agree. We *do* hold the land in common; we have a joint responsibility, and God rightly expects our full cooperation in administering his estates with care and conscientiousness, with sound sense and foresight. Waste is the very last thing we want. But to *avoid* waste and lack of productivity, you need order, organisation, planning, agricultural *policies*. You can't just leap in and start digging anywhere, you know. You have to *know* what you're doing. But one man's horizon is limited; he can see his own field and hedges but not the next county; he can tramp to his local market town, but what of the overseas export-trade? Who is to take the *over*view? You need someone to control the overall cycle, to look after the total output and input. Mere random effort isn't going to be very productive, now is it? So you need someone to do the *planning*, to take decisions in the interests of the whole community. But what's the point of decisions if nobody carries them out? So you need to be able to *persuade* people, for their own good — (*slight afterthought*) — and for God's as well, of course. So you have to establish some kind of *order* in the world — that's all that 'authority' is: a matter of giving orders to complex activities. Now, alright, you don't *need* to have kings and princes and lords and barons and earls and all the rest of it, for that. But what's the *alternative*, Ollie? You can't just turn the whole thing over to secretaries, you know. I mean, who *believes in* a bureaucracy, faceless civil servants, anonymous administrators? They might be perfectly *competent* at the job — I'm not disputing that — but who's going to *obey* a mere secretary? You get a letter signed 'Joe Blogg' or whoever, telling you you've got to increase production by 5 per cent or the country will suffer. Well! You look at it and you think: (*Cockney accent*) 'Joe Blogg, 'oo the 'ell's 'e?' Excuse the cavalier language, Ollie, I'm throwing myself into the part; always did have a penchant for amateur dramatics, a royal weakness. 'Joe Bloggs. 'Oo the 'ell's 'e to boss *me* around? I'm just as good as 'e is. I can make me own mind up, ta very much.' And you light your pipe with the letter and watch the signature burn with satisfaction. And the country suffers. But you don't know it, because you're puffing away on your pipe in clouds of complacent tobacco smoke. *But*: think what happens when you get a lovely parchment scroll, with a nice coat of arms and an imposing motto nobody can translate, and it crackles under your hand as you slowly decipher the elegantly illegible script, until finally you make out, at the bottom, amid a medley of seals and stamps and squiggles, a noble scrawl that reads: 'Lord Privy Seal'. And you don't know what a Privy Seal is, whether it comes from the loo or the zoo, but you know it's a Lord anyway, and by the time you've spent all that time and effort working the damn thing out you reckon it *must* be important, otherwise you wouldn't have wasted your time and ruined your eyesight. So you do as you're told. You go off and plough a few extra furrows before breakfast, and the country prospers nicely, thank you.

Now, that's all there is to it, Ollie. I really think you're barking up the wrong tree with all this stuff about the Fall. It's *you* that's got human nature all wrong. *Nobody* wants to be just a number on a file, a unit in a collective — which is where your bout of enthusiasm for levelling would lead. And nobody wants to be pushed around by some nameless Secretary of the State — I bet you don't even remember the name of your own secretary, and nobody else will, I'm sure. Whereas a title lends dignity not only to the man who has it, but to everyone he deigns to address, particularly if he condescends to remember them by name ... it's an old aristocratic trick, and it

always works. We *all* have our pride, you know. (*pause*)
Well, Ollie, I'm sure you'll think this over very carefully.
Let it sink in and you'll soon change your mind. And —
now, this is something I wouldn't say to just anyone, you
know — if in a few days' time, or even a few weeks, you
think you can see your way to helping Us (*the royal We*)
in Our difficult task of imposing a little order on things —
and it's a thankless job, I can tell you — you want to see
my desk, absolutely littered with letters and papers and
... Well, if you'd like to give Us a hand, to be a Lord
again — not Lord Protector, mind you, but, say, Lord
Hartlepool or Lord Windermere or somewhere like
that — no, they are a little wet, aren't they (*a little
joke*) — well, let's say, Ditchling or Gravesend or ... we'll
find somewhere. Anyway, just you drop in to see me, and
we'll have a quiet chat about it. But bring a bit of ready
cash with you, won't you, because there *are* expenses
involved in these things, you know. Any rate, I'm sure I
can pull a few strings, drop a few words in the right ears,
get the wheels moving discreetly, you know. Now,
promise me you'll think seriously about it?

P: Erm ... I will ... Sire (*he half moves to take his hat off,
a bit embarrassed*)

C: Good. Now just one other little thing I want to say to
you — before the audience is finished. It's important, and
I want you to remember it — if you can. (*absolutely
straight face in what follows*) One day, believe you me,
when I'm just remembered in the history books, if at all,
as a silly old buffoon, a merry monarch and licensed
lecherer, and so on, there'll be a big beautiful statue of
you standing just outside the Houses of Parliament, that
Mother of free parliaments the whole world over. And
that statue will mark *you* out as one of the great founders
of human liberties, as the architect of parliamentary
democracy in its finest hour. And every young boy with
the glint of freedom in his eye will pause before that
statue and gaze upon it thoughtfully. And he will turn his
young face upwards, to the older and wiser face of his
father, and ask: 'Daddy, of whom is that statue?' And the

father will smile down upon his son, and say: 'That, son, is Oliver Cromwell.'

(*Impressive cadence, pause, the audience is clearly over. 'Cromwell' looks deeply moved and thoughtful. Finally he gives a slight, rather self-conscious bow, takes his hat off, and backs slowly out of the circle of light. C watches him go, with a serious, even reverent, expression. Once P is out of sight, C continues*)

C: And the son will say: 'Daddy, who was Oliver Cromwell?' And the father will reply: 'I dunno, son. I just read the name on the plaque.' (*pause. Then, absolutely cold-steel voice, adult and contemptuous politician*) Good-bye, Lord ... Oliver ... Putty. (*pause. Then breaks into gleeful laughter and childish chant*)

Há, ha, há, há, ha!
We won the wá-ár
We won the wá-ar
I'm the king of the cástle.
I'm the king of the ca-//

During song, P's spot on A fades out fast, but there is still a faint light remaining at //

At or just before // OLD MAN *crashes stick onto table-top. Spot at B (C's) snaps off. In the blackness, we hear a faint, surprised 'Oh!' from C. Spot on A finally dies too. Only the light on C is left, now sharp white.* OLD MAN *impassive, grim.*

Sound	*Screens*
Very faintly we hear a female voice reciting 'Paradise Lost', Book IX, from Eve's speech, line 795ff so that lines spoken lead to 'Experience', with words now clearly audible, at point indicated:	A: *Portrait of Charles II in full robes* *then* B: *Portrait of Cromwell* A: *Charles replaced by 'Laughing Cavalier'* B: *Cromwell replaced by slide of copse of trees* A: *Cavalier replaced also by copse*

'Experience, next to thee I
  ow
Best guide; not following
  thee, I had remained,
In ignorance, thou openest

Wisdom's way,
And giv'st access, though
  secret she retire
And I perhaps am secret;
  Heaven is high,
High and remote to see from
  thence distinct
Each thing on earth; and
  other care perhaps
May have diverted from con-
  tinual watch
Our great Forbidder, safe
  with all his Spies
About him. But to *Adam* in
  what sort
Shall I appear? shall I to him
  make known
As yet my change, and give
  him to partake
Full happiness with mee, or
  rather not,
But keep the odds of Know-
  ledge in my power
Without Copartner? so to
  add what wants
In Femal Sex, the more to
  draw his Love,
And render me more Equal,
  and perhaps,
A thing not undesirable,
  somtime
Superior; for inferior who is
  free?
This may be well: but what if
  God have seen
And Death ensue? then I
  shall be no more,
And Adam wedded to
  another Eve

*Sides: tops of trees
Total effect of audience
being in clearing in
summer wood, the only
light, now dimmed, is on
C, and from the slides.*

*Screens remain with
forest-clearing effect
until:*

Shall live with her enjoying,
   I extinct:
A death to think. Confirmd
   then I resolve,
Adam shall share with me in
   bliss or woe:
So dear I love him, that with
   him all deaths
I could endure, without him
   live no life.

Silence.

Screens go blank.
Suddenly, very briefly
and almost subliminally:

LOUD, SHARP SNAKE
HISS (very brief)

A: *very large, extreme*
close-up of Python's head
raised to strike, front.
Sides: *body of huge*
snake
B: *immense coils of snake*
in close-up, fill screen

Silence.

Screens blank again.

A man's voice recites Paradise
   Lost, *IX, 896*:
O fairest of Creation, last
   and best
Of all Gods works, Creature
   in whom excelld
Whatever can to sight or
   thought be formd,
Holy, divine, good, amiable,
   or sweet!
How art thou lost, how on a
   sudden lost,
Defac't, deflowrd, and now
   to Death devote?
Rather how hast thou yielded
   to transgress

Screens now show
autumn trees, which are
gradually replaced by
dead winter trees as
speech proceeds.

The strict forbiddance, how
  to violate
The sacred Fruit forbidden!
  som cursed fraud
Of Enemies hath beguil'd
  thee, yet unknown,
And mee with thee hath
  ruind, for with thee
Certain my resolution is to
  Die;
How can I live without thee,
  how forgoe
Thy sweet Converse and
  Love so dearly joind,
To live again in these wilde
  Woods forlorn?
Should God create another
  Eve, and I
Another Rib afford, yet loss
  of thee
Would never from my heart;
  no, no, I feel
The Link of Nature draw
  me: Flesh of Flesh,
Bone of my Bone thou art,
  and from thy State
Mine never shall be parted,
  bliss or woe.

Silence.

Very faintly at first, but increasing in volume we hear boys' voices singing: 'My Beloved Spake', from Musica Deo Sacra *(1668).*
'My beloved spake unto me, and said unto me, Rise up my love, my fair one, and come away, For lo the winter

Screens change to spring trees, then once again to full summer; longer shots, now of Greenwich Park, with the Royal Naval College visible in distance and River Thames beyond.

229

is past, the rain is over and gone. The flowers appear on the earth, the time of the singing of birds is come, and the voice of the turtle is heard in our land. The fig tree putteth forth her green figs, and the vine with her tender grapes, give a sweet smell. Arise my love, my fair one, and come away.

Pause. Then: from Purcell's opera 'Dido and Aeneas', end of Act I: begin with Belinda's soprano, at:

Bel: See your Royal Guest appears
       How God like is the form he bears.
Aen: When Royal Fan shall I be blest
       With cares of Love, and State distrest.
Dido: Fate forbids what you pursue,
Aen: Aeneas has no Fate, but you.
       Let Dido smile, and Ile defie
       The feeble stroke of Destiny.
Chor: Cupid only throws the Dart
       That's dreadful to the Warrior's heart
       And he that Wounds can only cure the Smart.

During the song (c. 4 min), screens A and B move in closer on Royal Naval College, through formal gardens and porticos, until by end of song we seem to be on the landing area in front of the classical frontage. (4 min film)

As the opera proceeds, screens A and B give impression of moving onto river.

A: shots (film?) move downstream

B: moves upstream, showing bridges, St Paul's, National Theatre, Whitehall, Houses of Parliament, and finally shot of Buckingham Palace, followed by Bank of England.

A: meanwhile, overlapping shots of merchant and royal navy ships, then maps of colonies

A: prints of imperial battles, until finally A shows map of globe as at 1911, showing British Empire territories in red.

Aen: If not for mine, for
Empire's sake
Some Pity on your
Lover take.
Ah! make not in a
hopeless Fire
A Hero fall, and Troy
once more Expire.

Bel: Pursue thy Conquest,
Love — her Eyes
Confess ,the Flame her
Tongue denies.

Chor: To the Hills and the
Vales,
to the Rocks and the
Mountains,
To the Musical
Groves,
and the cool shady
Fountains.
Let the Triumphs of
Love
and of Beauty be
shown,
Go revel ye Cupids,
the dance is your own.

Side-screens: *begin with
Red, White and Blue;
gradually Red takes over,
a deep blood-red, until
strips of red behind
audience.*

*Music of dance. Over the
fading music of the dance the
extract shown on B is read out:*

*As global map comes up
on A, B shows extract
from* Encyclopaedia
Britannica, *1911 edition,
entry: British Empire.
Date is given at foot of
quotation.*

'The land surface of the earth
is estimated to extend over
52,500,000 square miles. Of
this area the British Empire
occupies nearly one quarter,
extending over an area of
about 12,000,000 square miles.
By far the greater portion
lies within the temperate

zones and is suitable for
white settlement. The area
of the territory of the
Empire is divided almost
equally between the southern
and northern hemispheres,
the great divisions of Aus-
tralasia and South Africa
covering between them in the
southern hemisphere
5,308,506 square miles while
the United Kingdom, Canada
and India, including the
native states, cover between
them in the northern hemisphere 5,271,375 square miles.
The alternation of the
seasons is thus complete, one
half of the Empire enjoying
summer while one half is in
winter."//

At // OLD MAN *smashes furiously on table with stick. All lights
go out except his own. Silence.*

*(If absolutely necessary, there may be an interval at this point. If
so: at* // *all lights go out, including* OLD MAN's, *except red
strips on side screens. These remain lit in darkness for a few
moments, then house lights fade slowly up; the red strips remain
lit during the interval. When audience re-assemble, house lights
down, red strips fade.* OLD MAN *either remains in seat
throughout interval, or vacates it and re-sits during blackouts.*
OLD MAN's *light snaps on to start Part 2.)*

Pause. OLD MAN *taps with stick on ground, twice, not too
loudly but fairly sharply.*

   *Spots fade slowly up on A and B simultaneously. Light at C
fades down slightly. Lighting is now more diffuse, and slightly
dimmer than before. Duskish.*

   In A spot is seated L; *he straddles the chair, its back towards B,
his hands gripping the struts of the back, his face above the top of*

232

the chair-back. He is dressed in a rumpled, grey-black pin-stripe suit, which could be that of a clerk, a Soviet official, or a prison suit. He is fairly small, but powerfully built, at least late fifties, perhaps older; a weary, lined face, but his body is relaxed. He reminds one of Lenin — there is a photograph of Lenin, hunched on the steps to the platform at the Third Comintern Congress, 1921, his head on his hands, preparing a speech, available to both delegates and platform. L has the same characteristics. He looks across at B with tired but still alert and even twinkling eyes.

In spot B is seated T. He, too, sits across the chair, his hands also grip the back-struts, but with an air more of being capable of forcing them apart rather than being imprisoned behind them; he is however also relaxed. A powerful frame, an expressive and mobile face, looks in his late forties but is probably older. He reminds one of Trotsky, perhaps a pince-nez. T is dressed in a brown well-worn tunic and trousers, perhaps with boots. He could be in uniform, or prison dress, or perhaps even a peasant.

The exchange that follows is spoken quietly, though not whispered. They have known each other a long time, do not need to say everything. They respect each other, are even friends, though they disagree and have argued violently together. Argument is now past, but if it became necessary on some future occasion each might have the other executed; each knows this, and accepts it: it is part of why they respect each other. They would prefer to be talking over a bottle of wine, but that is impossible; the darkness between them is perhaps that of a prison corridor.

T begins. It is not clear whether they have already been talking for some time.

T: You remember the night after the storming of the palace?
L: Yes, very well. My back still aches from the memory. We slept on bare boards in the committee room.
T: You quoted Engels to me — on the Peasant War in Germany.
L: Yes. I remember the passage. *(pause)* 'The worst thing that can befall the leader of an extreme party is to be compelled to take over the government in an epoch when the movement is not yet ripe for the domination of the

233

class which he represents, and for the realisation of the measures which that domination would imply. He necessarily finds himself in a dilemma.' *(pause, sadness in his voice.)* Finish the quotation. I can't.

T: 'What he *can* do is in contrast to all his previous actions, to all his principles and to the present interests of his party; what he *ought* to do *cannot* be achieved ... *(pause)* Whoever puts himself in this impossible position is irrevocably lost.'

L: *(pause)* Had *we* lost — before we even began?

T: We began long before. And the war is not over, even yet. *(pause)*.

L: Yes. But which war is being fought now?

T: Class against class. We are still in history.

L: But not the history we wished to make.

T: No — but our wishes do not determine history.

L: We knew that. That was what we wished to change. *(pause)*

T: We made another beginning.

L: And a new failure. The horrors multiplied, as before.

T: We were too few.

L: *(correction)* Our enemies were too many. They controlled the world. One-sixth was never enough. *(almost an in-joke; T smiles.) (pause)*

T: We were too young. The forces we fought were centuries.

L: Centuries of blood. We demanded peace.

T: We had to pay the price of peace. It *is* expensive.

L: We could not afford the cost. We were too poor.

T: That was why we fought.

L: And lost?

T: Others will win. Those who come after. They will not be quite so poor.

L: And they too will quote Engels, as before?

T: *(smiles)* They may even quote you, too, by then.

L: *(smiles)*

OLD MAN *bangs stick on table. Both* T *and* L *look briefly at him — the first characters to do so — as their spotlights go out. In the darkness we hear* L, *humorously)*

L: Can I quote you on that?

(only OLD MAN's *light is on; he sits still; pause)*

Sound	Screens
We hear a male voice announcing, then reciting, Brecht's poem, 'To those who come after':	*Side-screens: red strips. Screen B: large black letters: TWENTIETH-CENTURY BOOK OF THE DEAD.*

i

Indeed I live in the dark ages.
A guileless word is an
   absurdity.
A smooth forehead betokens
A hard heart. He who laughs
Has not yet heard
The terrible tidings.

Ah, what an age it is
When to speak of trees is
   almost a crime.
For it is a kind of silence
   about injustice.
And he who walks calmly
   across the street,
Is he not out of reach of his
   friends
In trouble?

It is true: I earn my living
But, believe me, it is only an
   accident.
Nothing that I do entitles me
   to eat my fill.
By chance I was spared. (If
   my luck leaves me
I am lost.)

They tell me: eat and drink.
   Be glad you have it!

Screen A: in succession, numbers appear, in red:
1. × 5. × 10. ×10. ×10. × 10. × 10. ×10. × 10. × 10.
Each number appears larger than previous. The running total is given also:
5. 50. 500. 5000. 50,000. 500,000. 5,000,000. 50,000,000. 500,000,000.

But how can I eat and drink
When my food is snatched
  from the hungry
And my glass of water
  belongs to the thirsty?
And yet I eat and drink.

I would gladly be wise.
The old books tell us what
  wisdom is:
Avoid the strife of the world,
  live out your little time
Fearing no one,
Using no violence,
Returning good for evil —
Not fulfillment of desire but
  forgetfulness
Passes for wisdom.
I can do none of this:
Indeed I live in the dark
  ages'.

Silence.   *Screens fade.*

Pause. OLD MAN *taps with stick on ground, twice. Spots
A and B fade up, dimmer than before. L and T seated as before.
Perhaps a night has passed. Pause.*

L: I was reading your diary again last night.
T: *(smiles)* That smacks of self-indulgence.
L: Do you remember what you wrote in 1901, the first
    day of January?
T: My good resolutions, I suppose. I hope I kept them!
L: No, not resolutions. Retrospection, and introspection.
    You were looking back on a century, and forward to the
    next.
T: I was young, very young — twenty-two. I still believed
    that the Roman Calendar divided history. I had forgotten
    that the Communards shot all the clocks in Paris once.
L: Shall I remind you of what you wrote?

236

T: *(smiles)* I tremble for my reputation. But — as a historian — yes.

L: *(quotes from memory)* 'Dum spiro, spero. The nineteenth century has in many ways satisfied and has in even more ways deceived the hopes of the optimist ... It has compelled him to transfer most of his hopes to the twentieth century. Whenever the optimist was confronted by an atrocious fact, he exclaimed: "What, and this can happen on the threshold of the twentieth century!" When he drew wonderful pictures of the harmonious future, he placed them in the twentieth century.

    And now that century has come! What has it brought with it at the outset?

    In France — the poisonous foam of racial hatred; in Austria — nationalist strife; in South Africa — the agony of a tiny people, which is being murdered by a Colossus; on the 'free' island itself — triumphant hymns to the victorious greed of jingoistic robbers; dramatic 'complications' in the east; rebellions of starving popular masses in Italy, Bulgaria, Rumania. Hatred and murder, famine and blood ...

    It seems as if this new century, this gigantic newcomer, were bent at the very moment of its appearance, to drive the optimist into absolute pessimism and social despair. — Death to Utopia! Death to faith! Death to hope! Death to love! thunders the twentieth century in salvoes of fire and in the rumbling of guns.

    — Surrender, you pathetic dreamer. Here I am, your long-awaited twentieth century, your "future".

    No, replies the unhumbled optimist. You — you are only the *present*'.

T: *(pause. Then kindly)* A young man's rhetoric. A young man's optimism — I was too influenced by moods in those days. I remember now: things had finally taken a turn for the better in 1901; I'd just finished three years in jail — and only had ten years in exile left to face. I felt relatively free in 1901.

L: And now?

T: (*slight gesture around*) Oh, I'm used to jails. We both are.
L: I meant, are you still an optimist?
T: History is not built on hopes.
L: Parties sometimes are.
T: It was your Party I joined. Because it was built on clear, sharp analysis, not on hopes.
L: On hopes too. Was the analysis wrong, after all?
T: (*pause*) No. It was correct. At the time.
L: I had too little time. A few days. The decision had to be taken.
T: And followed through. By other decisions. Some of those were wrong.
L: Such as?
T: (*grins*) You shouldn't have died.
L: (*laughs*) That was hardly *my* decision.
T: (*smiles*) Necessity is no excuse, comrade.
L: (*serious again*) Do we need excuses? We need explanations.
T: Yes. Explain. One thing I never fully understood.
L: If I can.
T: You loved playing chess so much. And music. Why did you give them up?

L: Because I loved them so much.

(OLD MAN *bangs with stick; L and T look at him; both lights stay on*)

L: I had no time to spare.
(*Lights on L and T fade out. Light on* OLD MAN *remains. He looks more feeble.*)

Sound	Screens
Female voice heard: Bertolt Brecht: *To those who come after* I came to the cities in a time of disorder When hunger ruled. I came among men in a time of uprising	*Screens during poem show dates, facts and figures:* 1899–1902: *South Africa: Boer War: 10,000 dead.*

And I revolted with them.
So the time passed away
Which on earth was given to
me.

I ate my food between
massacres.
The shadow of murder lay
upon my sleep.
And when I loved, I loved
with indifference.
I looked upon nature with
impatience.
So the time passed away
Which on earth was given
me.

In my time streets led to the
quicksand.
Speech betrayed me to the
slaughterer.
There was little I could do.
But without me
The rulers would have been
more secure.
This was my hope.
So the time passed away
Which on earth was given
me.

Men's strength was little.
The goal
Lay far in the distance,
Easy to see if for me
Scarcely attainable.
So the time passed away
Which on earth was given
me.

1900: *China: Boxer
Rebellion: 10,000 dead.*
1902 – 4: *Korea: Russo-
Japanese War: 100,000
dead.*
1911: *North Africa:
Italo-Turkish War:
15,000 dead.*
1912 – 13 *South-East
Europe: Balkan Wars:
100,000 dead.*
1914: *Turkey: Armenian
massacres: 1,000,000
dead.*
1910 – 20: *Mexican
revolutions, civil wars,
USA interventions:
USA-Mexico wars:
2,000,000 dead.*
Etc.
*At 1917, include:
Russian Revolution:
The Tsar and his family.
Include Easter 1916.
Side-screens either red, or
both show: 500,000,000.*

Poem ceases.

*Figures on screens cease
and fade. They need not
have reached the present.*

Pause. OLD MAN *taps, twice, on floor with stick. Lights fade up on A and B, fairly dim now, as is* OLD MAN's *light. L and T are seated as before. Perhaps another night has passed. Their voices are even quieter now.*

L : I've been thinking about your question last night. (*pause*) Will you explain something to me?
(*pause*)

T : Yes, if I can.
(*pause*)

L : After my death, you acted strangely.

T : How so?

L : You let that (*slight pause*) Secretary beat you. He was no more than that. A party bureaucrat. Yet you, a general of genius, let him outflank you.
(*pause*)

T : We fought with different weapons. He gripped the party apparatus in his fist.

L : What weapon did you choose?

T : I held a pen.

L : You wrote. A book?

T : Yes.

L : On what?

T : On revolution — and on literature.

L : In those desperate days you took time off to write on *literature*?

T : Yes — and revolution. It *was* the right time.

L : Why? Explain.

T : (*pauses, then speaks slowly and analytically, at first*) Our cadres were destroyed. The old Party shattered. We had lost too many comrades in the war against the Whites. The new blood was of an old type: the careerist, the ambitious, the bureaucrat; the inexperienced, the uneducated, the illiterate. The old Party could not survive *that* change of personnel. The machinery was intact, but the old *men* had gone into the dark. The *new* man was a creature of the machine. And the mind of the machine was narrow, single-minded, seeing only a single track before it into the future: along straight and familiar tram-lines. There could be no wavering; to question was to hesitate, to query was to oppose, to argue was to sabotage. The machine must move inexorably on, crushing a path for itself. There were dark decades ahead. (*slight pause*) The Opposition would be defeated. We knew that, very early. We *must* oppose, but we must *also* bury our seeds deep underground, where the machine could not reach. (*slight pause*) The machine would take our words and bend them, mouth our meanings but change them, shout our slogans but ignore them. (*slight pause*) Others' words would have to speak for us, the slippery, evasive, allusions of the poet, the probing portraits of the novelist, the precise, quiet, gestures of the dramatist. New minds would have to grow, in silence and in absorption, in the margins of manipulation. One day, they would reach back, and recover the truths we knew. They would outflank the machine — when its work was done.

L: (*pause*) It is not minds that re-make history.
T: (*agreeing*) No. The machine comes first. But mind matters.
L: That was your analysis. Was it correct?
T: At the time, I did not know. Other possibilities seemed present.
L: And now?
T: I am disappointed.
L: Why? Has it not happened?
T: In part, it has. But still in isolation. One-sixth was not enough, whatever happened. We needed allies. They have failed us.
L: They have been defeated?
T: A few, yes. So far.
L: And the many?
T: Some have drawn back from the brink. Have mouthed our meanings, but ignored them. Have whispered our slogans, but only when it was safe to do so. Have

murmured our words — but have been afraid of our deeds. (*pause*).

L: What are they afraid of?

T: (*pause, then firmly*) Of being compelled to take over the Government in an epoch when the movement *is* ripe for the domination of the class which they represent and for the realisation of the measures which that domination implies.

L: Why are they afraid?

T: Because what they *ought* to do *can* be achieved. But what they *can* do is in contrast to all their previous actions, to all their principles, and to the present interests of their party.
(*pause*)

L: Who are 'they'?

T: (*smiles*) You, and I, and the others.
(*pause*)

L: But the future cannot be built on fear.

T: I know. Neither fear nor courage saves us.

L: (*pause, understands*) So you remain an optimist.

T: Yes.

(OLD MAN *bangs stick on table. Lights stay on.*)

L: They are coming.

T: Are you prepared?

(OLD MAN *bangs on table, louder. Lights stay on.*)

L: Yes. You have helped me. Thank you, comrade.

T: Goodbye, comrade.

(OLD MAN *bangs stick on table, even louder. Rises from seat to do so. Lights stay on.*)

L: ⸱I hope your freedom comes, soon.

(OLD MAN *bangs stick very loudly. L's light snaps off.*)

T: (*quietly:*) It will, one day.

(*T's light fades out.* OLD MAN *sinks back onto his chair, tired and almost feeble.*)

We hear various voices, some of which we might recognise from the previous scenes, reciting together, but clearly so that the

242

words are heard, the last section of Brecht's poem; the OLD
MAN's *light remains on, but the screens are blank.*

> You, who shall emerge from the flood
> In which we are sinking,
> Think —
> When you speak of our weaknesses,
> Also of the dark time
> That brought them forth.
> For we went, changing our country more often than our
>   shoes,
> In the class war, despairing
> When there was only injustice and no resistance.

> For we knew only too well:
> Even the hatred of squalor
> Makes the brow grow stern.
> Even anger against injustice
> Makes the voice grow harsh. Alas we
> Who wished to lay the foundations for kindness
> Could not ourselves be kind.

> But you, when at last it comes to pass
> That man can help his fellow man,
> Do not judge us
> Too harshly.

Pause. OLD MAN *is slightly slumped at the table. Perhaps he is
almost asleep, or sick. His stick scratches a few times on the
floor.*

*Psychedelic colours start revolving on the four screens. Over
loud-peakers, but not too loud, comes a record: 'Hey Jude',
sung by the Beatles. Faintly reddish light diffuses over acting
area, but concentrated on spots A, B and C. Enter casually, from
opposite ends,* GIRL *and* BOY, *teenagers, the girl perhaps 16 or
17, the boy perhaps 17 or 18. Both are dressed in cheap but
fashionable gear: working-class kids on a night out, each alone;
they have ended up in a fairly tatty cafe with a juke-box. Boy is
black.*

During the first few bars of the music, G *turns her chair
around and sits on it, taps her feet to the music, perhaps adjusts*

her hair, re-does her lipstick, etc. B sits astraddle his chair, and leans on the back of it, looking towards G, pretending he isn't trying to catch her eye; she pretends she doesn't know that he is trying to catch her eye.

Music continues. OLD MAN bangs stick, once, not loudly, impatiently, on table. B and G both look at OM, then at each other; they exchange grins about him: 'what's eating him' attitude.

G takes out cigarette. B saunters off his chair and goes forward to light her fag. She lets him get half-way across — and lights her own. Smiles sweetly at him: mouths 'Thanks anyway', then ignores him. B is stranded between A and B, almost alongside OM's table. B unsure of his next move, hesitates. By now music has reached final chorus and goes into up-tempo dance rhythm. B starts to dance (he dances well): motions to G to come and dance with him. She hesitates.

Suddenly, OM crashes stick on table in exasperation. B jumps, thrown out of his dance. G laughs at him. He grins. Both look at OM. OM thumps again, much more feebly, on table. The music fades; we hear click of stylus leaving disc. Screens fade. Lighting diffuses to normal light.

B turns to OM. Asks, not aggressively, in working-class Liverpool accent:

B: What's up, grandad? Don't yer like the music?

OM: *(peevish, grumpy; also Liverpudlian working-class)* Dat's awright — bit loud tho'. I want me pint. Where is it?

(B looks puzzled by this. Looks over to girl, seeking enlightenment. Shrugs. G gets up and comes over to old man.)

G: *(kindly)* This is a caff, old fellah, not a pub.

OM: *(pause, as it sinks in)* Bloody 'ell! — 'Scuse me langwidge, luv. I've been sittin' 'ere fer hours, waitin' fer me pint.

(B and G share smothered laughs.)

B: *(kindly)* You want the pub next door, Dad.

OM: *(explains)* I can't see so well dese days. I thought I was in it. Wondered what the hell was goin' on.

G: You poor ol' thing. Come on. I'll give yer a hand.

(G takes old man by the arm, taking the stick in her own hand, as B also takes an arm.)

B: Come on Dad, up you get!

(*They help the old man to his feet, and start to guide him out, using exit nearest to theatre bar. As they leave playing area, boy speaks to girl over old man's bent back:*)

B: Eh luv, can I buy yer a pint when we get there?

G: (*looks at him, grins:*) If you buy *him* one as well.

B: (*grins*) Right, y'er on!

They leave. By this time playing lights are almost at normal house-lights level. House-lights blend into them. All is as it was at the beginning — except that there are now two extra chairs.

Acknowledgments

For use of copyright material, acknowledgments and thanks are due to the following:

Spike Milligan, for an excerpt from the Goon Show, 'A Punch up the Conker'; Oxford University Press, for an extract from Isaac Deutscher, *The Prophet Armed: Trotsky 1879-1921* (1954); Chatto & Windus: The Hogarth Press and W.W. Norton & Co., for passages from volumes 7 and 10 of *The Standard Edition of the Complete Psychological Works of Sigmund Freud*, translated from the German under the General Editorship of James Strachey; Allen & Unwin and Liveright Publishing Corporation for passages from Sigmund Freud, *Introductory Lectures on Psychoanalysis*; Jonathan Cape, A.D. Peters & Co., and the Estate of Arthur Koestler, for a passage from Arthur Koestler, *Darkness at Noon*; *The Guardian* newspaper for passages from the issue for September 15th 1983; The Bodley Head and William Morrow & Co., Inc., for an extract from Robert M. Pirsig, *Zen and the Art of Motorcycle Maintenance*; Faber & Faber Ltd. and Harcourt Brace Jovanovich Inc. for passages from *Four Quartets* by T.S. Eliot; Harcourt Brace Jovanovich Inc. for the translation by H.R. Hays of the poem by Bertolt Brecht, *An die Nachgeborenen* ('To Posterity'); New Left Books for a passage from T.W. Adorno, *Minima Moralia*, translated by Frank Jephcott.

The author sincerely apologises to any holder of copyright material used in the book for which permission has inadvertently not been sought or obtained, and to any genuine critic whose name has, coincidentally, been taken in vain.

246

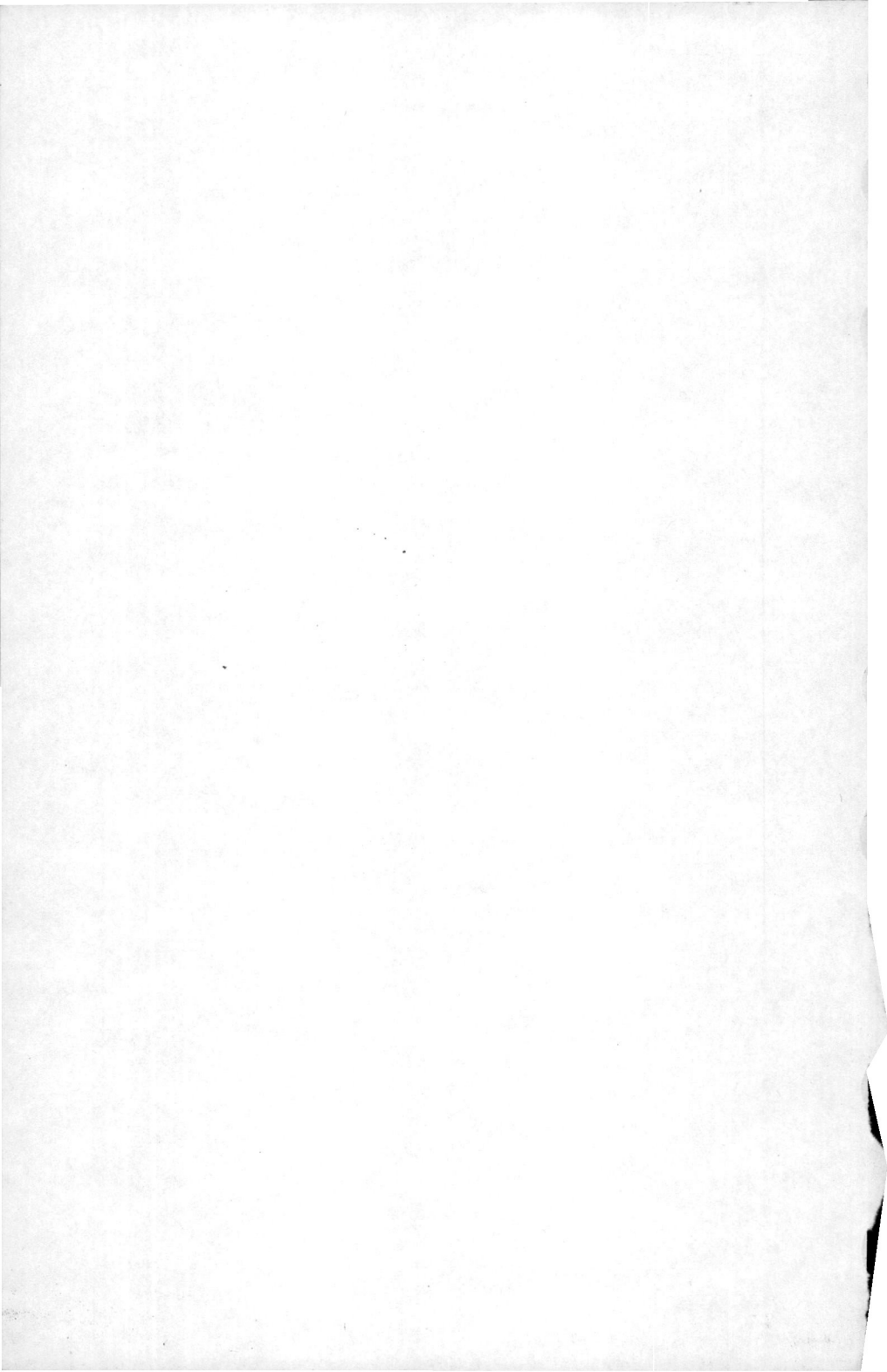